KU-466-073

The Victorians

Queen Victoria, after the portrait by Winterhalter in the Houses of Parliament

THE VICTORIANS

Sir Charles Petrie

Bt. C.B.E. M.A.(Oxon.) F.R.Hist.Soc.

President of the Military History Society of Ireland, Corresponding Member of the Royal Spanish Academy of History.

1960

EYRE & SPOTTISWOODE

LONDON

First published 1960

Printed in Great Britain
by Billing & Sons Ltd
Guildford
Cat. No. 6/2387

Contents

Illustrations

PLATES

IN THE TEXT

ENDPAPERS

Preface

Like the *Stuarts* and *The Four Georges* of which it is the successor this volume makes no pretence of being a complete history of Great Britain during the period which it covers. It is solely concerned with the changing conditions that marked the reign of Queen Victoria, and if a good deal of space has been devoted to religious and political problems this is because an understanding of them has been considered a necessary background to any account of the social transformation of the age under review. At the same time some events which occupy much space in modern history-books have received scant attention, and others have been omitted altogether, in the attempt to depict the lives of our grandfathers and grandmothers alike in their gravity and in their gaiety; in other words, as they were, and not always as posterity has chosen to see them in retrospect.

CHARLES PETRIE

November, 1959

CHAPTER I

What was Victorianism?

It has for so long become customary to divide the past into periods that there is a real danger of taking these periods too seriously, and what is known as the Victorian Age is assuredly no exception. Most educated people have a definite idea of what they mean by Victorianism, but it did not commence with the Queen's accession in 1837, nor did it cease with her death in 1901. The aftermath of the Georgian era lasted at least until the Crimean War–Lord Cardigan of Balaclava fame was a complete Georgian type–and it would be difficult to refute the assertion that Victorianism received its death-blow, not in 1901, but with the outbreak of the First World War. The period was marked, and to no small extent influenced, by the predominance of the railway, which was a much greater social factor than is always realized, and when the train gave place to the motor-car Victorianism was on the decline. The First World War registered the triumph of the internal combustion engine, and with this triumph a new age began.

All the same, the Victorian Age is a very elastic term to denote an extremely dynamic society: it was certainly 'no cycle of Cathay'. In 1841, the date of the first census in the Queen's reign, the population of the United Kingdom was 26,730,929, and was in the main agricultural; in 1901 it was 41,458,721, and was largely industrial, and this increase was in spite of the fact that the figure for Ireland had dropped by nearly four million in the intervening years. In many ways there was almost as great a gulf between the conditions existing on the Queen's accession and those that obtained at her death as there has been between those of 1901 and those of 1960. A brief summary of the changes in the capital alone well illustrates this point, and as we shall see in due course what was true of London was equally true of the big provincial cities.

Among the six million people who flocked to the Great Exhibition in Hyde Park in 1851 there must have been not a few who had been born in the City, for its resident population at that date was still over a hundred and twenty thousand, and in many ways it bore more resemblance to what it had been in the past than to what it was to become by the end of the nineteenth century. Old London Bridge, with its shops and houses, had gone, but Temple Bar still stood to mark the boundary between the City and Westminster; the schools of Charterhouse and St. Paul's had not yet moved elsewhere; and the construction of Cannon Street and Holborn Viaduct lay in the future. It is true that the penny post had been introduced, but the streets were devoid of the now familiar pillar-boxes which were introduced later at the suggestion of Anthony Trollope, the novelist, who was also a distinguished Civil Servant at the Post Office. Those condemned to death were still hanged in public, outside Newgate, for it was not until 1868 that public hangings came to an end.

Although the resident population of the City was very little less than it had been at the beginning of the century, people were already beginning to live further afield. The parents of Joseph Chamberlain were a case in point. For generations the Chamberlains had lived in Milk Street, off Cheapside, but when Joseph's father and mother were married in 1834 they settled in Camberwell, where in due course the statesman was born; later they moved to Highbury. Everywhere suburban villas were springing up amidst fields and orchards, and the chief reason for this migration was that new facilities were making it possible for men to live away from their work. Southwark Bridge, for instance, shortened the way to the southern slopes. The four-wheeled cab had been on the streets for the best part of a generation, and the hansom made its appearance in 1834. The omnibus, too, was a familiar sight in the streets at the time of the Great Exhibition. The first bus to run in London was that started in 1829 by M. G. Shillibeer, and it went from the Yorkshire Stingo at Marylebone to the Bank; it was drawn by three horses abreast, carried twenty-two inside passengers, and the fare for the journey was a shilling. Incidentally, this vehicle, though speedy, proved too large for use in traffic, and it was superseded by a smaller type, while in due course seats made their appearance along the centre of the roof.

The movement away from the City was first directed to such places as Camberwell and Clapham, and then to Canonbury and Highbury, as we have seen in the case of the Chamberlain family. Kensington came later, in the seventies and eighties, for most of what is now the Royal Borough was built in the decades following the Great Exhibition; previously market-gardens had formed its predominant feature, and in any event it was too far away. If this exodus was stimulated by the provision of improved means of communication, it also created a demand for even further improvement. The traffic problem in the City is probably as old as the City itself, but it became especially acute during the second half of the nineteenth century. In an attempt at alleviation Cannon Street was built in 1854, and Holborn Viaduct seventeen years later, but it was not until the coming of the underground railway from Paddington to Farringdon Street in 1863 that the pressure upon the streets became modified to any extent.

These material changes were reflected in the social scene. For long City men and women kept themselves to themselves, and during the earlier years of Queen Victoria's reign West End society was little affected by those who had their interests to the East of Temple Bar. The aristocracy, new and old, with its hangers-on, had its being in Belgrave and Grosvenor Squares, and it was fashionable to despise trade and commerce, which was, incidentally, a somewhat illogical attitude in view of the fact that 'society' was largely composed of the children and grandchildren of the 'nabobs' and profiteers of the Revolutionary and Napoleonic Wars. Nor, in those days, did City men lunch in the clubs of Pall Mall and St. James's Street; few of them were members, and anyhow they would have felt out of place there. As the nineteenth century drew to a close a change took place, and Anthony Trollope in *The Way we Live Now*, which was published in 1875, gives a satirical account of the way in which the City was beginning to permeate the West End. There were several reasons for this, of which the most important was the rapid growth of London as a whole. Camberwell and Clapham were declining in the social scale, and as the internal combustion engine was still in the future Leatherhead and Hitchin were too far away; so the City man who could afford to do so took a house in Westminster, Chelsea, or Kensington, and thus made the acquaintance of those with whom his father would never normally have come in contact.

These developments, however, did not only affect the rich. There was a big expansion of London to the North and East, and if the new districts opened up there were not fashionable they were undeniably populous. The City clerk imitated the City magnate, and moved out, generally of course, to areas served by railways which had their London terminus within easy reach of the place where he was employed. Thus the 'daily breader' came into existence, and the resident population of the City was shown by each successive census to be shrinking rapidly.

In this connection, tribute must be paid to the Prince of Wales, later King Edward VII, for breaking down the division between the Court and the aristocracy on the one hand, and the commercial classes on the other. Queen Victoria's social outlook was doubtless the result of her husband's influence, and that was typically German. She would never have sat down to dinner with a playwright as Louis XIV had done with Molière, but her son revived the older, and more generous, traditions of the monarchy. It is true that when he went yachting with Sir Thomas Lipton the snobs gibed at the incongruity of a monarch 'going for a sail with his grocer,' but it was typical of the manner in which he showed those who had made their

Typical Victorian Domestic Building: Belgrave Square

A Victorian Slum: Gareth Place, Southwark, now destroyed

own way in the world that they would not be treated like pariahs. Sometimes, of course, there were misunderstandings, and it is told that on one occasion when the King said to Lipton, 'I want to give you an Order', Sir Thomas misconstrued the Sovereign's intentions, and whipped out a note-book and pencil. All the same, the City continued to have a very definite life of its own. Some of the most sumptuous entertaining in the world centred round the Mansion House and Guildhall, and the halls of the various Livery Companies. Clubs catering for all tastes came into existence, although the City of London Club, the foremost of them, had been founded so long ago as 1832. Innumerable chop-houses and other eating-places, many of them dating from the eighteenth century or even earlier, continued to exist, and the problem of getting a satisfactory meal in the City was by no means the difficult one it was subsequently to become.

Nor was the Victorian Age static where the Temple and Fleet Street were concerned. The removal of the Royal Courts of Justice from Westminster Hall to their present site in the Strand in 1873 brought the legal centre of the kingdom to the very gates of the City, and in due course this had its effect upon the Inns of Court, though they tended to become less residential as the nineteenth century drew to its close. As for Fleet Street, it became in the reign of Queen Victoria what it was subsequently to remain. To give a list of the London daily and evening papers which flourished, say, in the year of the Diamond Jubilee would be to mention many a forgotten name; similarly, more than one well-known contemporary sheet was unknown at the turn of the century. *The Daily Mail* made its appearance as early as 1896, but *The Daily Express* was still below the horizon, and it seems a long time since *The News Chronicle* was entitled *The Clerkenwell News*.

The development of the newspaper was, indeed, one of the outstanding achievements of the Victorian Age, for it was not until 1840 that the publication of reports, papers, notes, and proceedings of either House of Parliament, by order or under the authority of that House, was absolutely protected, and also the reproduction in full. *The Morning Chronicle* is credited with being the first paper to employ a regular staff of Parliamentary reporters who actually took their places in relays in the gallery of the House of Commons, while it was *The Morning Herald* which established correspondents in the chief European capitals and in all the larger centres of population in the British Isles. It is no exaggeration to say that during the earlier part of the Victorian Age journalism in Great Britain was dominated by *The Times* under the proprietorship of various members of the Walter family, and especially during the editorship of John Delane which lasted from 1841 to 1879. During his regime it was not unjustifiably observed by Archdeacon Denison that 'if Scripture said one thing in England and *The Times* newspaper another, five hundred out of every five hundred and ten people would believe *The Times*.' As the century drew to its close, however, competition from *The Daily Telegraph* began to make itself felt, for that paper ushered in a new era in British journalism by the organization of exploration parties, and also by making the fullest use of the brilliant critiques, and articles on social life, literature, and art by George Augustus Sala.

One thing, however, did remain unchanged throughout the whole of the Victorian Age, and that was the pre-eminence of the City of London as the financial centre of the world. British investments abroad reached a figure of almost astronomical proportions, and in one way or another the City administered these vast assets, for the amount spent in Victorian England in proportion to the amount saved was the smallest in any recorded epoch, while the City's prestige was further enhanced by the position of London as the chief port of the British Isles. There had never been anything like it since the fall of Rome.

If the Victorian Age was far from being static where London was concerned then the capital was only typical of the whole country, for it was not only in respect of material matters that changes were in the air. Towards the end of the century there were to be heard the first rumblings of the storm that very soon was to sweep away the erstwhile governing class. For generations the landed gentry had fought with the utmost ferocity

The Hustings at Stepney Green: The General Election of 1852

for its position and its possessions; in its defence one King had been sent to the scaffold, another was driven into exile, and a foreign dynasty was placed upon the throne; at the other end of the scale any attempt to disturb the existing order was crushed with equal ruthlessness, and when, not long before the accession of Queen Victoria, the wretched labourers of Wessex had burnt a few ricks to call attention to the fact that they were starving, seven of them were hanged, four hundred were imprisoned, and four hundred and fifty-seven were transported. 'My father', Mr Millbank observed to Coningsby, 'has often told me that in his early days the displeasure of a peer of England was like a sentence of death to a man.'

As the years passed, however, the franchise was gradually extended by ambitious statesmen desirous of stealing a march on their rivals at all costs, and the members of the governing class perceived that if they wished to preserve their influence, then their service to the State could no longer be confined to having a good luncheon four times a year at Quarter Sessions, and sitting on the local Bench once a month on a non-hunting day. The whole paraphernalia of Local Government began to compel their attention, if from no other instinct than that of self-preservation. Parliamentary elections were ceasing to be a choice between a Tory and a Whig landlord; the squire was as often as not opposed by a Radical, who was not ashamed to confess that he was out to demolish the existing order altogether, and to lay his hands on the very Ark of the Covenant in the shape of the hereditary principle. The spirit of the pleasant age that was passing was well expressed by the Eton boy who said, 'Don't bother about farming or politics; all father's tenants have to do is to walk a foxhound puppy and vote for the Conservatives'. On the other side was the member of the Cavendish family who refused to allow his tenants to keep ducks 'because they quacked, and made a noise like a Tory voter'. By the end of the century leaflets, pamphlets, and all the other horrors of what the nineteenth Lord Willoughby de Broke described as 'that terrible thing called propaganda' had been brought into full play, and the comfortable evening at home had with distressing frequency to give place to the village meeting, so that there was not a little wisdom in the remark of the legendary *grande dame* that unless these privations were cheerfully borne 'the eight o'clock dinner would ruin the Conservative Party'.

Yet until the Queen's death there were many of the governing class who still lived the life of their fathers and grandfathers. A typical member of it would make it his custom to change his seat of government from his country house to his London house on the same date every year. He would see that his eldest son obtained a commission in the Household Troops, or he would use his influence to get him into the House of Commons. The younger sons divided the family living, the cavalry and infantry of the Line, and the Navy between them, having received from their father a sufficient allowance to make them independent of their not too exacting professions. This arrangement formed a convenient setting for the enjoyment of field sports in the autumn and winter, and of other delights in the summer. It is true that there may have been a certain period of boredom for 'the sad Meltonian' in the spring, but this was shortly relieved by the festive Yeomanry Week, followed by the London Season with Epsom, Ascot, Newmarket, and Goodwood, to say nothing of a few country-house cricket parties.

At this point it may be neither useless nor uninstructive to see what the Victorians said about themselves, and their remarkable complacency was reflected in the article which Sir Walter Besant wrote for the Diamond Jubilee number of the *Illustrated London News* when he contrasted the England of 1897 with that of 1837. 'The Broad Atlantic', he said, 'has, indeed, become a mere pond. The wooden vessel looks almost as antique as the caracks of the Armada. Iron has come to rule supreme; steam has made the picturesque sails of sixty years ago as old-fashioned almost as the trireme. Thus in 1840 the steamers belonging to England numbered but 600; to-day they have increased to nearly 8,500; the steam tonnage has increased from 98,807 to 6,121,555 in this year of Jubilee, against a total tonnage of nearly nine millions.' Sir Walter found equal cause for satisfaction with the railways, as when he pointed out, 'In 1837, the Queen could not have possibly reached Aberdeen on her way to Balmoral under forty-five hours; to-day she could cover the 540 miles in twelve hours–the quickest long-distance journey in the world'.

Sir Walter was quite lyrical when he came to deal with the Queen's soldiers. 'In Africa they have planted the Queen's colours on the mountains of Magdala, and marched twice into Coomassie. They have quelled the unruly tribes of the Niger, broken the power of the brave savages South of the Zambesi, subdued an Egyptian rebellion on the Nile, and inspired with a wholesome dread of the British name the death-despising hordes of the Sudan; and the Queen's troops are prouder of no victories than those of Tel-el-Kebir, El-Teb, Tamai, Abu-Klea, Kirbekan, Hasheen, and Tofrek'. One would have thought that he might have mentioned the Alma, Balaclava, and Inkerman, if not the Sikh Wars and the Indian Mutiny, but in 1897 war to the British meant a colonial campaign and nothing else. Those were the days of the legendary cavalry subaltern, secure in an allowance from his father, who received a letter from his regimental bankers to the effect that there was a sum of one hundred pounds standing to his credit, and asked, 'Who is this fellow who says that he has a hundred pounds of mine?' On it being pointed out to him that this was probably his pay, he exclaimed, 'Good God! I didn't know that we were paid for this job.'

Yet, apart altogether from the extension of the franchise, the old order was being steadily undermined without those concerned having any perception of what was afoot. Fish proverbially go rotten from the head downwards, and the same was true in this case. There was much church-going, and a great deal of lip-service was paid to the Deity, but Oxford and Cambridge had passed into the hands of the freethinkers. The story already ran that in Balliol chapel Jowett used to interpolate *sotto voce* the words 'used to' after 'I' and before 'believe', so that he could still recite the Creed. Yet Jowett was one of the outstanding figures of the Victorian Age:

My name is Benjamin Jowett:
All there is to know I know it.
I am the Master of Balliol College,
What I know not is not knowledge.

Mr Douglas Woodruff well summed up the Victorian age when he wrote, 'The governing class in England reproduced the characteristics of high French society under the *ancien régime*, believing that it could quite easily have the best of both worlds, draw all the practical advantages that came from settled habit and custom in English society, like the extreme reverence for the law of property, and at the same time feel advanced, believing that the present challenges to all conventional morality could be trusted to remain inside the covers of books. . . . It was a governing class which spared itself effort too readily, most of whose members were content to be intellectually and morally passengers, and many of them disloyal passengers, with, over them all, the motto from their already neglected Old Testament, "Yet a little sleep, a little slumber, a little folding of the hands to sleep, so shall thy poverty come as one that travelleth, and thy want as an armed man".'[1]

At the same time the aristocracy rapidly became more *bourgeois* during the reign, and therefore more respectable. Before the Queen had been very long on the throne it was already far removed from the days when Lord Barrymore and his brothers were known as 'Hellgate, Newgate, and Cripplegate', while their sister rejoiced in the nickname of 'Billingsgate'. It also tended to approximate more to the landed gentry from which as a class it had for centuries been distinct. There were several reasons for this change. One of the most potent was the much better example set by the Royal Family than in earlier years when Society was dominated by Queen Victoria's 'wicked uncles', of whom the Duke of Wellington said that they were 'the damnest millstone about the necks of any government that can be imagined. They have insulted two-thirds of the gentlemen of England.' It was of them that Shelley wrote, 'Princes, the dregs of their dull race who flow through public

[1] *The New English Review*, vol. XIV, pp. 539 and 550.

scorn'. Compared with their enormities, the peccadilloes of Albert Edward, Prince of Wales, were of very small importance, and in fact tended rather to his popularity than otherwise.

Another reason for the growing respectability of the upper classes was that they increasingly tended to marry into the *nouveaux riches* of the Industrial Revolution. The peerage had impoverished itself under the inspiration of 'The First Gentleman of Europe' both as Regent and King, and to recoup itself it looked to the daughters of the successful manufacturer. Now however hard an employer such an individual might be to his own workpeople, he was the last person to approve of the sort of life that was led at Carlton House or the Pavilion at Brighton, and his son-in-law had in consequence to watch his paces. In the next generation the transformation was complete, so that by the end of the century the average British aristocrat was very far removed from his hard-drinking, hard-living ancestor of two generations earlier. Where the Irish peerage was concerned it is true that more latitude was allowed even down to our own times, and the story is told that Stanley Baldwin was dining quietly at the Carlton Club one night with a well-known Scottish duke when there entered the coffee-room a tall man with tow hair, whiskers, and over-dressed in a fancy fashion. The duke at once remarked that the newcomer was an Irish earl. 'How do you recognize an Irish earl?' asked Baldwin. The duke replied, 'My father told me that when you saw a man come into the club with a velvet collar, two or three of his flies open, and if he had forgotten to pull the plug, you could be sure he was an Irish earl'. Elsewhere, however, a preservation of outward appearances became the order of the day, and it is significant that the last Head of an Oxford College openly to acknowledge an illegitimate child died in 1903.

Last, but by no means least, of the factors in the transformation of the behaviour of the governing class was Arnold's establishment of the modern Public School System. The conditions prevailing before his reforms may be guessed from Mr Turner's account of life at Westminster. Bishop Short wrote, 'When I was a boy at Westminster the boys fought one another,

The Police among the Cockfighters, 1865

they fought the Masters, the Masters fought them, they fought outsiders; in fact we were ready to fight everybody'. Mr Turner continues, 'Lord de Ros kept fighting cocks in the space between the floor of the dormitory of his boarding-house and the ceiling of the room below, and even Lord John Russell remembered employing one of the hours which should have been devoted to the study of writing and arithmetic with the writing master in Dean's Yard, in watching a fight between young Belcher and another famous pugilist'.[1] Readers of *Lavengro* will remember how on one occasion Borrow was conducted to a kind of cockpit 'not far from the Abbey church of Westminster', where dog fights and fights between a dog and a bear took place, and how the proprietor 'Joey' remarked that the young gentlemen from the School 'comes here in shoals, leaving books, and letters, and masters, too. To tell the truth, I rather wish they would mind their letters, for a more precious set of young blackguards I never seed.' Westminster was typical of the Public Schools of the day, and the scope of the revolution effected by Arnold can easily be imagined by the fact that at the end of the century the spirit animating the leading educational establishments was that expressed by Newbolt in the poem beginning, 'There's a breathless hush in the Close to-night'. Possibly the pendulum had swung too far in the opposite direction.

There were, however, occasions when a detailed knowledge of the Westminster slums came in useful in later life, and a case in point was Lord de Ros himself. The attitude of the crowd was so hostile to George IV at his Coronation that as the Banquet in Westminster Hall drew to a close he had to be told that it would be dangerous for him to attempt to return home by the ordinary route. In this dilemma Lord de Ros, then a subaltern in the Life Guards and one of the Escort, offered to pilot the royal carriage through the Tuttle Fields, of which he knew every inch from his Westminster days. The offer was accepted, and the King, 'horribly nervous and . . . constantly calling to the officers of the Escort to draw well up to the carriage

[1] Turner, L. E.: *Westminster School, A History*, pp. 37–38.

windows', returned by way of Millbank, the Five Chimneys, the Willow Walk, and Five Fields, now Eaton Square, to Carlton House. Those were, incidentally, the days when snipe could be shot in Belgrave Square, so marked was the contrast with the end of the century in matters small as well as great.

This is not to say that there were no wicked Peers even in the heyday of the Victorian Age, but there were nothing like so many as there had been, and they wanted finding. One of the finest specimens was the fourth Marquess of Ailesbury, who burnt the candle at both ends so furiously that he died, in 1894, at the age of thirty. He was a nobleman of low tastes, bad character, and brutal manners, of whom Lord Rosebery remarked that 'his mind was a dunghill, of which his tongue was the cock'. His career, though short, was by no means devoid of incident. In 1887 he was expelled for life from the Jockey Club for fraud in connection with the running of his horse 'Everitt', and in 1892 he went bankrupt for £345,462 of which £244,211 was unsecured. When he died it was said that his death was only mourned by the Radicals who thus lost, for their propaganda, a most eligible example of a hereditary legislator.

There were also to be found in clubs and drawing-rooms almost to the end of the century a number of old men who had acquired a reputation, often fictitious, for wickedness solely on account of their companions of earlier days. In many a respectable Victorian family there was an elderly and somewhat mysterious uncle whose appeal to the younger generation was assuredly not diminished by the fact that 'he had done things for the Regent at Brighton'.

A school of modern writers has done its best to paint the Victorian Age as one of drab respectability, and relative to the days of the Regency this may have been the case, but it was not so in any absolute sense, for it witnessed three of the greatest sensations in modern English history, namely those associated with Dilke, Parnell, and Tranby Croft: as for the accusation of dullness this was certainly not true, though it was not an age of exhibitionism like the present.

One of the men who relieved it from the charge of being dull was Lord Charles Beresford, and of the many stories told about him two will suffice to point the moral in question. The first relates to a bet with Walter Long, the statesman, who subsequently became the Viscount Long of Wraxall, regarding an exploit in Hyde Park. The only persons who have the right to drive up Rotten Row are the Sovereign and the Duke of St. Albans, the latter in virtue of his office as Hereditary Grand Falconer, but Beresford bet Long five pounds that he would do so between eleven and twelve on a certain morning. On the day in question Long kept a sharp look-out from eleven o'clock onwards, and just before noon he saw the watering-cart wending its way along the Row as usual; something prompted him to scan closely the man who was driving it, and there was Lord Charles who had bribed the driver to change clothes with him.

The second incident is a testimony to his quickness of repartee. One day at a race meeting the Prince of Wales greeted Sir Edward Sassoon with the remark, 'Hullo, Sassoon, your nose seems to get bigger each time I see you'. Whereupon Beresford observed, 'Can you be surprised, Sir, seeing how often he has to pay through it?'

In fact there were probably more wits about in Victorian times than there are to-day, and one of the greatest was Sir William Gilbert. Soon after *Ruddigore* was produced in 1887 he met the Bishop of London, Frederick Temple, outside the Athenaeum, and was taken to task for giving publicity to the word 'ruddy', which the Bishop maintained was indistinguishable from 'bloody'. Gilbert demurred, and added, 'Because I admire your lordship's ruddy countenance it does not follow that I like your bloody cheek'. Another time Gilbert went into a theatre where one of his operas was in rehearsal, and asked the first person he saw for the leading lady. 'She's round behind, Sir William,' was the reply. 'I know that,' remarked Gilbert, 'but I want to speak to her.' On yet a third occasion he was walking down the Haymarket at night just as the theatres were coming out when a somewhat ill-favoured young man rushed up to him with the words, 'Call me a cab'. 'Growler,' was the instantaneous reply. 'What do you mean?' said the young man angrily. 'Well, I could hardly call you handsome, could I?' observed Gilbert.

Even the Bishops of those days were not without a sense of humour, notably Mandell Creighton, the last great scholar to fill the see of London. It is said that when he was trying to secure some uniformity of worship in his diocese a High Church rector stuck out for the use of incense of which the Bishop disapproved. 'I have a cure of souls, my Lord,' he protested. 'I see,' Creighton replied, 'and you want the smoke to cure them.'

The Victorian Age was, indeed, very far from being one of uniformity, and as it recedes into the historical background it is easier to distinguish the lights and shades on the canvas. There was a world of difference between the men and women of 1837 and those of 1901, and of this transformation the Queen herself was the outward and visible sign. As a child she had known the men of the Regency and the Europe of Metternich; when she died Sir Winston Churchill was already a Member of Parliament and Mr Harold Macmillan was within a few years of going to Eton. Not only were the material changes during the period immense, but there had been a revolution in outlook. When she came to the throne her subjects were much what they had been under her grandfather; when she died the first whisperings had been heard of the Welfare State. Yet, there was one characteristic which gives a unity to the period, and that characteristic was its middle-class smugness: never has a people been so middle-class and so smug as were the English in the Victorian Age, or, in consequence, so little inclined to look ahead, and that in spite of the revolution which was taking place in their midst.

To survey the Victorian scene objectively in retrospect is to be driven inevitably to the conclusion that its dominating feature was the rise and importance of the middle-class, however unconscious that middle-class may have been of the fact at the time. The term is not an easy one to define, but the sociologist knows what he means when he uses it. The upper middle-class by the end of the century was not readily distinguishable in its way of life and in its outlook from the aristocracy, for although the latter was snobbish to a degree, yet its members were, quite prepared to welcome anyone who had enough money to live like themselves. Indeed, that was one of the most amazing aspects of the period; no doubt it had been the same in previous centuries, but not in quite so self-satisfied and pretentious a way. At the other end of the social scale there was a much greater distinction between the lower middle-class and the working-class, for the social rise of the skilled worker, which is so prominent a feature of English social life to-day, was still in the future. In effect, class distinctions in the middle strata of society were very rigid down to the First World War, and even to-day they are by no means extinct, whatever may be said or written to the contrary.

The late C. F. G. Masterman defined the middle-class, which he called 'The Suburbans', in this way:

> They are the peculiar product of England and America; of the nations which have pre-eminently added commerce, business, and finance to the work of manufacture and agriculture. It is a life of Security; a life of Sedentary occupation; a life of Respectability; and these three qualities give the key to its special characteristics. Its male population is engaged in all its working hours in small, crowded offices, under artificial light, doing immense sums, adding up other men's accounts, writing other men's letters. It is sucked into the City at daybreak, and scattered again as darkness falls. It finds itself towards evening in its own territory in the miles and miles of little red houses in little silent streets, in number defying imagination. Each boasts its pleasant drawing-room, its bow-window, its little front garden, its high-sounding title–'Acacia Villa' or 'Camperdown Lodge'–attesting unconquered human aspiration.
>
> There are many interests beyond the working hours: here a greenhouse filled with chrysanthemums, there a tiny grass patch with bordering flowers; a chicken-house, a bicycle shed, a tennis lawn. The women, with their single domestic servants, now so difficult to get, and so exacting when found, find time hang rather heavy on their hands. But there are excursions to shopping centres in the West End, and pious sociabilities, and occasional theatre visits, and the interests at home. The children are jolly, well-fed, intelligent English boys and girls; full of curiosity, at least in the earlier years. Some of them have real gifts of intellect and artistic

> skill, receiving in the suburban secondary schools the best education which England is giving to-day.[1]

Mr Masterman was, of course, thinking primarily in terms of London, but his remarks are *mutatis mutandis* also true of the other large centres of population.

The great dividing line between the upper middle-class and that immediately below it was the possession of a carriage, and to become carriage-folk was the great ambition of those who had not reached such heights; it might be that the coachman was in reality not much more than a groom, and that he was expected also to look after the garden and do odd jobs about the house, but there he was on the box, for all the world to see, when occasion demanded. What income was required to live in this state is difficult to decide, for it depended a good deal upon time and place. At the turn of the century it was generally reckoned that a couple who married on £600 a year would be able to keep a carriage and two maids. When the author's father married in 1880 his bride, who was an orphan, had an annual income of £800, and in the West of Ireland, whence the bridegroom hailed, it was considered that he had married an heiress.

Of the circumstances of the upper middle-class, and of the ease with which it might be entered by those with the necessary financial resources, the late Lord Mersey of Toxteth has given an account in the case of his grandfather, who was born in 1814 and died in 1880: he was the son of a cloth manufacturer in Wigan, but at an early age he migrated to Liverpool where he became a clerk in a shipping-office:

> My grandfather was a man of untiring industry, and though for many years oppressed by what my father used to call 'grinding' poverty, by work and saving he managed bit by bit to get enough money to start on his own feet, so that by 1848, when he was thirty-four, he had become the owner of a small schooner named the 'Speed'. Trading as a general merchant he bought and sold cargoes, he began to make money on the Liverpool Exchange,

[1] *The Condition of England.* Mr Masterman was writing in the reign of King Edward VII, but what he said was equally applicable to the later years of the Victorian Age.

and he became a member of the Town Council and of the Mersey Docks and Harbour Board. But for a long time misfortune dogged him. He was persuaded to make one of his brothers-in-law captain of the 'Speed'. On a journey to South America the captain sold the cargo and traded with the proceeds for his own profit. Communications were slow; and it was months before the news reached Liverpool. My grandfather determined to go and rescue his ship, and in 1853 and again in 1854 he made what was then a prodigious journey across the Atlantic to New Orleans, across the Isthmus of Darien and up the Pacific coast to California. After four months' travelling he reached San Francisco. He drove to the docks and asked for news of the 'Speed'. He was told that it was even then sailing out of the Golden Gates for the Pacific; and he was just able, after crossing the Atlantic Ocean and the American continent, to descry the masts of his ship for the last time.

This loss was a terrible blow. He came back to Liverpool to find himself almost ruined, and he had eventually to go through the Bankruptcy Court. But his courage was undaunted; and his friends stuck by him. In 1855 he was entertained at dinner by the Mayor and a number of his admirers in the Town Hall, and was presented with a service of plate 'by numerous friends in testimony of their admiration of his talents and of his indefatigable and spirited exertions to promote the welfare of Liverpool during his career as a member of the Town Council, Dock and Pilots Committees.'

After paying his debts, my grandfather resumed his business as a general merchant; he acquired another ship, and again began to do well. During the American Civil War he made large purchases of rosin and turpentine, continuing to buy as their prices rose, until he held large stocks. At the right moment he sold, and so laid the foundations of his fortune. When the war began he was worth some £10,000; when it ended, more than three times that amount. In the panic of 1866 his securities suffered serious depreciation–he put down his carriage and moved to a smaller house–but they soon recovered, and he then began to invest in insurance shares. In these also he made considerable profits, so that his reputation as a financier became high; and when he died in 1880 he was worth over £120,000. . . . He was a generous man, though after he became prosperous he rarely spent more than half his annual income, a policy which my father also pursued for most of his life.[1]

Such was the career of the man whose son became President

[1] *A Picture of Life, 1872–1940*, pp. 2–4.

A Victorian Interior: The Horn Room, Osborne House

The Development of the Omnibus, 1829, 1865, and 1900

of the Probate, Divorce, and Admiralty Division, a Viscount, and a member of the Privy Council. The aristocracy of the Victorian Age may have been snobbish in its outlook, but it never became a caste.

There was, indeed, as will be seen on a later page in the case of Glasgow, quite a brisk two-way traffic where the upper middle-class was concerned, but that cannot disguise the fact that this was confined to a small minority of those concerned, and in the class immediately below society was overwhelmingly static. Its members for the most part passed their lives in the environment in which they were born, and recruitment from the working-class was relatively infrequent compared with more recent times.

The Victorian middle-class may have been outwardly smug, but it was very far from being sure of itself. It had none of the weapons at its disposal which those above and those below it had readily to hand. The Conservative Party of those days was the champion of the landed classes; the Liberal Party catered for the manufacturing interest; and the nascent Labour Party was almost entirely recruited from the working-class with whose claims it was exclusively concerned. In effect, the middle-class was quite unorganized, and in consequence nobody either respected or feared it; such was the position at the end of the Victorian Age, but within a few years that same middle-class was to give proof of what it was capable when it flung from power the Progressives who had dominated the London County Council for twenty years. Despised as its members might be by those above them, their ideas were all towards the top of the scale; they were proud of identifying their interests with those of Kensington, and indignant when others identified them with those of Poplar. They tended to vote Conservative rather than Liberal not so much because Conservative principles made a special appeal to them as because Conservatism was supposed to be the party favoured by the Court, society, and the wealthy and fashionable classes. One result of this was that they became the butt of the rest of the community, and contemporary literature, like the contemporary stage, abounded with jokes at the expense of those who transferred their residence from Upper Tooting to Belgravia, or discussed the respective social advantages of Clapham and Herne Hill.

The middle-class man was both suspicious and frightful of those below him. 'The vision of a "Keir Hardie" in caricature–with red tie and defiant beard and cloth cap, and fierce, unquenchable thirst for middle-class property–has become an image of Labour Triumphant which haunts his waking hours. He has difficulty with the plumber in the jerry-built houses needing continuous patching and mending. His wife is harassed by the indifference or insolence of the domestic servant. From a blend of these two he has constructed in imagination the image of Democracy–a loud voiced, independent, arrogant figure, with a thirst for drink, and imperfect standards of decency, and a determination to be supported at someone else's expense. . . . Every hour he anticipates the boiling over of the cauldron. He would never be surprised to find the crowd behind the red flag, surging up his little pleasant pathways, tearing down the railings, trampling the little garden; the "letting in of the jungle" upon the patch of fertile ground which has been redeemed from the wilderness.'[1]

This attitude, and the similar feelings which it inspired in the working-class, explains the bitterness which marked such clashes as that in the West End of London on February 8th, 1886, when, after a meeting of the unemployed in Trafalgar Square under the auspices of the Social Democratic Federation, the rougher elements unexpectedly found the surrounding district at their mercy, and there was a certain amount of looting before the police gained the upper hand. Much the same sort of thing took place in the same area on November 13th, 1887, and, later still, the industrial disputes which immediately preceded the First World War were generally marked by extreme bitterness. It was the companionship in the trenches during that conflict which made the various classes in the community realize that no one of them had a monopoly of virtue or vice, and since

[1] Masterman, C. F. G.: *The Condition of England*, pp. 66–67.

The Charge of Mounted Police in the Riots in Trafalgar Square, November 13, 1887

then, in spite of the injection of the Communist virus into the body politic, class-consciousness in England has on the whole been kept within reasonable bounds.

In the rural areas the Victorian Age had almost as bad a record as in Ireland, though for very different reasons. The mechanical inventions, and particularly the improvement in the means of production and transport, had given powerful assistance to the process which had been going on since the end of the eighteenth century, and led to a further transfer of population from the villages to the towns, so that by the end of the reign seventy-seven per cent of the inhabitants of the United Kingdom were resident in urban districts. While the towns and their suburbs shared a rapid increase at each decennial census the purely agricultural areas were almost stationary or actually retrogressive. 'There is no social life at all', wrote a Somerset clergyman. 'A village which once fed, clothed, policed, and regulated itself cannot now dig its own wells or build its own barns. Still less can it act its own dramas, build its own church, or organize its own work and play. It is pathetically helpless in everything.'[1]

The opening up of new countries, and the development of oceanic and railway transport, combined to bring into England the supplies of cheap foreign food and raw materials which were as valuable to the manufacturers as they were detrimental to the agricultural interest. The acreage under wheat and other grain crops declined steadily, and the labourers left the land to seek employment in the mills and factories. National prosperity, as measured by manufacturing production and the statistics of imports and exports, was at a higher level in 1873 than it had ever before attained, for in that year Great Britain was called upon to make good the destruction of capital caused by the Franco-Prussian War; but in the years that followed a succession of bad harvests told heavily on agriculture, and prices were further depressed by the extension of wheat growing in the United States, whence grain was poured into England.

There was no permanent recovery in the countryside after

[1] Marson, C. L.: *The Commonwealth.*

this. In 1874 the area under wheat in the United Kingdom was 3,821,655 acres, as against about 4,000,000 fifteen years earlier, while twenty years later it had fallen by considerably more than half. Other arable crops had also declined, though admittedly not to quite the same extent. The supplies from the United States and the improved transport in due course brought down the price of corn, which up to the later seventies was higher than it had been immediately after the abolition of the Corn Laws. How it varied per quarter during the reign can be seen from the following figures:

1849	40s. 3d.
1874	55s. 9d.
1877	56s. 9d.
1887	32s. 6d.
1894	23s. od.

When it is also taken into account that the average freight rate per quarter by steamer from New York to Liverpool fell from 5s. 6d. in 1871 to 10d. in 1901, it is easy to see why, although the general wealth and productive activity of the country were growing apace, the agricultural interest had no share in this expansion.

The English countryside during the latter half of the Victorian Age was the countryside of Richard Jefferies. The wonder was not why so many people left the land, but why anyone stayed on it. There had once been real life in rural England, but it was slowly brought to an end, first by Puritanism, and then by the enclosures. Since the Queen's death the situation has changed again with the coming of the cinema, television, and the motor-car, not to menton a realization by successive governments of the fact that to allow agriculture to decay is a form of national suicide; but it is too early yet to say what the future holds in store for a countryside, if not urbanized, at any rate well on the way to becoming suburbanized. However this may be there can be no doubt that in the last decade of the nineteenth century rural England had reached its nadir.

Finally, the break-up of the big estates had not yet begun, and power still rested in the hands of the upper class, so that while it is true to say that the emergence of the middle-class was one of the main features of the Victorian Age in the urban areas it was nothing like so important in the rural districts where the minority of twenty-three per cent resided. There the development was slower, and it was not until after the Second World War that the farmer took the place of the squire as the dominant figure in the countryside, but by then the Victorian Age was becoming little more than a memory.

The London Coffee Stall, 1851

CHAPTER II

The Victorian Monarchy

The heritage to which Queen Victoria succeeded was, as we have seen, not an easy one. It is a by no means uncommon mistake to assume that the decline of the power of the Crown began with the last illness of George III, but such was not, in fact, the case. Both the sons who succeeded him exercised more direct influence upon politics than the first two sovereigns of their dynasty had done, and William IV even went so far in 1834 as to dismiss a ministry that had a majority in the House of Commons. As for George IV, it is necessary to distinguish carefully between his behaviour as a man and as a monarch. In the former capacity there is, indeed, little that can be placed to his credit. He betrayed in turn everyone who was foolish enough to trust him, and he was equally faithless as a husband, a lover, and a friend. His conversation was so objectionable that the Duke of Wellington, who was not squeamish in these matters and whose loyalty was above suspicion, once said, 'He speaks so like old Falstaff, that, damn me, if I was not ashamed to walk into a room with him'; and in the year of his accession to the throne the Duke declared him 'degraded as low as he could be already'.

On the other hand the King's intelligence was far above the ordinary, and he entertained a very high opinion of his prerogative, which he was determined to do nothing to diminish. The history of his relations with Canning throws a great deal of light upon the position of the Crown at that period, and, incidentally, reflects the highest credit on the minister in question for a devotion to principle with which he is not usually credited. George disliked Canning personally, and at one time he suspected him of committing adultery with his wife; he also disagreed with Canning's policy, particularly where the recognition of the revolted Spanish colonies in America was concerned. For years there was a struggle between the two men, but though George tried to hamper Canning at every turn the statesman never cast any doubt upon the King's right of interference; all he maintained was that it should be exercised in a constitutional manner, for the Sovereign was continually endeavouring to utilize his position as King of Hanover to oppose the official policy of his British ministers. He was also by no means above playing the members of the Cabinet off against one another. Yet so highly did Canning think of the power of the Crown in spite of his differences with the reigning monarch that when he formed his ministry he endeavoured to enlist it in his support by reviving the post of Lord High Admiral for the Duke of Clarence.

That William IV did nothing to weaken the prerogative is proved by his action in 1834; but if the power of the King of England was undiminished when he died three years later, the prestige of the monarchy was become very considerably dimmed, and it was freely predicted that Queen Victoria would be the last British sovereign. If a monarch is to be the effective representative of the nation he or she must, in a civilized community, be the object of respect. George III had always retained his hold upon the affection of his subjects, and the fact that they respected him far more than they did most of his ministers had much to do with the success of his efforts to revive the power of the Crown. With his two successors it was otherwise. Enough has been said of the character of George IV to show that loyalty to him personally was an impossibility, and though William was more estimable in private life, his whole outlook was that of a retired ship's captain. In his time it was customary for the King when holding a Court to give his right hand to each lady to assist her to rise from the low curtsey she dropped to him; then, drawing her close to him, the Sovereign implanted a kiss on her cheek. William IV was the last monarch to avail himself of this privilege, which he thoroughly enjoyed, so much so, in fact, that anything which interfered with the unction of it greatly irritated him. The curled plumes worn by the girls in their hair were so long that they drooped over the face, and the King was often heard swearing to himself when his lips encountered feathers instead of the roses and cream of a débutante's cheek. The paint on the faces of the married women made him swear even more audibly. 'It makes my lips stick together so,' he was heard to complain. The throne had lost its dignity, and there was a reversion to the days of the first two Georges, without, however, the same necessity for the governing class to support the dynasty at all costs in case a worse thing befell.

The accession of Queen Victoria was to prove the turning-point in the modern history of the British monarchy, and it is well to realize that at that date the Crown still wielded very great direct power. The King could not, it is true, govern against the wishes of the House of Commons, for the simple reason that if he did so he would soon find himself without the necessary funds to carry on the administration, and the Royal veto had not been used since the House of Hanover came to the throne; but twice within a generation a ministry that had a majority in the Commons had been dismissed, while Governments that wished to bring forward measures of which the monarch did not approve had been forced to resign; and all the lesser prerogatives, such as those of mercy, the making of treaties, the creation of peers, and the nomination to official appointments, were still intact. Moreover, the state of affairs had so far been admitted by the leading statesmen of the day, though it is permissible to suspect that a good many of them anticipated with pleasure the accession to the throne of an inexperienced girl as certain to increase their opportunities of playing the old party game uncontrolled by the Crown acting in the interest of the nation.

The position, then, when Queen Victoria came to the throne was that a monarch who wished to exercise considerable personal influence upon the work of government would have found both the letter of the law, and a number of recent precedents, favourable to such a course. The monarchy, it is true, was a Parliamentary one, for George I and his descendants had only reigned by virtue of an Act of Parliament, namely the Act of Settlement of 1701; this measure deliberately passed over the superior hereditary rights of all the descendants of Charles I, and vested the succession in the Princess Sophia of Hanover, being the nearest Protestant heir to James I, and in her heirs being Protestants: a protest against this violation of her rights on behalf of the Duchess of Savoy had been read in the House of Lords on April 14th, 1701, but no action had been taken. The title of Queen Victoria to the Crown therefore rested on the statutory rights created by Parliament in 1701, which gave a final ratification to the principles of the Revolution settlement as laid down in 1689. On the score of heredity, therefore, the descendants of Charles I had a better claim than the new Queen; how many of them there were in 1837 it would be difficult to say, but nine years after her death there were estimated to be over a thousand.[1] On the other hand, since the Revolution the power of the Crown had not been further reduced by statute in any way, and the various monarchs who had occupied the throne since that date had put very different constructions upon their rights under the Constitution. William III personally conducted the country's relations with its neighbours, and also commanded its armies in the field. Anne often attended meetings of the Cabinet as well as the debates in the House of Lords, and she always claimed the right to appoint ministers according to her own choice, and from any party. Of the Hanoverians, the first two had been content to allow the Royal power, for the most part, to be exercised by the ruling oligarchy, but the last three had successfully prevented any usurpation of their prerogative.

Of recent years there has been a tendency to assume that the power of the monarchy has declined since the death of Queen Victoria, rather than during her reign, but such an assumption

[1] *Cf.* Robertson, C. Grant: *Select Statutes, Cases, and Documents*, p. 152.

has little foundation in fact, and it probably arises from a confusion of thought between power and prestige. She raised the prestige of the Crown to a greater height than it had attained since the fall of the Stuarts, but its active influence was steadily diminishing during her reign. The reason for this is not far to seek, and it is to be found in her political education. What her views, if any, of the place of the Crown in the Constitution may have been before her accession it is difficult, for lack of sufficient evidence on the point, to say, but once she was Queen she passed under the influence of the Whig Lord Melbourne, whose theory it was that monarchs should be seen but not heard. His knowledge of women is attested by the fact that the suspicions of at least one husband were aroused on this score, and he exerted it to the full in his relations with the young Queen. The result was that she came to believe that the Whig doctrine of monarchy was the only possible one for her to adopt, and although the woman often rebelled against the restrictions which the acceptance of this doctrine imposed, the Queen always yielded to them in the last resort.

It is not uninteresting to reflect that her upbringing might have been very different had George Canning not died at the age of fifty-seven ten years before her accession: in that case it might have been he, not Melbourne, who would have been her mentor. Canning would not, it is true, have brought her up to be a monarch of the old Stuart type, but with his firm belief in the necessity of maintaining the balance of the Constitution he would have taught her to take a much more exalted view of the prerogatives of the Crown than Melbourne would ever have tolerated.

Throughout the Queen's reign, then, the power of the Crown was continually on the decline, and a careful perusal of her published letters reveals this fact very clearly. As Sir Sidney Lee says: 'Many times did she write to a minister that "Never would she consent" to this or that proposal: yet her formal signature of approval was always at his service at the needful moment.'[1] Bagehot declared that an English monarch 'must

[1] *King Edward vii*, vol. II, p. 34.

sign his own death-warrant if the two Houses unanimously send it up to him',[1] while Gladstone undoubtedly spoke for the Liberalism of his day when he wrote, 'The ideas and practice of the time of George III, whose will in certain matters limited the action of the ministers, cannot be received otherwise than by what would be on their part nothing less than a base compliance or shameful subserviency dangerous to the public weal and in the highest degree disloyal to the dynasty. It would be an evil and perilous day for the monarchy were any prospective possessor of the Crown to assume or claim for himself a preponderating, or even independent power in any one department of the State.'[2]

The Conservative standpoint at any rate after Disraeli had made his own opinions the official views of his party, was slightly different in theory, though almost identical in practice. It was the prestige, rather than the power, of the Crown which was increased when the Queen was made Empress of India, and Disraeli, who was a good deal of a charlatan but who nominally held the neo-Tory views of Canning concerning the throne, did nothing to arrest the decline of its power, while the Marquess of Salisbury was a pure Whig in these matters. If the Queen had fewer differences with her Conservative than with her Liberal ministers, it was merely because she was generally in agreement with their policy, not because they allowed her more independence of action. The methods of her two greatest ministers were different, for Gladstone addressed her as a public meeting, and Disraeli as a woman, but their attitude towards the Crown as an institution was the same: the Conservatives were certainly more attached than their opponents to the Imperial idea, but that was all.

Nevertheless, during the Victorian Age there was no legislative diminution of the power of the Crown, which was still considerable as even Bagehot admits:

> It would very much surprise people if they were only told how many things the Queen could do without consulting Parliament, and it has certainly so proved, for when the Queen abolished

[1] *The English Constitution*, ch. III. [2] *Gleanings of Past Years*, vol. I, p. 233.

> purchase in the Army by an act of prerogative (after the Lords had rejected the Bill for doing so), there was a great and general astonishment. But this is nothing to what the Queen can by law do without consulting Parliament. Not to mention other things, she could disband the Army (by law she cannot engage more than a certain number of men, but she is not obliged to engage any men); she could dismiss all the officers from the General Commander-in-Chief downwards; she could dismiss all the sailors too; she could sell off all our ships of war and all our naval stores; she could make peace by the sacrifice of Cornwall, and begin a war for the conquest of Brittany. She could make every citizen in the United Kingdom, male or female, a peer; she could make every parish in the United Kingdom a university; she could dismiss most of the Civil Servants; she could pardon all offenders. In a word, the Queen could by prerogative upset all the action of civil government within the government, could disgrace the nation by a bad war or peace, and could by disbanding our forces, whether land or sea, leave us defenceless against foreign nations.[1]

In one respect this statement requires qualification, and that is where the prerogative of pardon is concerned. It had originally been the duty of the Sovereign personally to consider every death sentence, and in cases where a reprieve was not granted to sign the warrant of execution addressed to the sheriff, but in the exercise of the prerogative of mercy he always acted on the advice of his ministers. George IV was the exception to most rulers, constitutional and otherwise, and in 1830 one Peter Comyn, a man of some position in County Clare, was convicted of arson in that he had burned his own house down; as this was a capital offence he was duly sentenced to death. Comyn, however, seems to have been popular in his own district, and his neighbours got up a petition to the King asking that he should be reprieved. George was greatly moved by this, so without consulting his ministers he wrote to the Lord-Lieutenant directing him not to proceed with the execution, but to substitute for it some lighter sentence as he might think fit.

This at once precipitated a constitutional crisis, for unknown to the King the Lord-Lieutenant had already decided, on the advice of the Irish law officers, to let the law take its course, so

[1] *The English Constitution*, Introduction.

when the Royal instructions reached him he applied to London for guidance. The Prime Minister was Wellington who, as we have seen, was not partial to George anyhow, and the Home Secretary was Sir Robert Peel. They both declared that the King's action was unconstitutional inasmuch as he had not beforehand asked the advice of the minister responsible for the exercise of the prerogative of mercy: Peel wrote to the Sovereign to this effect, and also intimated that he would resign if Comyn were not hanged. At this point further evidence was produced to the effect that Comyn had not only committed arson, but also perjury, in that he had sworn that his house had been set on fire by three men who subsequently proved to be perfectly innocent. Wellington then had an audience of the King who in consequence withdrew the order of reprieve, and Comyn was duly hanged. Partly to prevent a repetition of this unfortunate situation, and partly out of sentimentality, when the Queen came to the throne seven years later an Act of Parliament was passed providing that no report in regard to persons under sentence of death should be made to her, her heirs, and successors, and since then the prerogative of mercy has been exclusively with the Home Secretary.

Bagehot omitted one important asset enjoyed by the Crown, and it was that in the latter part of her reign the Queen, owing to the accumulated experience of so many years, was able to exercise very considerable personal influence over her ministers; for she could quote from her own experience precedents relating to events that had occurred before some of them were even born, and this gave her an enormous advantage in her dealings with them. For example, when Campbell-Bannerman was Secretary of State for War he took some Army scheme to the Queen for approval, and explained that it was an entirely new one. 'No, Mr Bannerman,' was the reply, 'Lord Palmerston proposed exactly the same thing to me in '52, and Lord Palmerston was wrong.'

Because the Queen was venerated in her last years this does not mean that such was always the case; indeed, not even Winston Churchill has experienced such vicissitudes in the matter of popularity. When she came to the throne she was eyed askance by the Tories who regarded her as a Whig puppet, not, it may be added, without considerable justification, for she regarded the Tories with disfavour and suspicion. For Melbourne she had the affection of a girl for her father, and Greville noted in his *Journal*, 'If Melbourne should be compelled to resign her privation will be the more bitter on account of the exclusiveness of her intimacy with him. Accordingly, her terror when any danger menaces the Government, her nervous apprehension at any appearance of change, affects her health, and upon one occasion during the last Session she actually fretted herself into an illness at the notion of their going out.' In May, 1839, the Whig administration, its majority in the House of Commons having fallen to five, decided to resign. The Queen was distraught. To quote Greville once again, 'Her agitation and grief were very great. In her interview with Lord John Russell[1] she was all the time dissolved in tears, and she dined in her own room and never appeared on that evening.' This attitude on the part of the Sovereign was the origin of the Bedchamber Plot.

In due course Sir Robert Peel was sent for to form a new ministry, and during the ensuing audience he told the Queen that the ladies of the Court, appointed by Melbourne, must be changed. She objected strongly, and said, 'They are my personal friends, and not party politicians. Why should I be required to part with them?' Peel replied that one of his chief problems would be Ireland, and that he could not be satisfied that he would have fair play if the wife of the Whig Lord-Lieutenant, and the sister of the Whig Chief Secretary, were in the most intimate daily intercourse with the Sovereign as Ladies of the Bedchamber. The Queen, however, refused to give way, and Peel left Buckingham Palace without having been commissioned to form a Government.

The next step in this extraordinary crisis was that the Queen wrote a letter to Melbourne, which he read out the next day at a meeting of the retiring Whig ministers; the relevant passages

[1] Then Leader of the House of Commons.

ran as follows: 'Do not fear that I was not calm and composed. They wanted to deprive me of my ladies, and I suppose they would deprive me next of my dressers and my housemaids. They wished to treat me like a girl, but I will show them that I am Queen of England.' Melbourne and his colleagues were not slow to take this opportunity of combining sentimentality with self-interest to remain in office, and on the Prime Minister's advice the Queen wrote to the Leader of the Opposition, 'The Queen, having considered the proposals made to her yesterday by Sir Robert Peel to remove the Ladies of her Bedchamber, cannot consent to a course which she considered to be contrary to usage and repugnant to her feelings'. It was all very much in the style of George III, and it is little wonder that the mob shouted 'Mrs Melbourne' at her. The whole affair created a sensation, and the Tory ladies were heard to say that when they did get into Buckingham Palace they would see to it that the young thing was kept in her proper constitutional place. The incident is certainly revealing, for 'what a testimony to the personal power of the Sovereign, and the extent to which party ends were served by Court intrigues, even as late in the nineteenth century, that a whisper in the ear of Queen Victoria, by her lady attendants, while she was having her hair done, should be regarded as fraught with trouble for a Tory Ministry'.[1]

There was a marked change in the Queen's attitude towards her Ministers after her marriage with Prince Albert in 1840, and the Conservatives could no longer complain of her bias in favour of the Whigs: she ceased to be a partisan, and became, instead, the critic and counsellor of her different Ministers irrespective of their party affiliations. As a result, she became more popular, and this popularity was enhanced by the Crimean War and the Indian Mutiny, for at such times there is always a tendency for Englishmen to rally round the throne. With the Prince Consort's death another change came, for the Queen withdrew from public life for many years, and this was resented by her subjects; indeed, it is a curious commentary upon the character of the English people that this retirement

[1] MacDonagh, M.: *The English King*, p. 206.

on the part of the Sovereign should have been followed by the growth of a definite, if short-lived, republican movement. The long mourning for a man who had never been popular in the land of his adoption aroused a feeling of resentment, which was not lessened by the subsequent overthrow of the Second Empire across the Channel.

To some extent the way for the republican movement had been paved by Thackeray, who lashed the House of Hanover with scorn in his lectures on *The Four Georges*, the reading of which prompted Walter Savage Landor to write:

I sing the Georges four,
For Providence could stand no more.
Some say that far the worst
Of all the four was George the First,
But yet by some 'tis reckoned,
That worser still was George the Second.
And what mortal ever heard,
Any good of George the Third?
When George the Fourth from earth descended,
Thank God the line of Georges ended.

When the French Empire fell the working classes, too, began to feel the time had come for them to do something, so on Sunday, September 19th, 1870, the Phrygian red cap was hoisted on poles in Trafalgar Square to the singing of the *Marseillaise*, and orators hailed the coming of the Republic of England. As a result of this demonstration a number of republican clubs were founded in London and the provinces, and Charles Bradlaugh, who had thrown himself wholeheartedly into the movement, published a pamphlet entitled *The Impeachment of the House of Brunswick*. It was couched in a peculiarly offensive style, and Bradlaugh did not hesitate to attack altar as well as throne, comparing the Trinity to a monkey with three tails. From his point of view, however, this was a tactical blunder, for however little interest the English may take in the practice of religion, blasphemy of this nature is always repugnant to them.

In a short time Sir Charles Dilke, whose father had received his baronetcy for services to the Prince Consort, John Morley, and Joseph Chamberlain made their appearance upon the republican platform, and Chamberlain declared at a meeting in Birmingham, 'I do not feel any great horror at the idea of the possible establishment of a republic in our country. I am quite certain that sooner or later it will come'. John Richard Green, the historian, held the same views, and with questionable taste he gave expression to them by sneering at the Queen for her anxiety when the Prince of Wales was seriously ill with typhoid fever. On March 19th, 1872, Dilke moved in the House of Commons for an enquiry into the Civil List, and he was supported by that most paradoxical of characters, Auberon Herbert, who in his youth had founded the Canning Club at Oxford. When the division was taken, the motion was rejected by 276 votes to 2, for its only supporters, in addition to the tellers, Dilke and Herbert, were Sir Wilfred Lawson, the temperance reformer, and George Anderson.

This outbreak of republicanism proved to be a mere flash in the pan. The upper and middle classes were, with the exceptions already quoted, solid in their support of the monarchy, and among the lower orders the overthrow of the throne only appealed to a few extremists, chiefly foreigners. The fact was that a monarchical reaction set in before the republicans had time to get their campaign properly started, and they were never afterwards able to make any effective headway. The nation took a different view from John Richard Green, and the recovery of the Prince of Wales awoke a widespread feeling of sympathy for him and for his mother. Then, again, the state of republican France, and of Spain, which was at the moment indulging in its favourite pastime of trying to exist without the Bourbons, was not such as to encourage Great Britain to conduct an experiment in republicanism. The Royal Family, too, had been by no means blind to the threat contained in the movement, and its members began once more to show themselves in public in the way that the people loved. As the years passed, and the Conservatives came into office, the Imperial conception of the Crown began to develop, and it was realized that the establishment of an English republic would spell the end of the British Empire. In these circumstances there were clearly no votes to be gained by a continued devotion to republicanism, and so, ere long, Dilke kissed hands upon appointment to a post in the ministry; Chamberlain gave the Prince and Princess of Wales the warmest of greetings when they visited Birmingham, of which city he was then Mayor; and Morley finished his career as a peer of the realm. Republicanism seemed but an evil memory at the Diamond Jubilee in 1897, when the Empire rallied round the throne in a demonstration of loyalty to Queen and Motherland, which had never been seen before, and was never to be seen again, a demonstration, it may be noticed, organized by the man who had not felt 'any great horror at the idea of the possible establishment of a republic', namely Joseph Chamberlain.

At the same time it must be admitted that in restoring the prestige of the monarchy the Queen was inclined to look for inspiration to contemporary Germany with its rigid class distinctions. When a débutante attending a Drawing Room entered the Throne Room, where her name was called out by the Lord Chamberlain, she found herself in the presence of a little stout body in a plain dress relieved by the blue of the Garter Ribbon worn across her breast. There were groups of brilliant figures in the room, such as members of the Royal Family, ambassadors and ministers, and the ladies and gentlemen of the Household, yet somehow, amid this glittering throng, the little old lady in black stood out prominently with the throne as her background. As the débutante approached the Queen extended her right hand, which the lady being presented, placing the back of her own ungloved hand underneath, kissed as she curtseyed. Occasionally there was a variation in the procedure, when the Queen, instead of giving her hand to be kissed, kissed the débutante herself on the forehead or cheek: those favoured in this way were the daughters of dukes, marquesses, or earls.

This custom was not, of course, foolproof, and at one Drawing Room the wife of a knight was announced, and the Queen by inadvertence was about to salute her as if she were a member of this privileged circle, when a Gentleman-in-Waiting, shocked out of his good manners by the impending breach of etiquette, called out in a voice that echoed through the room, 'Don't kiss her, Your Majesty; she's not a real lady'.

Apart from these formal occasions kissing of an official nature fell out of fashion during the Victorian Age. The Queen exchanged kisses with Napoleon III when he visited England for the first time as Emperor, and when she made him a Knight of the Garter at Windsor she kissed him again on both cheeks: this was done with great ceremony in the presence of the assembled Court, but we are told that all the same there were irreverent giggles among the young Maids of Honour. Earlier, George IV had been in the habit of kissing Cabinet ministers on resignation, but this custom lapsed, and it was not revived by the Queen's successors.

To the very end of the reign the honour of presentation at a Drawing Room or Levee was undreamed of except by those who were already included in what was called fashionable society, and it was confined chiefly to the families of the aristocracy and country gentry, and the higher ranks of the Church and the Fighting Services. Distinguished members of the medical and legal professions were also regarded as entitled to the privilege, but to literature and the stage, and more so to trade, the Queen showed a face of reserve. Those engaged in manufacture and commerce on a large scale were not debarred, but the line was strictly drawn at retail trade, however extensive its operations, though the daughters of wealthy commercial men were not excluded from Drawing Rooms if their education, social associations, and moral character were above suspicion.

Four years before the end of the reign came the Diamond Jubilee of which it was the apogee. Stephen McKenna has summed up this last phase of the Victorian Age very well in the sentiments which he put into the mouth of George Oakleigh in *Sonia*. 'One thing that the Boer War ended was the Jubilee phase, the Victorian position of England in the world. Seated at a first-floor window halfway up Ludgate Hill I watched the little old Queen driving to the service of thanksgiving at St. Paul's escorted by troops drawn from every quarter of the globe. The blaze of their uniforms has not yet quite died from my eyes. I awoke with quickly beating heart to some conception of the Empire over which she ruled, some realization of the gigantic growth in our wealth and power during the two generations that she had sat the throne. Then followed the Naval Review. It was as though we flung a mailed gauntlet in the face of anyone who should venture to doubt our supremacy. For more than two years after that England basked in the consciousness of invincibility. . . . It needed the severest of our first Transvaal reverses to remind us that the Jubilee pageant was over, and our lath-and-plaster reputation being tested by fire and steel.'

By the end of her reign the Queen had become a legend, for it is a curious fact that while the actual powers of the monarchy declined the Sovereign herself drew further away from her subjects than had any of her predecessors on the throne; perhaps, indeed, the two events were not unconnected. It was to no inconsiderable extent the coming of the railways which made this development possible–there was no scope for the V.I.P. when travelling had to be done by road. Such being the case it was out of the question for Queen Victoria to know England as Louis XIV, for example, had known France. From infancy he had travelled, often in the most uncomfortable circumstances, over the length and breadth of the country, and in the days of the Fronde he had been driven from place to place as the fortunes of war swung this way or that, and he knew how the ordinary Frenchman lived. Louis had spent hours talking to the landlord of a wayside inn while a broken axle was receiving attention, and he had sheltered in farm-houses when torrents of rain rendered impossible further progress along a flooded road. With the improvement in the means of communication such sources of information were closed to Queen Victoria. At the same time she was one of the most consummate actresses who ever sat upon a throne, and 'The Widow of Windsor' was her own creation. When the late Sir Archibald

Boyd-Carpenter, the son of her favourite bishop and then a young man, was about to go out to the South African War, she sent for him, and to his great surprise in view of her notorious disapproval of smoking presented him with a cigar-case. 'As you are well aware,' said the Queen, 'I dislike smoking, but I know that when you young men are out on the veldt you will smoke whether I like it or not, so when you do smoke I want you to think of a lonely old woman at Windsor.' Of one thing, too, there can be no doubt, and it is that Queen Victoria was a very different woman when she ascended the throne from what she was when she died, for as a young girl there was more than a dash of her cousin, Princess Charlotte, in her composition. The change was due to the Prince Consort.

Of her devotion to him there can be no question, and she was broken-hearted when he died in 1861. 'It was the first grief he caused me,' she used to say in later years; and as she herself lay dying her last words were a cry of 'Albert, Albert, Albert.' Yet she was almost alone in her affection for him. He was a man of high ideals and many intellectual interests, while he did much to promote science, learning, philanthropy, and public decorum. To the British of all classes, however, he was an insignificant German princeling, wholly unworthy to marry a Queen of England. Unhappily for him his manners were stiff, reserved, and a little pedantic. He took no interest in sport, and from the point-of-view of many people this failing was not atoned for by his serious and scholarly character. As a result he was persistently disparaged, and he was sometimes even suspected of being a traitor. It was widely believed at the time of the Crimean War that Palmerston detected him in the betrayal of State secrets to Russia, while two London morning papers actually announced that he had been arrested by order of the Government on a charge of High Treason, and was about to be sent to the Tower. In consequence an immense crowd assembled on Tower Hill to gloat their eyes on the Prince loaded with chains, and shout their execrations at him.

Even to-day it is the upper classes who to no inconsiderable extent influence public opinion where members of the Royal

Family are concerned, and a century ago this was much more the case. The Prince, like the Duke of Edinburgh, was interested in everything–geology and art, building and mechanics, they were all one to him, and these interests demanded friendships outside the ranks of the governing class. The British aristocracy, on the other hand, was still much under the influence of Lord Chesterfield's dictum that 'a man of fashion, who is seen piping or fiddling at a concert, degrades his own dignity. If you love music, pay fiddlers to play for you, but never play yourself. It makes a gentleman appear frivolous and contemptible.' When the Prince entertained artists and scientists he had to look outside the ranks of the aristocracy, and this caused much raising of eyebrows; so much so in fact that the King of the Belgians wrote to the Queen, 'The dealings with artists, for instance, require great prudence. They are acquainted with all classes of society, and for that very reason dangerous.' On the other hand, with the serious middle-class to whom he talked of schools and docks, of architecture and warehouses, he slowly but surely became an undoubted success. He went, for example, to Liverpool in July, 1846, and standing beside the Mayor he was assured that the people of Merseyside appreciated the zeal he was displaying in promoting the best interests of mankind. His solidity appealed to them, and they felt that they understood him. 'With Mayors and Councillors he could talk of welfare and progress–religion, science, and philanthropy.'[1] It was the upper and lower classes that never appreciated him.

In retrospect it is possible to see how the very fact that he was a foreigner, and as such was able to regard the problems of his adopted country more objectively than could any Englishman, enabled him to exercise a moderating influence upon both the Queen and her advisers. For example, after the suppression of the Indian Mutiny an outcry for vengeance arose, and Lord Canning, the Governor-General, writing privately to the Queen on September 25th, 1857, said, 'There is a rabid and indiscriminate vindictiveness abroad, even among many who ought to set a better example, which it is

[1] Bolitho, H.: *Albert the Good*, p. 153.

impossible to contemplate without a feeling of shame for one's countrymen'. In reply, the Sovereign said that she shared 'his feelings of sorrow and indignation at the unchristian spirit shown, alas, to a great extent here by the public towards Indians in general, and towards Sepoys without discrimination'. This attitude was due, she explained, to the horror of the 'unspeakable atrocities perpetrated on innocent women and children', and for these 'stern justice must be dealt out to all the guilty'; but to the faithful natives the greatest kindness should be shown. 'They should know that there is no hatred to a brown skin–none; but the greatest wish on their Queen's part to see them happy, contented, and flourishing.' Would the Queen have taken quite the same view in the pre- or post-Albert period? It is at least doubtful.

On another occasion the tact and judgment of Prince Albert probably averted a war between Great Britain and the United States. In November, 1861, during the American Civil War the British mail steamer 'Trent' was boarded by the Federal vessel 'San Jacinto', and two Confederate agents, Slidell and Mason, who were on their way to England, were taken out of her. This affront to the British flag naturally aroused the greatest indignation in England, and Palmerston decided to send to Washington a stiff demand for the immediate release of the Confederate envoys. This despatch was in due course submitted to the Queen, who showed it to the Prince, then lying on his deathbed. He toned it down, and in its revised form it was adopted by the Government. When it was presented by the British ambassador, Lord Lyons, to the American Secretary of State, Seward, the latter said before he opened it, 'Everything will depend on the tone of it'. Happily, the note smoothed the way to peace instead of provoking war. When the crisis was over, and the Prince Consort was dead, Palmerston wrote to the Queen, 'There can be no doubt that the alterations made in the despatch to Lord Lyons contributed essentially to the satisfactory settlement of the dispute. Those alterations were only one of innumerable instances of the tact and judgment, and the power of nice discrimination, which excited Lord Palmerston's constant and unbounded admiration.' That was monarchy at its best.

On the other hand, had the Prince Consort lived for another twenty or thirty years the development of the Constitution might have been very different, for his conception of the rôle of the Crown was poles asunder from that of contemporary statesmen. From the beginning he left nothing undone to fit himself for the position which he regarded as properly his, namely that of 'permanent private secretary and adviser to the Queen', and in a private memorandum found among his papers after his death he wrote: 'Why are princes alone to be denied the credit of having political opinions, based upon an anxiety for the national interests, their country's honour, and the welfare of mankind? Are they not more independently placed than any other politician in the State? Are their interests not most intimately bound up with those of their country? Is the Sovereign not the natural guardian of the honour of his country? Is he not necessarily a politician?' In effect, the Prince desired that the Queen should rule as well as reign, which may be sound doctrine, as all true monarchists must agree, but how it would have been received by the Conservative and Liberal Parties in the seventies and eighties is another matter.

Bagehot's comments on the position of the Prince Consort are not without interest:

> It is known, too, to every one conversant with the real course of the recent history of England, that Prince Albert really did gain great power. . . . He had the rare gifts of a constitutional monarch. If his life had been prolonged twenty years, his name would have been known to Europe as that of King Leopold is known. While he lived he was at a disadvantage. The statesmen who had most power in England were men of far greater experience than himself. He might, and no doubt did, exercise a great, if not a commanding influence over Lord Malmesbury, but he could not rule Lord Palmerston. The old statesman who governed England, at an age when most men are unfit to govern their own families, remembered a whole generation of statesmen who were dead before Prince Albert was born. The two were of different

> ages and different natures. The elaborateness of the German prince–an elaborateness which has been justly and happily compared with that of Goethe–was wholly alien to the half-Irish, half-English, statesman. The somewhat boisterous courage in minor dangers, and the obtrusive use of an always effectual but not always refined, common-place, which are Lord Palmerston's defects, doubtless grated on Prince Albert, who had a scholar's caution and a scholar's courage . . . Prince Albert did much, but he died ere he could have made his influence felt on a generation of statesmen less experienced than he was, and anxious to learn from him.

On at least one occasion he interfered in the working of the Constitution in a way which would probably be regarded as improper in the present Duke of Edinburgh. It was in December, 1852, when Lord Derby on resigning the Premiership volunteered the suggestion that the Queen should send for Lord Lansdowne. 'I interrupted Lord Derby', the Prince has left on record, 'saying that, constitutionally, it did not rest with him to give advice and become responsible for it, and that nobody, therefore, could properly throw the responsibility of the Queen's choice of a new minister upon him.' Whether Derby relished this lecture upon the niceties of constitutional procedure may be doubted, but Lansdowne did not become Prime Minister.

There was also a strongly religious basis to the Prince's conception of kingship. He could not, circumstanced as the Queen was, believe in Divine Right, but he did hold the view that the monarchy should be a moral agency like the Church. The Sovereign should be seen as the personification of honour, virtue, and justice, and should be at once an example and a blessing to his subjects. When, on November 9th, 1841, the future Edward VII was born, the Prince felt that his chance had come to educate an heir apparent along his own lines, and he set about the task with a will. In this, as in everything else, the Queen agreed with him, though with the added determination that her eldest son should in no way resemble his great-uncle George IV of scandalous memory.

The Prince of Wales, as he was soon to become, early gave

rise to a dispute in military circles, for the precise moment of his birth was 10.48 a.m. It was customary when the Sovereign gave birth to a child for the officer in command of the guard at St. James's Palace to receive promotion. Now the guard was changed at 10.45 a.m., so the new guard had marched into Palace Yard, and taken over its duties three minutes before the birth. On the other hand the officer in command of the old guard claimed that as his sentries were still on duty at 10.48 it was he, not his successor, who should be promoted. The knotty point was referred to the Commander-in-Chief, Lord Hill, for a decision.

King Edward VII has been compared with Shakespeare's Prince Hal, who became the model monarch Henry V, and there is something in the comparison, though it must be remembered that even in his feverish youth he never allowed his pleasures to interfere with the performance of his duties. What, too, is often forgotten in this connection is that no Prince of Wales ever had to serve so long an apprenticeship for monarchy as he did, for at the time of his accession he was in his sixtieth year. His education was of the most deplorable and unsuitable kind, under the well-intentioned, but wholly misguided, direction of his father and Baron Stockmar. Queen Victoria not only inherited that attitude of suspicion towards the Heir Apparent which marked all the monarchs of the House of Hanover, but, as has been shown, she was obsessed with the fear that her eldest son might come to resemble her uncles in general, and the so-called First Gentleman of Europe in particular. Unhappily, in her attempt to prevent such a development she adopted, like so many parents in every walk of life, the very method most calculated to produce the result she was at such pains to avoid.

The boy's education was certainly no case of spare the rod and spoil the child, for often, when he committed some slight act of disobedience, his mother, then and there, in the presence of the ladies and gentlemen of the Court, would put him across her knee, and whack him with her slipper. Such treatment may well be justified in the case of a child, but the tragedy was that she continued to treat him as a child long after he had ceased to be one. When he came of age, shortly after his father's early death, she refused to allow him to have any regular and responsible employment, so that he was compelled to expend his enormous energies, and to dissipate his great and growing powers, on a number of petty, and in some cases unworthy, pursuits. Such, rather than any real tendency to vice, was the explanation of the Tranby Croft scandal and of the Prince's appearance in the Mordaunt case, of which more anon. Yet he travelled widely, both abroad and in what was then the British Empire; he took the lead in many notable philanthropic movements, especially those which had as their objects the provision of houses and hospitals for the poorer classes; and he did a great deal to raise the tone of sport. From politics, however, he was excluded. In vain one Prime Minister after another, Liberal and Conservative alike, implored the Queen to give him some work to do, whether it was to learn the routine of Government departments, to go through the discipline of the Army, to administer India, or, above all, to live in Ireland as his mother's representative. The Queen was adamant in her refusal, 'evidently haunted', to quote the late Professor Hearnshaw, 'by the fear that Albert Edward if allowed any independence would develop the undesirable filial features of one or other of the four Georges'. Queen Victoria was unquestionably a great monarch, but she was a poor mother to her eldest son. In the circumstances the astonishing thing is not that he kicked over the traces so much, but that he did it so little.

What is inclined to be forgotten is that the Prince of Wales was a very complex character. He inherited in almost equal proportions the frivolity and the buffoonery of the House of Hanover, and the seriousness and devotion to duty of the House of Coburg. His own special characteristic was a charm of manner for which one would have to go back to Charles II for a parallel, and which he has not transmitted to any of his descendants. These hereditary influences explain why he could spend a day upon the most boring public duties without giving the least indication of boredom, and in the evening amuse himself in sliding down a flight of stairs on a tea-tray or baiting some poor toady with billiard cues. What else could be expected of one who was at once the son of the Prince Consort and the great-nephew of George IV, and who had been treated like a school-boy at an age when most of his contemporaries were grown men of the world?

Like all prominent members of a Royal Family, especially in England where snobbery and class-consciousness are so inextricably mixed, the Prince of Wales alternated between adulation and criticism, and the lowest point his reputation reached was during the Mordaunt case in 1870 and the Tranby Croft case in 1890, of which some account must be given in any description of the Victorian Age.

In February, 1870, Sir Charles Mordaunt brought a divorce suit against his wife, and in this two co-respondents, both friends of the Prince, were cited, while in the husband's petition he declared that his wife had confessed to misconduct with the heir to the throne himself. The Prince was duly subpœnaed and appeared in the witness-box, and a dozen letters from him to Lady Mordaunt were produced in court, but they contained nothing that any man might not have written to another man's wife. The imputation against him therefore rested entirely on the alleged confession of Lady Mordaunt, who had long been queer in the head and at the time of the trial was a certified lunatic, and it was dismissed as being unfounded. All the same a certain amount of opprobrium stuck to the Prince, and when he next appeared at Epsom there was some hissing.

Like his grandson King Edward VIII, the Prince of Wales considered his private life to concern nobody except himself: he was no wilder than his friends and contemporaries, but the difference was that they had work to do while he had not, and this fact encouraged the hereditary Hanoverian tendency to dissipation and, on occasion, somewhat vulgar horseplay. So his popularity waxed and waned over the years, until in 1890 it reached its nadir in the Tranby Croft Case.

He was staying for the St. Leger meeting of that year with a Mr Arthur Wilson, a shipowner of Hull, at his house at Tranby

Croft, near Doncaster. One of his favourite games was baccarat, and he had certainly intended to play it during the evenings after the races for he took with him a box of counters, representing values from five shillings to ten pounds. On the first evening of his visit a table was got up, and the Prince took the bank himself. During the play a son of the house thought he saw Sir William Gordon Cumming, Regimental Lieutenant-Colonel of the Scots Guards, cheating by the device known as *la poussette*. This meant that if he received good cards he pushed more counters over the white line drawn round the table to mark off the area of staked money from that of the unstaked, but if he received bad cards he withdrew the counters under cover of his hands. Young Wilson communicated what he thought he had seen to his neighbour, Berkeley Levett, who was also in the Scots Guards, and they both watched Gordon Cumming very carefully, with the result that they saw him do it again. Before going to bed that night Wilson informed his mother, and next morning before going to the races two other members of the house party, namely his sister and brother-in-law, were also told.[1]

There were five people now in the secret, and on the following evening when baccarat was again played, they all agreed that they had seen Sir William cheat once more. On this they proceeded to inform two more people, Lord Coventry and General Owen Williams, and these two, although they had themselves seen nothing suspicious, accepted the evidence of the other five. It is a moot point whether in view of the presence of so august a guest young Wilson would not have done better to have kept his mouth shut in the first instance, but his blunder was venial compared with that of the seven of them who proceeded to tell the Prince, and thus to place on him the responsibility for all future proceedings.

This should surely never have been done, and the situation was made worse by the step which he took, for he required Sir William on pain of exposure to sign a declaration promising

[1] The best account of this unsavoury affair is to be found in Lord Russell of Liverpool's, *Though the Heavens Fall*, pp. 83–99.

never again to play cards for money. Two more men, who had hitherto known nothing about it, were called in as signatory witnesses, and Sir William was informed that if he signed the document the others promised never to reveal what had happened. In acting in this manner the Prince broke a regulation in not insisting that the accused should ask for a military enquiry since he had been accused of dishonourable conduct. What happened was that the unhappy man signed, all the while protesting his innocence. On the whole incident Lord Russell of Liverpool has commented, 'It would seem incredible that an officer of such a distinguished regiment, who had been acquainted with the Prince of Wales for over twenty years and a personal friend for over ten, should swindle his future Sovereign by cheating at cards, not only in the presence of two of his oldest friends and sitting within a few feet of his hostess and other members of her house-party, but in a manner which could hardly be expected to escape detection'.[1]

However this may be it was not long before it became clear that Sir William had signed to no purpose, for in due course he received an anonymous letter from Paris which showed that his secret had been betrayed, and he therefore brought an action for slander against the five people who alleged that they had seen him cheat. The Tranby Croft Case, as it was generally termed, was one of the most famous in English legal history, and the Prince was cited as a witness. Just as he was leaving the witness-box a juryman asked him whether he believed Sir William to be guilty or innocent. It was an awkward position, for if he believed him innocent he would surely never have been signatory to a paper that really proved he was not: if he believed him guilty, he should have insisted that the matter be reported to the Commander-in-Chief. What the Prince did reply was to say that he was forced to believe the testimony of so many witnesses who swore they had actually seen him cheat. That settled it: after a case lasting a week the jury were only absent from the box for thirteen minutes, and they found for the defendants.

[1] *Op. cit.*, p. 94.

This case was the signal for one of those outbreaks of hypocrisy which at regular intervals distinguish the British Press, and the Prince, his friends, and the amusements in which they indulged, particularly cards, were painted in the blackest colours. *The Times* considered it a pity that the Prince had not signed a declaration similar to that extracted from Sir William Gordon-Cumming; the *Nottingham Express* declared that the British Empire was humiliated; and the *Liverpool Courier*, described a game of baccarat as 'a gambler's orgy'. Needless to say the Churches joined in the cry, and, as Lord Russell of Liverpool rightly says, 'pride of place' must go to the Venerable Dr Douglas of Montreal: 'Another year has brought sadness and sorrow to the bosom of our gracious Queen and a diminished spirit to meet the responsibilities of her high position; while over the throne the black shadow of a ghastly spectre has fallen. Among us has risen a second George IV in the heir to the throne of this vast Empire. He has been convicted of being concerned in an infamous abomination, and the awful spectacle is presented of the heir to the throne publicly acknowledging complicity in gambling transactions.'

It only remains to add that the one sensible person at Tranby Croft was the host who went to bed, and the only person implicated who was deserving of any praise was the lady who married Sir William on the very day after the adverse verdict was given, and was snubbed by her family for so doing. On June 12th a notice appeared in the *London Gazette* erasing Gordon Cumming from the Army, 'the Queen having no further occasion for his services'; on the 16th the secretary of the Carlton Club announced his resignation to the committee; and on May 20th, 1930, he died at his home in Scotland, where he had lived in retirement ever since his trial.

Apart from the attitude of the Press the Prince came badly out of the affair. 'More than once before the barometer of public opinion had sunk to stormy: the Mordaunt case, his rumoured debts, his associates, the conduct of his private life as garnished up in the gutter-press, had threatened tempest, and now it came. He was made the scapegoat on whom was

The Prince Consort as Colonel of the Grenadier Guards reviewing British troops in 1854. In the background is the Emperor Napoleon III

'A Quiet Round Game' from the cartoon in *Truth*, December 1891

laid the iniquity of all, and if it had been he who had conspired to watch the suspect, or if it had been he who had been detected cheating, he could not have been subjected to more bitter vituperation.'[1] There was also a great deal of hypocritical talk about the example set by the Prince and his friends, and this was compared most unfavourably with that of the Queen, but it is difficult to resist the conclusion that most of what was, and is, said about Royal influence on the nation's morals is very wide of the mark.

The Queen and the Prince Consort had for twenty years given an example of a dutiful, godly, and serious life, but there is no real reason to suppose that they, or for that matter Queen Elizabeth II and the Duke of Edinburgh, affected the moral tone of the country, or that adultery, drunkenness, and gambling were greatly diminished in those two decades owing to their moral splendour. They set the tone of their immediate circle, for they saw to it that the Court should be composed of people of the utmost respectability, but it is hard to believe that their domestic devotion restrained the amorous inclinations of a citizen of Windsor towards his neighbour's wife; that a heavy drinker at Ballater corked up his whisky-bottle because the Queen was abstemious; or that there was less betting at race-meetings because the Queen never put a shilling on a horse. Moral reforms and deteriorations are moved by large forces, and they are mostly caused by reactions from the habits of a preceding period. Backwards and forwards swings the great pendulum, and its alternations are not determined by a few distinguished folk clinging to the end of it. No doubt the influence of the Marlborough House set was wider than the Queen's and the Prince Consort's had ever been, because their circle was strictly limited and water-tight, and for the last forty years of her reign the Queen had no social influence of any sort thanks to her determined seclusion of herself; but to attribute to the Prince and his friends any responsibility for a widespread laxity of morals is to make far too much of their rumoured disregard of them. 'Nobody coveted his neighbour's wife because

[1] Benson, E. F.: *King Edward VII*, p. 158.

Lord Charles Beresford had liberal ideas on the subject, any more than Nelson corrupted the morals of the Navy because he was popularly supposed to be very good friends with Lady Hamilton.'[1]

The fact is that the Prince of Wales was a man of high spirit and boundless energy, and fettered as he was by his mother's orders it was only natural that he should on occasion break out in questionable directions. Yet he worked hard where he was allowed to work at all, and where the welfare of the working-classes were concerned he was indefatigable, as he proved in the case of the Housing Commission and the Aged Poor Commission. It was the same in his advocacy of the Deceased Wife's Sister Bill, and he twice presented petitions in the House of Lords in its favour. This was a measure which cut across party loyalties, though the votes of the bishops in the Upper House were solid against it. In face of this opposition it was not until 1896 that it passed the third reading in the House of Lords, and then, as the Archbishop of Canterbury bitterly remarked, 'only because the Prince whipped up a number of sporting young peers who had never previously attended a debate in their lives'. All the same, it was not until 1907 when the Prince had become King Edward VII, and his Liberal friends were in office, that the Deceased Wife's Sister Bill became law.

There was also a great humanity about him which a later generation has to no inconsiderable extent forgotten. One year at the Grand National his horse, Ambush, was leading the field when he crashed into the last fence, and hung on the top. The Prince came to the front of his box, with his glasses to his eyes, and an equerry was sent running down the course. 'Is the man hurt? Is the man hurt? Find out if the man's hurt,' came echoing in that deep voice which was so well known on the racecourse. 'No, sir, the man's all right,' reported someone, and after that, to quote an eye-witness, 'the Royal owner seemed to lose all interest'. When Ginistrelli won the Derby at 100 to 1 with Signorinetta he led in the winner dressed in his homely tweeds and his sombrero. In consequence he was in a state of

[1] Benson, E. F., *op. cit.*, pp. 160–161.

consternation when he was told that the King wished to congratulate him. 'But I cannot go! Look at my clothes! I cannot go in this clothing! Cannot I go when I have fresh clothes?' cried the bewildered old gentleman, but he was quickly put at ease by the congratulations of King Edward, who insisted on a glass of champagne to the health of the mare.

One asset the Prince certainly possessed, and that was the ability to learn by experience, so when he himself had sons he took care to see that they came under a very different regime from that to which he had been subject. He determined that they should have the companionship which had been denied him, and when the Duke of Clarence was thirteen and the future King George V was eleven, he had them sent to train as naval cadets for a couple of years in the 'Britannia'. After that they went off without any equerries, and only one tutor to look after them both, for a couple of cruises that lasted three years. All this was in marked contrast with the regime imposed on him when he had gone to Rome in charge of Governor Bruce and his tutor, spent the morning in study, relaxed in the afternoon in museums and the Forum, wrote his diary when he returned, and entertained distinguished people twice a week at dinner. He had not been allowed to visit foreign embassies or even to see the King of Italy for fear of the effect upon his morals–he was young Lord Renfrew intent on the study of archaeology. His sons were treated very differently, for they were put up in a palace in Cairo by the Khedive when they visited him, and they were received in state by the Emperor of Japan. On their return the Duke of York went back to the Navy, which was to be his profession, and the Duke of Clarence was given a couple of years at Cambridge where he lived in college in the ordinary way in marked contrast with the life of his father at Christ Church, where he resided in a house hired for the purpose, and was not allowed to smoke.

The other members of the Royal Family were legacies from the past. Foremost among them, and by no means the least able, was 'wicked Uncle Ernest', whom the Queen's mother, the Duchess of Kent, always suspected of the intention to murder her daughter. Until the birth of the Princess Royal he was Heir Presumptive to the throne. He was very unpopular in England where he was widely suspected of having murdered his valet, and he was extraordinarily indifferent to the feelings of others. 'Ernest is not a bad fellow', said his brother, William IV, 'but if anyone has a corn, he will be sure to tread on it.' On the death of William IV he succeeded to the kingdom of Hanover, where the so-called Salic Law prevailed, and his first act on arrival was to declare invalid the Constitution which had been granted by his brother in 1833, and this made him more unpopular still in Liberal circles in England. All the same he soon ingratiated himself with his new subjects, and when practically every throne on the mainland of Europe was rocking in 1848 he had singularly little trouble. He died in 1851, at the age of eighty, and was succeeded by his son, George V, who was expelled by the Prussians in 1866 for his adherence to the Habsburgs in the Seven Weeks' War.

There was certainly no love lost between Uncle Ernest and the Prince Consort, and when he came to England for the wedding of Princess Augusta of Cambridge there was a scene between them. 'It almost came to a fight with the King', the Prince Consort wrote to his brother. 'He insisted on having the place at the altar, where we stood. He wanted to drive me away and, against all custom, he wanted to accompany Victoria and lead her. I was to go behind him. I was forced to give him a strong punch and drive him down a few steps, where the First Master of Ceremonies took him and led him out of the Chapel. We had a second scene, when he would not allow me to sign the register with Victoria. He laid his fist on the book. We manœuvred round the table, and Victoria had the book handed to her across the table. Now the table was between us, and he could see what was being done. After a third trial to force Victoria to do what he commanded, but in vain, he left the party in great wrath. Since then, we let him go, and, happily, he fell over some stones in Kew, and damaged some ribs.'

A more attractive character as an uncle was the Duke of Sussex. Melbourne had pressed his appointment as Lord-

Lieutenant of Ireland. Like so many members of the British Royal Family there was a streak of eccentricity about him, and in his Will was the following clause: 'I desire that on my death my body may be opened, and should the examination present anything useful or interesting to science, I empower my executors to make it public. And I desire to be buried in the public cemetery at Kensal Green in the Parish of Harrow, in the County of Middlesex, and not at Windsor.' This last instruction put the cat among the pigeons where the sticklers for protocol were considered, but after some hesitation his wishes were respected; the body lay in state in Kensington, and was buried in the Kensal Green Cemetery. The Duke's matrimonial affairs were also somewhat complicated, for his first marriage in 1793 to Lady Augusta Murray, daughter of the fourth Earl of Dunmore, was declared void under the Royal Marriage Act. He married a second time, on this occasion to a widow, who was created Duchess of Inverness, with remainder to her heirs-male.

Most of the Queen's relatives died off during the earlier part of her reign, with the exception of her cousin, the second Duke of Cambridge, who with the best will in the world was liable to be an embarrassment at times. He had been born in 1819, and he had had a good war record in the Crimea, so in 1856 he was appointed Commander-in-Chief, a post which he held for the next thirty-nine years. He clung with singular pertinacity to this position, and he resisted with all his powers any attempt at the establishment of a Parliamentary control such as administered the affairs of the Navy through the Board of Admiralty. He was, in effect, a soldier of the most antique mess-room type, judging the efficiency of a regiment by its speckless appearance on parade, and making seniority in the service the sole passport to promotion. He did not want new ideas to unsettle the Army, for the organization that won the battle of Waterloo was good enough for him, and these reforming young officers like Wolseley, whom he detested, must wait their turn. Nor did the Duke take kindly to officers who came from the commercial classes, and the story is told that when he was inspecting a Dragoon Guards regiment a member of the Gunter family, the confectioners, worked his horse up into a lather: the Commander-in-Chief noticed this, and shouted to the wretched officer, 'What have you done to that horse? Ice him, damn you, ice him.' It was not until he was seventy-six that the Duke was induced to resign.

As with the Prince of Wales, so with her other relatives with the exception of the Duke of Cambridge, the Queen would not allow them any responsibility. They were invariably treated with the respect due to their rank, but it was well known that they had no influence over her at all. It was, of course, a great deal easier for Queen Victoria to control the Royal Family than it has been for her successors. Royalty was not 'news' as it is now, and so she could do what she liked without the fear that there would be unpleasant reactions in the Press. If there was more hostility to the monarchy as an institution in some quarters than is now the case there was a great deal more respect for Royal personages; the age of lampoons and caricatures was over, and that of the columnist and the snap-shot had not yet arrived; in the interval they were regarded as a class apart, and within certain very broad limits the public was quite satisfied that the Queen should regulate their lives. Furthermore, the members of the Royal Family were not dogged by reporters and camera-men wherever they went. It may be that the light beat fiercely enough upon the Sovereign, but it did not beat nearly as fiercely upon her relatives as was later to be the case.

CHAPTER III

A Victorian Seaport: Liverpool

Liverpool was pre-eminently the seaport of the Victorian Age. It is true that London was a bigger port, but it was more than a seaport. The ships which sought London pushed their slow way up the devious course of the Thames until they reached the narrow anchorage below London Bridge, but the craft which were moored there had long left the sea behind. 'They lay to their anchors, picturesque additions to an animated scene, adding to the business of a capital occupied with almost every interest under the sun; but ships, crews, and cargoes formed only some elements of a marvellous and miscellaneous activity, and the sailors who wandered from the river bank were soon lost in a varied crowd.'[1] London as a port was in fact merged in London as a capital. Then there was Bristol, which had been Liverpool's great rival in the eighteenth century, but which she had vanquished by the time that the Queen came to the throne. In any case Bristol lay ten miles up a narrow and tortuous stream, and was the chief town of a rich valley of the West, its position in a fruitful agricultural district gave it a distinctly inland atmosphere in spite of its old and honourable connection with the sea. Its interests, too, were numerous, and by the end of the Victorian Age its manufactures were more important than its commerce.

From the beginning of its history Liverpool, by reason of its geographical situation, had been singularly isolated from the rest of England, and even from the rest of Lancashire. It had

[1] Roscoe, E. S.: *The English Scene in the Eighteenth Century*, pp. 107–108.

been content with its maritime highway, and it had not troubled to come into closer touch with the inland portions of the kingdom. Just as the French Canadian *habitant*, dwelling in the white villages which nestle under the solitary and impassable hills which border the St Lawrence, looks on that river not as an immense barrier, but only as a connecting-link with the world beyond the seas, so the Liverpudlian has for the last two centuries regarded the Mersey. To him the sea unites rather than divides, and especially was this the case in the early years of the nineteenth century, when he looked on the river as his outlet, rather than the miry tracks which led from Liverpool across the bleakest of countrysides to other centres of population.

A few statistics will prove the isolation of the city in the period immediately preceding the Victorian Age. In 1753 the only means of communication with London was by stage wagons, of which the quickest took ten days on the journey. It was not until 1760 that the first stage-coach to London made its appearance; it covered the distance in forty-eight hours, and was called, 'The London and Liverpool Flying Machine'. In that same year the road to Warrington was made practicable for carriages, but even fifteen years later one postman met the requirements of the whole city. In 1784 mail-coaches were started, but at first they carried only four passengers in addition to the guard and the coachman, each of whom was armed with a blunderbuss. Goods were conveyed by sea for the most part to the other ports of the kingdom.

In spite of the fact that the city had received its charter from John so long ago as 1208 its growth had been slow.

In the fourteenth century Liverpool played an important part in the later Irish wars. Twice the Viceroy and his army passed through the city; several times the shipping in all the ports on the West coast was ordered to be collected in the Mersey for the conveyance of troops; and hardly a year passed without the Great Heath being the scene of an encampment of men waiting for a fair wind. This was good for trade, since war, although often bad for the country as a whole, generally brings wealth to the ports of embarkation, for not only have armies to be transported, but they have to be supplied. So Liverpool shipping prospered, and the trade with Ireland increased.

On the other hand the fifteenth century spelt disaster. For the larger towns this was not the case, for York and Norwich began to compete with the looms of Flanders, and the merchants of Bristol began to challenge the mercantile supremacy of the German cities. For Liverpool the period was one of steady decay; her trade was too local in character and too insecurely established not to suffer greatly from the anarchy of the Wars of the Roses, which was nowhere worse than in Lancashire; her burgesses were neither numerous enough nor strong enough to keep the contending factions at arm's length as the towns of the South and East were able to do. Fortunately the two great local families, the Molyneuxes and the Stanleys, were both Yorkist, so that Liverpool was spared the misery of continued war between them which might have resulted in its total extinction.

By the end of the seventeenth century its population was only about 6,000, and there was still no mole or quay, though it was not to be long before the first dock was constructed. It may perhaps seem difficult to understand why with considerable advantages of position Liverpool was so long in establishing her supremacy, but it was only very slowly that the sources of her wealth began to be opened up. Until the seventeenth century all the main connections of England, both in trade and civilization, were with the opposite coasts of Europe. All her own wealth was concentrated in the South and East, while the North was desolate, savage, and very thinly populated. It was not until the eighteenth century that the mineral wealth of Lancashire began to be developed, or that the cotton industry got into its stride. It is not always remembered that apart from mines and climate Lancashire is a poor county; that until two hundred years ago she was one of the least important in the kingdom; and that if Liverpool was isolated from Lancashire the latter was isolated from the rest of the country by the Pennines on the East and by a series of marshes on the South.

Moreover, so long as the channel of the Dee estuary remained open and unsilted, and ships drew relatively little water, Liverpool was faced by a serious rival for the trade even of Ireland in Chester, which was also admirably placed for commanding the northern roads into Wales, and since it was an ancient city of the first military importance it had on its side all the advantages of prestige.

To some extent, it must be admitted that the causes of the final triumph of Liverpool were gifts from the gods, and were quite beyond her control, namely the discovery of the New World and the subsequent transference of the main English trade-routes from the North Sea to the Atlantic, and the rapid development of the cotton industry by the great inventions of the latter part of the eighteenth century.

> Yet the townsmen proved themselves worthy and able to make use of these opportunities when they came by the constant and successful struggle which they carried on against the nearer obstacles to their success. The driving of roads over the surrounding marshes, the making of canals, the deepening of shallow streams, the building of railways, the creation of safe harbourage in the finest docks ever built in England – these were activities in which the townsmen took their full share; and it was the vigour and enterprise which they showed in these regards which gave to them their ultimate victory over rival ports, such as Bristol, which started with every advantage.[1]

The closing years of the eighteenth century had seen steady progress, and the external aspect of the city was a great deal more prepossessing than it had been in 1780 when Samuel Curwen, an American loyalist, found the 'streets long, narrow, crooked, and dirty. . . . We scarcely saw a well-dressed person. . . . The whole complexion of the place was nautical, but so infinitely below all our expectations that naught but the thoughts of the few hours we had to pass here rendered it tolerable.' Before 1786 the principal streets were not more than six yards wide, and the paving was exceedingly rough. The houses which faced upon these streets were of infinite variety both in size and form, for rich and poor existed cheek by jowl,

[1] Muir, R.: *A History of Liverpool*, p. 5.

and even the wealthiest merchants lived above their cellar warehouses in Duke Street, Oldhall Street, and Lord Street. Towards the end of the century, however, they began to desert the old houses, and transfer themselves to residences further afield. Rodney Street was well built up before the Regency began, and John Gladstone, the father of the statesman, was settled in his house before 1798; St Anne Street, too, contained a number of good houses; and in 1801 the Mosslake fields began to be laid out as well as Bedford Street, Chatham Street, and Abercromby and Falkner Squares. The country mansions of the merchant princes were also to be found dotted about what was still the countryside, such as Everton Hill and Toxteth Park, and even further afield in Childwall and Allerton.

There was unfortunately a less pleasing side to this expansion, for new districts rose with mushroom rapidity for the housing of the poorer inhabitants. In those days no regulations existed to ensure that these houses should be healthy and substantial; they were erected back to back, with no proper provision for air and light, and with no adequate sanitation; and they were often so jerry-built that in 1823 a violent wind blew many of them down, though this misfortune did have the salutary effect of impressing upon the Council the necessity of taking some precautions. In this way there came into existence those terrible slums to the North and South of the city which it was to be the task of the late Victorians and their successors to remove.

As elsewhere, the houses deserted by the wealthier citizens were soon over-crowded by a swarming multitude of the poor, and the cellars which had once been used as warehouses became the homes of whole families. As early as 1790 a survey showed that there were 8,148 houses in Liverpool of which 1,728 had inhabited basements. In these cellars some 6,780 people dwelt, this figure representing almost four people to each one and considerably more than one-ninth of the total population of the city. In these circumstances it is in no way surprising that disease should be rampant, and in 1823 no less than 31,500 cases were treated in the dispensaries and the infirmary, that is to say about one in four of the citizens. The significance of these figures is enhanced when it is remembered that they excluded on the one hand those who consulted their own doctors, and on the other all those resident in the workhouse.

Though the local authorities made no attempt to alleviate or remove the conditions of sordid misery in which so many Liverpudlians dwelt, they did pay a good deal of attention to the beautifying of the central streets and public buildings, though it must be admitted that this was done with scant respect for the monuments of the past. The Castle had been demolished in 1725, and in 1819 the same fate befell the Tower. Thus vanished the last relic of mediaeval Liverpool, for the old church of St Nicholas had been rebuilt, and in 1810 even the seventeenth century spire had fallen and been replaced. So it has come about that modern Liverpool, one of the oldest local government authorities in the kingdom, can nowhere exhibit any outward and visible sign of her past. It has been argued, and may well be, that this is due to the fact that so many of the leading citizens have not been Liverpudlians by birth, and have concerned themselves little with its traditions in this respect.

The Town Hall, built in 1784, had been gutted by fire in 1795, but it was reconstructed with such taste that it is to-day one of the most beautiful Town Halls in the British Isles, and was so described by King Edward VII who must have sampled plenty of them in his time. Then there was put up the memorial to Nelson, which was the first public monument in the city. At the other end of Castle Street the Old Dock was in 1826 filled in, and on its site was erected a fine pillared and domed Custom House. On all sides the narrow and tortuous streets began to be systematically improved, and the first Improvement Act was obtained in 1785 with the immediate result of the widening of Castle Street, Dale Street, and Water Street. To Castle Street, at that time the premier thoroughfare, special attention was given, and the builders were required to conform to a uniform design in erecting houses on the West side. This was almost the only case in which the Council made any attempt to enforce dignity of design upon private builders, and the results were disastrous. To quote Professor Ramsay Muir once again, 'Neither in 1785 nor in 1825, nor at any later date, did the Town Council make any attempt to control the character or direction of the new streets which were being created with such rapidity during this age of growth, so as to make the town healthy or beautiful. A glorious opportunity was thus lost. For Liverpool, throned on her long range of hills, and looking over a magnificent estuary to the distant hills of Wales, might easily have been made one of the most beautiful cities in Europe, if due care had been taken to ensure that the streets running down the hill should command uninterrupted vistas. The fact that in modern Liverpool these fine prospects do not anywhere refresh the vision of the treader of pavements must be attributed above all to the lack of foresight of the governors of the town in the age when it was so rapidly extended.'[1]

Such was the position of Liverpool at the beginning of the Victorian Age, and the lines of her future commercial development were already laid down; from then until the death of the Queen the period was in the main marked by the increasing utilization of the openings already made. Like the reign itself, the history of Liverpool falls into two parts: during the first of these the country maintained that supremacy, amounting almost to monopoly, which she had obtained as a result of the Revolutionary and Napoleonic Wars both in the field of manufacture and of overseas trade. Until the Franco-Prussian War in 1870–71 Europe was in a more or less unsettled condition, either because of efforts to reconcile democracy and stability, or because of outbursts of nationalist fervour, and so no very great effort was made to foster or stimulate manufactures, commerce, and colonization. At the same time in the United States it was the period of 'Go West, young man', and the Union was mainly engrossed by the development of that vast area which stretched away to the Pacific; her industrialization had hardly begun, and of her principal exports, if tobacco went mainly to Bristol, it was by way of Liverpool that cotton

[1] *A History of Liverpool*, p. 280.

entered the United Kingdom; then came the Civil War, and for five years the outside world was forgotten. Thus the United Kingdom was left as the supreme industrial, commercial, and colonial Power in the world; she was at once its workshop and its market, and Liverpool, as the distributing centre for a great industrial district, profited accordingly; especially was this so when with the coming of Free Trade artificial restrictions on the movement of commerce were brought to an end.

It was, however, out of the question that this state of affairs could continue indefinitely, and that the rest of the world would permit their trade permanently to be dominated and controlled by the merchants of Great Britain. Political changes were also taking place, for Europe perforce settled down under the iron rule of Bismarck, and the end of the Civil War brought to the United States a realization of the magnitude of its own resources; so there began an era of fierce competition which continued unabated until Europe committed suicide in August, 1914. There was an eager rush to obtain control of the unoccupied parts and undeveloped markets of the world, and foreign governments began to foster native industries by protecting them by high tariffs, while foreign shipping tended to become subsidized. The really surprising thing about this era was that British trade was not merely able to survive, but actually continued to make progress.

All this was faithfully reflected in the history of Liverpool. The tonnage of her shipping rose from 1,768,426 in 1835 to 5,728,504 in 1870; that is to say it multiplied three-and-a-half times during the period of the unquestioned ascendancy of British trade. There was, perhaps, nothing very remarkable about this, but by 1905 it had risen to 15,996,387. This shows that the rate of increase had, indeed, slackened, but the relevant point is that the actual addition to the tonnage of Liverpool shipping made during the period of competition was more than twice as great as it had been during the earlier period when conditions were so much easier. What had, in fact, happened was that shipping as an industry had grown immensely following on the great increase of population in the new primary producing countries which wanted British manufactured goods. By the end of the Victorian Age the city was among the three or four greatest ports in the world; she conducted one third of the export and one quarter of the import trade of the United Kingdom; she owned one third of the total national shipping, and one seventh of the total registered shipping of the world; and of every ten ships that sailed the seas one hailed from Liverpool.

The changed conditions which the Victorian Age produced made their mark upon the city, and of these the outstanding was the substitution of steam for sail: the first liner, in a strict sense, was the *Britannia*, with which, in 1840, the Cunard Company inaugurated a regular fortnightly service to New York. The growing size of the ships necessitated the enlargement and perfecting of the dock system until it became one of the wonders of the shipping world. By the beginning of the twentieth century Liverpool possessed dock space to the extent of 570 acres on both sides of the river, and there was a lineal quayage of over thirty-five miles. In 1858 the Mersey Docks and Harbour Board came into existence to control this vast enterprise, a task in which it proved remarkably successful.

At the same time this concentration on shipping, and on shipbuilding across the river, had its dangers for Merseyside, though they were not to make themselves felt in their full force until the Queen had been in her grave for nearly thirty years. Liverpool and the surrounding district became dependent upon a single 'crop'. There was probably no city of equal size in the world in which, in 1901, so small a proportion of the population was maintained by permanent and stable industrial work. There were, needless to say, a number of minor industries, and several of these, such as matchmaking, depended upon low-paid and comparatively unskilled labour, but the principal occupation of the city and the basis of its prosperity was the handling of goods in transit. Now this work came in sudden rushes, and had to be done at high pressure, so it came about that a large proportion of the men employed had no permanent work, but were compelled by the nature of their employment to put up with long periods of idleness alternating with periods of sudden heavy labour. In this way the great development of steamships and docks during the Victorian Age brought it about that the city's prosperity largely depended upon casual labour, and so Liverpool had to deal with a social problem more acute than elsewhere; how acute was shown in the strike of 1911 when the troops had to open fire with the result that two people were killed and two hundred were injured.

To pass from the activities of the city to those who took part in them is to be impressed with the city's powers of assimilation, which were–and still are–unrivalled in the United Kingdom. Liverpool has always welcomed the stranger, and has been ready to pay its homage to merit. This power of assimilation is noticeable at all levels, and it is rare to find the man or woman who has come to work in the city who is not impressed by the atmosphere of friendliness to be found there. It is continually recruiting from outside, and that is certainly not the least of its assets where the upper and middle classes were concerned, but it is not easy to be quite so sure in the case of those below them in the social scale. As the Victorian Age progressed there was an Irish Question in Liverpool as well as in the British Isles as a whole, but it was of an economic, rather than a political, nature. 'Liverpool as a principal port of entry from Ireland received far more immigrants than either could or intended to settle down and make a living there. The result was that there was always a large floating population of recently arrived immigrants in a state of temporary destitution; and also that those who did settle down in Liverpool were largely the less skilled and enterprising ones who were unable rather than unwilling to make their way elsewhere.'[1]

The Irish have always been numerous in the city, and there were Irish names among the burgesses as early as 1378, but the great wave of Irish immigrants came over at the time of the Famine. Over ninety thousand of them entered Liverpool in the first three months of 1846, and nearly three hundred thousand in the twelve months following July, 1847. They were for the

[1] White, B. D.: *A History of the Corporation of Liverpool*, 1835–1914, p. 31.

Old Haymarket, Liverpool

St John's Lane, Liverpool

most part penniless and hunger-driven, and they were violently Anglophobe–in the circumstances they could hardly have been expected to be anything else–so it is little wonder that they proved a very turbulent element in the population, with the result that twenty thousand Liverpudlians were sworn in as special constables and two thousand troops were encamped at Everton. The Irish not unnaturally tended to live together in a distinct quarter, the Scotland Road area, and they supplied no inconsiderable proportion of the unskilled labour required at the docks.

It would be impossible to exaggerate the influence of Ireland upon Liverpool during the Victorian Age and, indeed, down to the present day. The steady stream of immigrants at all levels, from those who were to become Lord Mayors to those who were to remain dock labourers, meant that there was an Irish background to the lives of a large proportion of the citizens, and never was this more obvious than when the Irish Question became acute in the eighties. In the General Election of 1885 an Irish Nationalist was returned for the Scotland Division in the person of T. P. O'Connor, and he continued to represent it until long after the Victorian Age had come to an end; nor was this all, for at that same election none other than the infamous O'Shea came within sixty votes of being returned as a Home Ruler for the neighbouring constituency of Exchange, and from that date there was always a solid phalanx of Irish Nationalists on the Council.

One result of this Irish influence was to perpetuate the distinction between Liverpool and the rest of Lancashire with the possible exception of Preston, where the Irish element was also very strong. In this way the result of improved communications was offset, and in more than one town in the County Palatine Liverpool was referred to as 'a suburb of Dublin'; there was, indeed, some truth in the taunt, for there was more interest in what went on in the Irish capital than in the neighbouring city of Manchester. At the same time Liverpudlians always considered themselves somewhat superior to their fellow Lancastrians, and a favourite story on Merseyside was that of the guard of a coach, who, on being asked at his arrival in London how many passengers he had, answered, 'Four. A Liverpool gentleman, a Manchester man, a Bolton chap, and an Oldham fellow.'

The census returns of the period hardly indicate the nature and extent of the growth of population because they only relate to the population within the municipal boundary which, until 1895, remained fixed where it had been drawn in 1835 when Everton, Kirkdale, and the more populous areas of West Derby and Toxteth were added to the original township. It was not until 1895 that the districts of Walton and Wavertree, the rest of Toxteth, and another section of West Derby were incorporated in the city, while five years later the township of Garston was also included. At the Queen's death the population of the city was 716,000, but this was far from representing the total number of those economically dependent upon Liverpool. The Victorian Age saw Bootle develop from a rural township into an incorporated borough with a population of 58,000, and beyond Bootle it was marked by the appearance of a number of populous suburbs containing some 40,000 inhabitants in all in Seaforth, Litherland, Waterloo, and Crosby. On the other side of the river the Victorian Age saw Birkenhead rise out of nothing to a population of over a hundred thousand, while outside of its limits the district of Wallasey could claim 53,000 inhabitants, and Hoylake and West Kirby 10,000 more. To a greater or lesser extent these were all dormitories of Liverpool, and thus it would be no exaggeration to say that the population economically dependent upon her largely exceeded a million, having multiplied something like fivefold during the Queen's reign.

The *terminus a quo* of Victorian Liverpool was the Municipal Reform Act of 1835. As we have seen, unlike many other cities which had come into existence as a result of the Industrial Revolution it was an ancient borough whose charter had first been granted in the reign of John. This meant that for more than six centuries Liverpool had possessed a municipal corporation with a Mayor, Aldermen, and Councillors, and in the early part of its career it was genuinely representative of the citizen body whose representative it was in face of the outside world. As time went on, however, its organization became antiquated, and by 1835 it had collapsed. This was due to a variety of causes, not least among them being the fact that the system of representation, originally based on the mediaeval guilds, lost its *raison d'être* as the guilds themselves fell into decay.

The position in 1835 was that in theory the Corporation of Liverpool consisted of the whole body of the freemen of the borough, but by this date the freemen had themselves become a close corporation a few thousand strong. The position of a freeman was hereditary, and a number of privileges still went with it, among them being exemption from town dues and the lucrative right of the Parliamentary franchise. What an election was like in the Liverpool of those days can be gathered from a letter from Brougham to Grey in 1812:

> You can have no idea of the nature of a Liverpool election. It is quite peculiar to the place. You have every night to go to the different clubs, benefit societies, etc., which meet and speechify. This is from half-past six to one in the morning at least; and you have to speak to each man who polls, at the bar, from ten to five. It lasted eight days. I began my canvass three whole days before, and had nine nights of the clubs, besides a regular speech each day at close of poll. I delivered in that time 160 speeches and odd.[1]

On the Tory side there is the testimony of Stratford Canning, later Lord Stratford de Redcliffe, who, although a career diplomatist, was in the easy-going manner of those days helping his cousin, George Canning:

> On reaching Liverpool we found the town in an uproar. Party strife ran high; bitter speeches were exchanged on the hustings, and mobs were violent in the streets. Windows were broken, candidates pelted, and for more effective missiles resort was had without ceremony to the pavement and the area rails. Fortune finally declared in favour of Mr Canning, who was cheered, chaired, and feasted to the top of his bent. I cannot venture to say how many dinners were given to him and his friends by the Tory capitalists of Liverpool. I know that they were enough, with the help of turtle and punch, to imperil health far more than any riotous

[1] Brougham and Vaux, Lord: *Life and Times*, vol. II, p. 62.

assaults in the street. It was an uninterrupted jubilee of two or three weeks.[1]

The final state of the poll affords a good idea of the voting strength of the freemen in the early years of the nineteenth century:

Canning, Tory	1,641
Gascoyne, Tory	1,532
Brougham, Whig	1,131
Creevey, Whig	1,068
Tarleton (retd.)	11

The power of the freemen was, however, confined to the election of Members of Parliament, for they were not the governing body of the town, and they had no voice in the election or control of it. The effective representatives of the Corporation were the Mayor, Aldermen and Councillors, who constituted the real local authority. They held office for life, and filled vacancies by co-option.

There is a difference of opinion with regard to the old Corporation between the two of the great modern authorities on the history of Liverpool, namely Professor Ramsay Muir and Mr Brian White. The views of Professor Ramsay Muir have already been quoted, but Mr White is more generous:

> The prosperity of Liverpool, if not its very existence as a port, depended on its docks. These docks had been built on the initiative of the Corporation and were for many years entirely controlled by them, while in 1835 they still had a principal and final voice in their management. From 1786 onwards they had embarked on a policy of widening streets. In the same year they began to take an interest in the water supply of the town. In 1802 they promoted, though unsuccessfully, a Bill anticipating the provisions of the Health-of-the-Town Act of 1842 which marked the beginning of Liverpool's career as a pioneer of public health. In the field of education they had gone so far as to provide and manage two schools which were for their time among the most favourable examples of cheap elementary education. Where activities now municipal were being undertaken by other bodies the Council generally had some finger in the pie. In some cases it had actually set up, and in all cases were represented on, the

[1] Lane-Poole, S.: *The Life of Stratford Canning*, vol. I, pp. 185–186.

> bodies concerned. There are in fact few of the broad divisions of modern municipal activity in which the Liverpool Council had not before 1835 shown some interest or taken part.[1]

In support of this tribute to the Corporation's activities may be cited the fact that the Commissioners appointed in 1833 by the Government to enquire into the affairs of municipal corporations recorded that the Liverpool Council had administered its estate in an honest and efficient manner. On the other hand the policing of the town left much to be desired. For the purpose of guarding the Cotton Exchange the Corporation employed a force of 52 men, but a mere 170 had to suffice to preserve law and order elsewhere: they only operated at night, and were commonly known as 'Old Charlies'. For the most part they were 'so aged and feeble that the inhabitants could only account for their filling the post by supposing that when men were considered too decrepit for any other employment they were elected guardians of the public safety'.[2] In these circumstances it is little wonder that juvenile delinquency flourished – in 1836 it was reported that no less than 1,500 thieves under the age of fifteen were at work – while 3,600 prostitutes roamed the streets.

Whatever may have been the merits or demerits of the old system it became a thing of the past after the passage of the Municipal Corporations Bill which imposed upon all boroughs, with the curious exception of the City of London, one constitutional form of government. The governing body was henceforth to consist of a Mayor, Aldermen, and Councillors, and the last of these were to be elected directly by rate-paying occupiers; they were to hold office for three years, while the Aldermen were to be elected by the Councillors for six years, and the Mayor was to be elected annually, also by the Councillors. Such was the form of government which Liverpool was to know during the Victorian Age.

The first Council elected under the new dispensation was possessed of a crusading zeal where reform was concerned. Its

[1] *Corporation of Liverpool*, 1835–1914, pp. 10–11.
[2] Walmsley, H. M.: *Life of Sir Joshua Walmsley*, p. 17.

members began by getting rid of most of the old officers, though some of them were highly competent, and they cut down salaries unsparingly. They took over the functions of the old separate Watching, Lighting, and Cleansing Board, and they proceeded to reorganize the police force which was doubled in number. Hitherto its function had been almost entirely confined to the arrest of criminals, but henceforth the principle was laid down that it was the duty of the police not merely to punish, but to prevent, vice and crime.

Social Reform was another matter which early received attention, though the war on the slums was far from being won when the Queen died. The civic conscience awakened to the fact that there were hundreds of houses, not actually dangerous in the sense that they were in imminent danger of collapse, but in a wholly insanitary and uninhabitable condition. In order that this state of affairs might be terminated the Council applied for power to impose certain building regulations on all new buildings erected in the town, to close existing houses which were not merely dangerous but also filthy and unwholesome, and to appoint a Health Committee to regulate the sanitary condition of the town: the result was the Building Act of 1842, which was the pioneer of its kind in the kingdom and the model for other local authorities. In another cognate matter Liverpool also took the lead of all England, and that was the initiation of public wash-houses. The origin of this scheme must be credited to a lady of the name of Mrs Martin, who threw her own kitchen open to the women of the poorer streets to wash their families' clothes. News of this enterprise came to the ears of Mr William Rathbone, and he persuaded the Council to establish municipal wash-houses at a small charge: this was first done in 1842.

Nowhere was the Victorian Social Revolution more marked than in Liverpool, and there it was particularly noticeable in all that related to Public Health. In 1843 Dr Duncan, then a lecturer in the Royal Infirmary School of Medicine which was the precursor of the Medical Faculty of Liverpool University to-day, published a pamphlet which gave remarkable impetus to this cause. He showed that half the working-class population of the town lived in narrow closed courts, devoid of all sanitary amenities, or in equally objectionable underground cellars, while only the streets in which the well-to-do lived were provided with sewers. Of the lodging-houses in which no inconsiderable part of the poor resided he painted a most distressing picture, with many of their inhabitants sleeping on dirty straw. The density of population was a hundred thousand to the square mile, and this included the more spacious areas where the wealthy had their abode. This figure was the highest in the kingdom, so it was no wonder that the mortality was unparalleled, and that one person in every twenty-five was yearly stricken with fever. In short, Dr Duncan drew such a picture of squalor, disease, misery and vice as no self-respecting local authority could contemplate with anything approaching equanimity.

In any event the Victorians were more receptive to reports of this nature than are their more sophisticated Elizabethan descendants, and this particular one touched the conscience of Liverpool, which was indeed coming to be known as 'the black spot on the Mersey', on the raw and remedial action was at once undertaken. The powers conferred by the Building Act of 1842 were much extended by a new act obtained in 1846, and in that same year Dr Duncan was appointed the first Medical Officer of Health in England. He was, as might be supposed, far from letting the grass grow under his feet, and a great campaign was initiated against insanitary dwellings. The investigations which ensued fully confirmed the allegations in his report, for of 14,085 cellars examined in no less than 5,841 were found pools of muddy and stagnant water on the floors, and in one year Dr Duncan had over five thousand cellars condemned as unfit for human habitation and closed.

This was a mere palliative, and recourse was had to Parliament for further powers. By the Sanitary Amendment Act of 1864 the Corporation obtained authority for the Medical Officer of Health to bring to the notice of the Grand Jury any court or alley which he thought should be condemned, while the Council was empowered to alter or demolish any building so condemned after purchase or the payment of compensation to the owner. The powers thus obtained far surpassed those enjoyed by any other local authority in the kingdom, and it may confidently be claimed that the group of private acts from 1842 to 1864, supplemented by the by-laws which they empowered the Council to make, rendered Liverpool the pioneer in the field of Public Health. There would appear to have been a slackening of the pace under Dr Duncan's successor in the seventies, and in 1874 *The Times* went so far as to declare that the criminal statistics and the health statistics of Liverpool point to the same conclusion: 'Liverpool is a town whose leading inhabitants are negligent of their duties as citizens.' This was not wholly just, for the Council was, with much honest questioning and doubt, embarking upon a great change of policy, which involved a complete departure from the principles of even the most ardent reformers in the middle of the Victorian Age. Much that to-day is taken for granted in the field of Local Government was then regarded as revolutionary in the extreme. It was in those days considered to be the sole function of a governing body to maintain order, to protect the just rights of every citizen, and to punish actual crimes after they had been committed: anything beyond that seemed to the mid-Victorian mind to be an improper interference with the liberty of the subject.

The Corporation was now embarking upon a much more ambitious task, that is to say nothing less than the prevention, rather than the punishment, of crime, and of removing inducements to vice. One result of this new resolve was that the Council began to devote itself to the problem not merely of demolishing insanitary property under the powers obtained by the various local acts already mentioned, but also to that of replacing them by new houses for the displaced tenants. In 1869 only one block of cottages had been built for this purpose, and the new policy did not really get under way until 1885, when the large group of dwellings known as Victoria Square was erected, and by the end of the reign accommodation had been provided for over seven hundred families. Further schemes of a similar nature were under consideration as may be gathered from the fact that seven years later more than two thousand houses were municipally owned.

One of the obstacles in the path of the reformer of those days was that there was far too much drinking. It is sometimes complained that it is unduly difficult to get a drink in modern Liverpool, but there can be little doubt that a couple of generations ago it was too easy, and even more recently some of us can remember the state of Lime Street on a Saturday night. Ever since the eighteenth century, and perhaps earlier, the disproportionate number of public houses had been a subject of comment by every visitor. In the decade between 1831 and 1841 the number of licensed houses rose from 1,752 to 2,274, and for two years after 1863 the licensing bench entered upon the deliberate experiment of granting licenses freely to all who applied, without taking into account the number already in existence in any given locality. The prevailing principle of Free Trade held that no distinction should be made between beer-shops and bread-shops, and that open competition would rectify all evils. Unfortunately liquor goes to the head while bread does not, and the result was an increase of drunkenness which was to form a problem for many years.

With the rapid growth in the population and the consequent density in the older parts of Liverpool the question of transport became a problem of increasing importance, for only an improvement in this respect could render possible the transportation of thousands of the poorer classes to healthier conditions in the outskirts, and some account, however brief, of the activities of the Council in this respect cannot be omitted.

In actual fact Liverpool and Birkenhead were the first towns in Europe in which tramways were operated. One, George Francis Train, a U.S. citizen, obtained permission from the Birkenhead Commissioners in 1860 to construct an experimental tramway in the town, and the line was completed and opened for public traffic the same year. Liverpool lagged a few years behind, but in 1868 the Liverpool Tramways Company Limited was incorporated, and under powers of an Act of Parliament constructed a line between the Town Hall and the

Dingle. The new tramway soon proved so popular that Parliamentary powers were obtained for the building of two additional lines, one running between the Town Hall and the northern boundary at Walton, and the other between Kirkdale and Toxteth Park. In due course the new tramways and the older omnibus undertaking amalgamated under the title of the Liverpool United Tramways and Omnibus Company Limited. In 1875, when Liverpool had a population of 443,930 people this body provided by way of transport eight route miles of tramways, equipped with thirty cars, with an average seating capacity of thirty-eight, together with about a hundred-and-seven omnibuses of various types with an average seating capacity of thirty.

As evidence of the extent to which Liverpool has changed it will be noticed that neither at this date, nor for some years afterwards, did the tramway system extend to the Pier Head, and this was because of the narrow strip of water which connected the Canning Dock and the old George's Dock: this channel seems in the eyes of contemporary engineers to have constituted an insuperable barrier against any extension. Mann Island was a kind of wilderness or No Man's Land, and was paved with cobble-stones, while the site upon which the Royal Liver and Cunard Buildings were later erected was then occupied by the George's Dock and its sheds. These were the only buildings in the neighbourhood, except for the Old Baths and a couple of public-houses at the extreme South end of the Island, though there was also a round stone hut on the open space at the rear of the Landing Stage where the bus conductors paid in their cash. Incidentally, 'the space bounded on the North by Princes Dock, and West by the Landing Stage, on the South by Canning Dock, and on the East by St Nicholas' Place and Goree, was a locality much frequented by Crimps and Owls, which was the name given to ladies of a certain type, because of their habits which so much resembled that carnivorous bird, that sleeps all day, and seeks its prey at night. Many were the outrages committed in this locality on sailors returning from sea'.[1]

[1] Mallins, C. W.: *The Story of the Tramway*, p. 6.

In 1897 the undertaking was municipalized, and the first care of the Corporation was electrification. As a result on November 16th, 1898, an electric line was opened for traffic between South Castle Street and the Dingle, and by the end of 1902 the whole system had been electrified. Soon afterwards C. W. Mallins was appointed General Manager, and it may not be out of place to quote his terms of reference as an illustration of the attitude of the Council towards its new responsibilities:

> Shortly after my appointment as General Manager I had an interview with the Chairman of the Committee, the late Sir Charles Petrie, who very frankly outlined the policy to be adopted. There was no ambiguity in the language used by Sir Charles. He stated that the policy of the committee was to give the cheapest possible scale of fares to the public, and the best conditions of labour as well as the highest rate of pay to the employees, consistent with the financial stability of the undertaking. He further remarked that whilst the committee and himself were anxious to grant every reasonable facility and consideration, they were determined to have the tramway undertaking operated on sound commercial lines. Sir Charles further stated that in his opinion and that of the whole committee, the rate-payers, whose credit was pledged for the whole of the capital expenditure, and who would be called upon to make good any loss which might be incurred on the operation of the concern, should have every consideration; and that if any surplus was available, after providing for all statutory and other obligations, including reserve and renewal funds, and all other possible contingencies, such surplus should be allocated to the relief of rates. 'Now', he said, with his usual kindly smile, 'Your work is to accomplish all that. I am not in the least oblivious of the difficulties of your task, as you are following a very able man,[1] whom we all believe has developed the system to the fullest possible extent, and therefore, in our opinion, it has reached its maximum earning powers.' He then expressed the hope that I might be able to reduce the expenditure, which the committee considered was rather high. After which remarks I outlined a scheme which I felt I could recommend to the committee, embodying a revision of the stages and fares, as well as a general overhauling of the spending departments, to which Sir Charles agreed, remarking that it would have his support when I brought it before the committee.[2]

[1] The late C. R. Bellamy.

[2] Mallins, C. W.: *The Story of the Tramway*, pp. 53–54.

In view of the fierce political controversy which divided Liverpool opinion in those days it may be noted that Sir Charles Petrie, the Chairman of the Tramways Committee, was a Conservative, and Alderman Frederick Smith, the Deputy Chairman was a Liberal. The City Fathers did not allow party politics to obtrude too far in municipal affairs.

The subsequent development of the tramways took place after the Victorian Age had come to an end, but it followed on the lines stated above, and by the end of the First World War no less a sum than £1,062,800 had been allocated to the relief of the local rates. Furthermore, the efficiency of the transport system had been of enormous assistance to the expansion of the city.

It would, however, be a mistake to assume that the progress of Liverpool in the Victorian Age was wholly of a material nature: it is true that it was not until the reign of King Edward VII that the building of the Anglican cathedral, one of the glories of the city today, was put in hand, but since 1880 there had been a bishop to look after the citizens' morals. Perhaps, however, the greatest achievement in the latter part of the nineteenth century lay in the field of higher education with the establishment of the university, and the impetus was given by the Education Act of 1870. All over the kingdom there then began to grow up institutions called university colleges, and in due course the proposal was put forward that Liverpool should follow this example. At first there was a good deal of opposition, for in those days the pre-occupation of the leading citizens was money-making and good living, and the idea of making a commercial sea-port the seat of a university appeared to be rather a poor joke. The enthusiasts, however, refused to be daunted, and gradually the idea gained ground; William Rathbone threw himself into the work of collecting funds, and at last the scheme was formally launched at a town's meeting in 1879. The Corporation granted a site; £50,000 was raised by subscription; and in January, 1882, the University College was opened, albeit in a disused lunatic asylum in the middle of a slum district. From then it went on from strength to strength, though another twenty-one years were to elapse before it obtained from the Crown its charter as a fully organized and independent university.

Enough has been said to show that the full impact of the Victorian Social Revolution was felt in Liverpool, and the Queen's reign witnessed a complete change in the character of the city, not least in the spirit in which civic obligations were regarded, for this was even more remarkable than the growth of its wealth and the increase of its population. In 1837 the borough did little for its inhabitants, and it was little more than a place where they lived as best they might until they had made enough money to be able to leave it; but by 1901 it was no longer content merely to guard their lives and property, for it took care of them from the cradle to the grave. It was thus only fitting that the dignity to which Liverpool was attaining should receive official recognition, and by the first charter of Queen Victoria in 1880 it was granted that henceforth Liverpool should no longer be denominated merely a borough, but that it had earned the higher appellation of a city. Thirteen years later the matter was carried further, and by a second charter the plain Mayor of Liverpool became the Right Honourable the Lord Mayor of the City of Liverpool.

The progress of the city in the Victorian Age might, *mutatis mutandis*, be paralleled in that of many other large centres of population in the nineteenth century, but when one turns to Liverpool politics it is to be confronted with a thing apart, and to begin to understand the situation the influence and the proximity of Ireland must never be forgotten. Sectarian influences have always been strong, but they were never stronger than at the end of the nineteenth century when public opinion was roused by Gladstone's Home Rule proposals. The large Irish Roman Catholic population, centred in the Scotland and Exchange divisions of the city, had its counterpart in a strong Orange vote in Everton, Kirkdale, and West Derby, and this schism was reflected in politics, both national and local.

In the previous century Liverpool, unlike the rest of Lancashire in general and Manchester in particular, had been a

Whig stronghold, and it had displayed scant sympathy with the Jacobite cause in The Forty-Five. Then a change had come, and such prominent Tories as Canning and Huskisson had been among its representatives at Westminster. During the Victorian Age the Liberals from time to time acquired control of the Council, but this became increasingly rarer as the century drew to its close, and that for reasons peculiar to Merseyside.

The old Liverpool families, such as the Holts and the Rathbones, tended, as the heirs of the Whigs, to be Liberals, and as there was no Labour Party in those days the opposition to them, which came from a lower strata of society, was Conservative. The Liverpool Working Men's Conservative Association was formed as early as 1865, but it was not until Archibald Salvidge became its leader in 1892 that it became an effective force in local politics. Thereafter, by means which have not passed unquestioned, he converted it into a machine which enabled him within fairly wide limits to control the results of elections in Liverpool. The more important part of his career, incidentally, lies outside the Victorian Age, and until 1901 he was content to work in the background; indeed, even as late as the outbreak of the First World War he was not chairman of any committee of the City Council. Salvidge was, it must be confessed, a good deal of a rabble-rouser, and in the biography of him written by his son it is related that he once said to his family that it was his aim to give to the mass of the people of Liverpool the power which they had never before exercised. He is also alleged to have told the members of his Association that if they followed him he would make them Councillors, Justices of the Peace, and even Members of Parliament. However this may be, he was responsible for an organization which was diametrically opposed to the old families and everything for which they stood.

Mention has been made on an earlier page of the steady flow of immigrants at all social levels into Liverpool, and this, too, militated against control by the traditional Liverpudlian families; consequently these newcomers enjoyed a position which they would never have attained elsewhere, say in Bristol for example. They also often held views which it was not usual to find in Conservatives in other parts of the country as may be seen from the fact that two local leaders of Conservatism were Sir Thomas Hughes, who was a convinced Temperance Reformer, and Sir Charles Petrie, who was a strong Presbyterian and that at a time when the line of division between the Establishment and Dissent was very marked. It is true that Hughes soon had to resign for many reasons, but he was followed by Petrie, who retained the leadership until 1918, and who in addition to being a Presbyterian was an Irishman from County Mayo. The general situation was further confused by the fact that towards the end of the century there was a compact block of Irish Nationalists sitting in the City Council.

All this was complicated enough, but to make confusion worse confounded the Conservatives were divided among themselves on sectarian matters. With very few exceptions they were strongly opposed to anything that smacked of Popery, but the more extreme among them regarded with equal disfavour the Ritualists of the Established Church. The nineties constituted a period when Ritualism was strong, and when, as we have seen, the Bishop of London was much exercised about it in his diocese. So far as Liverpool was concerned the matter came to a head in 1898 with the introduction of the Church Discipline Bill; in consequence the last two years of the nineteenth century witnessed an outbreak of Protestant feeling on Merseyside, and the Laymen's League was formed to support the Bill. This organization had the full support of Salvidge, who deliberately made religion the key issue in local politics. 'The easiest road to immediate political success was to find an issue which demanded no practical policy . . . but one about which people felt strongly, and the opponents were certain to be in a minority. The Protestant campaign was a perfect answer to this problem. From a party point of view it was used with complete success, even to the point of making the Labour Party for a good many years an almost exclusively Catholic party. But from the side of municipal organization and activity it can hardly be judged so favourably'.[1]

[1] White, B. D.: *A History of the Corporation of Liverpool*, 1835-1914, p. 193.

In this self-imposed task of exacerbating religious differences Salvidge had the enthusiastic support of the Rev. George Wise who started what he termed a Protestant Crusade, and whose idea of propagating the Christian religion was to hold, in the Catholic districts, highly provocative meetings at which abuse was hurled at the Pope. Salvidge was never the man to do things by halves, and he was not content with raising the Protestant banner in Liverpool, for when, in 1899, there was a by-election in the neighbouring division of Southport he did not hesitate to throw the weight of his influence on the Liberal side to secure the return of a Liberal candidate who shared his religious prejudices as against a Conservative whom he did not consider to be sound on the sectarian issue.

In Liverpool itself the controversy soon came to centre round the figure of Walter Long, who represented West Derby and was also President of the Board of Agriculture. Unfortunately for him this crisis coincided with the period of weak leadership in local Conservative politics, for Sir Arthur Forwood had recently died, and his immediate successors did not command sufficient support among Liverpool Conservatives to ride the storm which Salvidge and Wise had raised. Indeed, it was not until the election of Sir Charles Petrie in 1906 to the chairmanship of the Liverpool Constitutional Association that the teeth of this political Protestantism may be said to have been drawn, and even since that date there have been occasions when official Conservatism and extreme anti-Romanism have come into conflict. In the present instance Long was far from being a High Churchman, but quite apart from his position as a Cabinet Minister he held the view very strongly that a Member of Parliament is a representative, not a delegate, and he refused to join the Laymen's League, or to promise to support the Church Discipline Bill. In the absence of a local Conservative leader with sufficient prestige to make his authority respected, Long was in an impossible position, and he took the only course open to him – he sought a seat elsewhere. Salvidge had triumphed. Nearly two generations have elapsed since these events took place, but the passage of time has only served to confirm the judgment of those who held that Long was badly treated, and that the loss to Liverpool was very great indeed. It only remains to add that Bristol accepted with delight the statesman whom the rival seaport had rejected.

As has already been suggested, the passions which Salvidge and Wise aroused were not easily allayed, and when, on the accession of King George V, it was proposed to modify the Coronation Oath, which in its existing form was highly offensive to members of the Roman Catholic Church, there was a storm of protest in Liverpool, and the following refrain sung at a by-election in Kirkdale did not a little to crystallize opinion in favour of the subsequently victorious Conservative candidate:

Vote for Kyffin-Taylor;
Let the Oath remain.
Keep the Empire Protestant:
We don't want Rome again!

Apart from Sir James Reynolds there were few Roman Catholics among the local Conservative leaders, which is hardly surprising in view of the way in which they were treated. On one occasion, for example, when it was desired to display a united front in the face of some measure of the Liberal Government of the day a meeting was held at which some of the leading Catholics in South Lancashire were specially invited to be present, but the desired effect was lost when, to the evident delight of the large majority of a vast audience, Sir Edward Carson referred to the reigning Pope, Pius X, as 'a damned Italian priest'.

Apart from Canning and Huskisson early in the century, it cannot be said that the representatives of Liverpool at Westminster were in any way remarkable, nor is this surprising when the case of Walter Long is taken into account; able men fought shy of a place where they were subject to the dictation of a caucus. If, however, the Conservatives who were elected were on the whole mediocre, some of their opponents who were defeated were men of greater calibre, such as Augustine Birrell, Oscar Browning, J. C. Bigham,[1] and John Redmond.

[1] Later Viscount Mersey of Toxteth: President of the Probate, Divorce and Admiralty Division.

What may, perhaps, be described as the 'new' Conservatism of Liverpool, which was evolved by Forwood and practised by Petrie, had municipalization as its basis, and the belief of its leaders was that the services which primarily concerned the rate-payers should be owned by the rate-payers. The Conservatism of the North of England and that of the South have always been as poles asunder, and some of the policies adopted in Liverpool in the closing years of the Victorian Age would even to-day, after two World Wars and the lapse of sixty years, be viewed askance by many a Conservative councillor in London. Especially is this the case with anything that resembles municipal trading, which is anathema in the South, but to which the northern Conservative can see no special objection. It was, indeed, seriously proposed not long before the First World War to establish a municipal zoo, and no opposition was encountered on doctrinal grounds, though one can well imagine what an uproar such a suggestion would create in, say, some London Conservative borough. 'As a result mainly of the writings of members of the Fabian Society and the activities of the Progressives in the London County Council, municipal trading came to be regarded both by its friends and enemies as the most immediate practical form of Socialism. This point of view was not taken very seriously in Liverpool.'[1] Indeed, in 1905 the local Conservatives claimed credit for the acquisition of the Tramways and of the Electric Supply Company as 'a daring and successful experiment in municipal Socialism'.

If Liverpool was, largely owing to its juxtaposition to Ireland, different in some respects from the other great cities of England during the Victorian Age it was like them in that it was the scene of a social revolution: the Liverpool of 1835 would have been recognizable in 1735, but it bore no resemblance to the Liverpool of 1901, either externally or in the outlook of its inhabitants. The same transformation was taking place in all the larger centres of population throughout the kingdom.

In effect, Liverpool, when the Queen died, was a singularly pleasant place in which to live, which certainly could not have

[1] White, B. D.: *A History of the Corporation of Liverpool*, 1835–1914, p. 166.

been said when she came to the throne. There was nothing narrow about its life, and as there was a steady flow of visitors on their way from or to the New World it was by no means isolated from the main currents of international activity. It had good theatres, which were regularly visited by first-class companies containing the leading actors and actresses of the day; lectures were frequent and well attended; there were ample facilities for the study of art, music, and letters: and the two local newspapers, the Conservative *Courier* and the Liberal *Daily Post*, could bear comparison with those published elsewhere. The inhabitants considered themselves to be citizens of no mean city.

CHAPTER IV

Victorian Ireland

Ireland in the middle years of the nineteenth century was prostrate after the disaster of the Famine. In Irish history there have been several breaks with the past such as the Flight of the Earls and the Treaty of Limerick, but probably the most far-reaching of all was the Famine, when the old Celtic civilization received a blow from which it was never to recover. In this connection it may not be out of place to quote three authorities, two of them Irishmen and the third a German, for Irish history has become so bedevilled with Irish politics that it is usually very difficult to get at the truth; therefore the more evidence the better when a statement has to be proved.

First of all, then, there is George Petrie,[1] writing in 1855 in *The Ancient Music of Ireland*:

> I called to mind that, but for the accidentally-directed researches of Edward Bunting, a man paternally of English race, and the sympathetic excitement to follow in his track which his example had given to a few others, the memory of our music would have been but little more than a departed dream, never to be satisfactorily realized; and that, though much had been done by those persons, yet that Moore's statement still remained substantially true, namely that our national music never had been properly collected.
>
> I could not but feel what must have been at no distant time the inevitable result of the change in the character of the Irish race which had been long in operation, and which had already almost

[1] B. 1789, d. 1866. Artist, collector of folk-music, and archæologist. Great-uncle of the author.

entirely denationalized its higher classes, had been suddenly effected, as if by a lightning flash, by the calamities which, in the year 1846–7, had struck down and well-nigh annihilated the Irish remnant of the great Celtic family. Of the old, who had still preserved as household gods the language, the songs and traditions of their race and localities, but few survived. Of the middle-aged and energetic whom death had yet spared, and who might for a time, to some extent, have preserved such relics, but a few remained that had the power to fly from the plague and famine-stricken land; and of the young, who had come into existence, and become orphaned, during those years of desolation, they, for the most part, were reared where no mother's eyes could make them feel the mysteries of human affections–no mother's voice could soothe their youthful sorrows, and implant within the memories of their hearts her songs of tenderness and love–and where no father's instructions could impart to them the traditions and characteristic peculiarities of feeling that would link them to their remotest ancestors.

The green pastoral plains, the fruitful valleys, as well as the wild hill-sides and the dreary bogs, had equally ceased to be animate with human life. 'The land of song' was no longer tuneful; or, if a human sound met the traveller's ear, it was only that of the feeble and despairing wail for the dead. This awful, unwonted silence, which during the famine and subsequent years, almost everywhere prevailed, struck more fearfully upon their imaginations, as many Irish gentlemen informed me, and gave them a deeper feeling of the desolation with which the country had been visited, than any other circumstance which had forced itself upon their attention; and I confess that it was a consideration of the circumstances of which this fact gave so striking an indication, that, more than any other, over-powered all my objections, and influenced me in coming to a determination to accept the proposal of the Irish Music Society.

Nearly seventy years later Douglas Hyde, in due course to be President of Ireland, confirmed in retrospect George Petrie's contemporary apprehensions:

Of the many linguistic miracles which the world has to show, few are more extraordinary than the snuffing out of the great Irish language which was spoken by, or at least known to, everybody of Milesian race down to about the year 1750, or even 1800. At the time of the Great Famine in 1847–8, it was the ordinary language of about four millions of people in Ireland. The Famine knocked the heart out of everything. After that it just wilted away until little more than three-quarters of a million, and the bulk of these aged people, knew anything about it. No one cared, no one troubled except, perhaps, Dr McHale, the Archbishop of Tuam. It just withered off the face of Ireland.

In 1760, Irish was so universally spoken in the regiments of the Irish Brigade that Dick Hennessey, Edmund Burke's cousin, learnt it on foreign service. In 1825, the Commissioners of Education in Ireland, in their first report laid before Parliament estimated the number of those who did not know any English at half a million, while a million more might know a little for trading purposes. Between 1861 and 1891 the language died out with such rapidity that the whole island contained in 1891, according to the census, less Irish speakers than the small province of Connacht had done thirty years before–that was something over three-quarters of a million.[1]

Finally, there is a very different witness, in fact no less a person than Frederick Engels himself, who wrote to Karl Marx on May 23rd, 1856:

In our tour in Ireland we came from Dublin to Galway on the West coast, then twenty miles North inland, then to Limerick, down the Shannon to Tarbet, Tralee, Killarney, and back to Dublin–a total of about four to five hundred miles in the country itself–so that we have seen about two-thirds of the whole country. With the exception of Dublin, which bears the same relation to London as Dusseldorf does to Berlin, and has quite the character of a small one-time capital, all English-built too, the whole country, and especially the towns, has the appearance of France or Northern Italy. Gendarmes, priests, lawyers, bureaucrats, squires in pleasing profusion and a total absence of any and every industry. . . . Strong measures are visible in every part of the country, the Government meddles with everything, of so-called self-government there is not a trace. Ireland may be regarded as the first English colony, and as one which because of its proximity is still governed exactly in the old way, and here one can already observe that the so-called liberty of English citizens is based on the oppression of the colonies. I have never seen so many gendarmes in any country, and the drink-sodden expression of the Prussian gendarmes is developed to its highest perfection here among the constabulary, who are armed with rifles, bayonets, and handcuffs. . . .

[1] *The Irish Language Movement: Some Reminiscences.*

> The landowners, who everywhere else have taken on bourgeois qualities, are here completely demoralized. Their country seats are surrounded by enormous, wonderfully beautiful parks, but all around is waste land, and where the money is supposed to come from it is impossible to see. These fellows ought to be shot. Of mixed blood, mostly tall, strong, handsome chaps, they all wear enormous moustaches under colossal Roman noses, give themselves the sham military airs of retired colonels, travel around the country after all sorts of pleasures, and if one makes an inquiry, they haven't a penny, are laden with debts, and live in dread of the Encumbered Estates Court.

Such was the background against which the Irish scene was set in the fifties of last century, and until the end of Queen Victoria's reign the drama that was played in Ireland was stark tragedy. At the same time English rule was characterized by a great deal of make-believe, and the chief piece of make-believe was the Viceregal Court: it was indeed a strange, theatrical institution, of which the influence affected everything in the country down to the commonest little tradesman, or that curious product of the age the 'Castle waiter', whose services aspiring hostesses thought it was a great comfort to secure, even for a higher fee than that paid to his less exalted brethren. At the apex of the pyramid stood the Lord-Lieutenant himself, who was usually a great English nobleman, often with Irish connections: few Lords-Lieutenant were themselves snobs, but the whole system of which they were the head reeked of snobbery. Everyone had their place in society according to their standing at Dublin Castle or the Viceregal Lodge in Phoenix Park, and because the Lord-Lieutenant crossed to England by Kingstown and Holyhead that route was considered much more aristocratic than the one from North Wall to Liverpool: even to-day it is by no means unknown to hear it referred to by older people as 'the old Viceregal route'. Nevertheless Dublin society of a century ago had one redeeming merit which was not shared by contemporary society in London, and it was that money alone could not purchase admittance–indeed, if it had, very few would have been admitted, for however prejudiced the views of Engels may have been on other points there can be no question but that he was right about the poverty of the bulk of the landed gentry. The Lord-Lieutenant's parties were frequently attended by those who had nothing but their birth to recommend them, with the result that at these functions victuals of all kinds had a habit of disappearing into pockets and hand-bags for future consumption. So prevalent did thefts of this nature become at one time that the chickens at the buffet were secured to the plates with elastic, and the story is told of one old dowager whose hand-bag shot back to the counter together with the bird which she was endeavouring to conceal in it.

The truth is that Dublin a hundred years ago was living on its past. It had not recovered from the blow of the Union, while outside, as we have seen, was a nation prostrate after the Famine. In the eighteenth century the Protestant Ascendancy had been a very serious affair indeed, and there was no make-believe in those days, as a single incident will suffice to indicate. In 1759 a Catholic girl of considerable fortune was urged by a suitor to change her faith, and to avoid him she fled to the house of a friend, who was in due course denounced to the authorities: at his trial the Chancellor very aptly summed up the existing state of affairs by declaring that the 'law does not presume a Papist to exist in the kingdom, nor can they as much as breathe here without the connivance of the Government'. Nor was there any make-believe about the Lords-Lieutenant of that period; they were there to govern the country in the interests of England, and if, like the 'good' Lord Fitzwilliam, as the Irish called him, they showed any disposition to sympathize with the grievances of the people of Ireland, they were speedily recalled.

By the time that Queen Victoria had completed the first twenty years of her reign all this was a memory; for the Irish Parliament had gone, Catholic Emancipation had come, and the Chief Secretary had replaced the Lord-Lieutenant as the really effective figure in the administration. When Ireland had her own Parliament, and still more when she had an independent Parliament from 1782 to 1800, the Chief Secretary had been to the Lord-Lieutenant what a Secretary of State is to the Crown, that is to say the exponent of the pleasure of the supreme executive. For some years after the Union the Lord-Lieutenant governed the country subject to instructions from London, and his Chief Secretary, sitting in the House of Commons, did no more than explain small matters of local government; so, when Sir Arthur Wellesley went to take command in Portugal in 1808 he did not give up the post of Chief Secretary, but deputed Croker to explain to the House such Irish business as might arise during his absence. The growing complexity of Irish affairs, the development of English interest in them, and the improvement in the means of communication with the coming of the steamship, the telegraph, and the railway, gradually effected during the Victorian Age a complete transformation in the relations between the Lord-Lieutenant and the Chief Secretary so that in 1905 Balfour, having been called upon to arbitrate in the dispute between Lord Dudley, the Lord-Lieutenant, and Walter Long, the Chief Secretary, laid it down that the real head of the Irish administration was the Chief Secretary. Admittedly that was in the reign of King Edward VII, but the same conditions had prevailed during the latter part of that of his mother.

Nevertheless, if the eighteenth century system had become a mere memory it was one to which a great many people still clung, and it was the basis of the prevalent make-believe. In these circumstances it is surely little wonder that two men, Oscar Wilde and George Bernard Shaw, who were both born in Dublin in the middle of the nineteenth century, should have become the greatest satirists of modern times. Those who rallied round the Lord-Lieutenant and the Castle were, in effect, whatever their origin, the English garrison of Ireland, and it became fashionable to ridicule anything that was Irish. 'Society' aped London, and despised the mass of the population – 'so Irish' was a favourite term of reproach, while religious differences were allowed to become a further cause of class distinctions. As Shaw himself put it, 'Imagine being taught that there is one God – a Protestant and a perfect gentleman – keeping Heaven select for the gentry; and an idolatrous imposter called the Pope, smoothing the Hell-ward way for the mass of the people, only admissible into the kitchens of most of the aforesaid gentry as "thorough servants" (*i.e.* general servants) at eight pounds a year'. As for the attitude of Victorian England itself this was well summed up by G. K. Chesterton when he wrote, 'Englishmen have never taken the trouble to understand Irishmen. They will sometimes be generous to Ireland; but never just to Ireland. They will speak to Ireland; they will speak for Ireland; but they will not hear Ireland speak.'

These social distinctions were reflected in the residential areas of the Irish capital. Dublin is divided by the River Liffey, and even to-day the South side is considered the more respectable, while in the fifties and sixties of last century it was respectability itself. There, in such exclusive residential suburbs as Ballsbridge, Rathmines, Rathgar, and Terenure, lived at least ninety per cent of Dublin's well-to-do Protestant population. There too, were to be found Dublin Castle, Trinity College, the two Protestant cathedrals, the National Gallery, St Stephen's Green, Grafton Street, and the Shelbourne Hotel. To cross what is now O'Connell, but was then Carlisle, Bridge, to quote the late M. J. MacManus, 'and rub shoulders with the Catholic residents of the North side was a thing that Protestant old ladies would no more dream of doing than their early seventeenth century ancestors would have dreamt of venturing beyond the city walls into the country of the ferocious O'Byrnes and O'Tooles. The Viceregal Lodge, to be sure, was in the Phoenix Park (which is North side), but that could be reached in a closed carriage by a roundabout route.'[1] The dividing-line was religion, not so much because there was exceptional religious bigotry as such, as on account of the fact that the richer Dubliners were Protestants, while the poorer ones were Catholics. The Catholic middle-class of to-day had hardly begun to emerge, and the Catholic gentry had long since taken refuge on the Continent, principally in France and Spain, or had changed their religion under the pressure of the Penal Laws. Apart, too, from any particular district, it was easy to tell a Protestant household, for a china model of the White Horse of Hanover would as

[1] *Shaw's Irish Boyhood.*

often as not be found behind the fanlight over the front door: even now, in the middle of the twentieth century, the custom is not wholly obsolete.

At the same time it would be a mistake to look at mid-Victorian Dublin solely through the eyes of Shaw. He was only twenty when he left Ireland, and was thus at a very censorious age, quite apart from the fact that his home life had been unhappy; he had no other recollection of Wesley College than as a 'damnable boy prison', and he declared that his years there were a sheer waste of time; and he found his work in an estate agent's office in Molesworth Street wholly distasteful. Shaw was, in effect, brought into contact with all that was worst in the Irish capital, but there was another side of which he was ignorant, or which he ignored. 'Dear old dirty Dublin' as the city was affectionately, and not inaccurately, called in those days had, as it still has, a charm of its own which was, perhaps, best appreciated by those of more mature years than the youthful G.B.S. Among them was Charles Kean, who never wearied of paying tribute to the spontaneous Irish wit; there was one story of which he was particularly fond, and it related to an actress in his company, who was obviously much advanced toward maternity; she was one day plaintively singing the song in *The Stranger*, 'I have a silent sorrow here', when, after an encore, a voice came from the gallery, 'Faix, and it'll soon spake for itself'.

Kean certainly did not err in his tribute to Irish wit: probably the greatest wit in nineteenth-century Ireland was the famous Father Healey, who was Parish Priest of Little Bray, and of whose witticisms innumerable examples are still going the rounds. One of the best concerns a conversation he is alleged to have had with Gladstone, and rests on the authority of the late Lord Quickswood. During the course of this conversation the English statesman declared that on a recent visit to Italy he had seen a notice on the door of a church in which the local priest offered to rescue souls from Purgatory for twenty-five *lire* a time. 'I ask you,' thundered the G.O.M., 'as a clergyman of the Church of Rome, what have you to say to that?'

At once came the reply, 'Tell me of any other Church, Mr Gladstone, that would do it at the price.' On another occasion he and the Protestant Archbishop of Dublin, Lord Plunket, had been spending the night in some provincial town on their respective duties, and the following morning the Archbishop suggested that they should walk from the hotel where they were both staying to the station to catch the train back to Dublin. Father Healey doubted if they had time, but Plunket looked at his watch, and said that they had. However, when they arrived at the station the train was just slipping out. 'I had great faith in that watch,' said the Archbishop sorrowfully. 'T'would have been better if you'd had good works in it,' replied the priest.

An aggressive Protestant was one day loudly proclaiming his utter disbelief in Purgatory. 'Well,' said Father Healey doubtfully, 'if you won't believe in Purgatory, you may go to Hell.' He hated theological controversy in everyday social intercourse, and he usually found a mild but pointed phrase with which to put an end to it. 'What, after all, is the difference between Catholic and Protestant?' asked someone of him suddenly; 'I've lived for sixty years in this world without discovering it.' 'Never mind, my dear fellow,' said Father Healey soothingly, 'you'll know all about it before you've lived sixty seconds in the next.' Perhaps if Shaw had seen a little more of the Irish life that lay behind the Irish wit he would have thought more kindly of his native city.

The outstanding fact about the Irish capital in those days was that it was a city in transition, and cities in transition are rarely attractive. All contemporaries bear witness to its charm before the Union, and Froude went so far as to say, 'Society was never anywhere more brilliant than in Dublin in the years which succeeded 1782. The great Peers and Commoners had cast their lot with the national life. They had their castles in the country and their town houses in the Irish metropolis. Their lives had a public purpose. They were conscious of high responsibilities; and if they were not always wise they had force and dignity of character. With the Union all was changed. The centre of political life had been removed to England, and the men who had intellect and ambition followed it.' How different was this state of affairs from that which obtained in 1850 can be gauged from an extract from *The Times* of May 30th, 1850, 'Two classes in Ireland stand arrayed in deadly hostility to each other; the proprietors of the land on the one side, the holders and tillers of it on the other. Sympathies for the misery of each other seem entirely to have left the breasts of both parties. The law, indeed, looks with different eyes upon the acts of the two bands carrying on this deadly fray.'

In England, Scotland, and Wales the Crown acted as a centripetal force, but in Ireland such was not the case, and the Union Jack was, as it still is, a party emblem. As for Queen Victoria, had she paid a quarter of the attention to Ireland that she paid to Scotland, some, at any rate, of the troubles of the last hundred years might have been avoided: as it was, during her whole reign, she spent less than five weeks in Ireland, while her visits to Scotland covered nearly seven years.

Until very recently the English have always been extremely jealous where their monarchs were concerned, and have been most unwilling to allow them to leave England.[1] Ireland and Scotland have suffered in this respect, and no *de facto* British Sovereign visited either country from the Revolution of 1688 until the reign of George IV. The so-called 'First Gentleman of Europe' broke with this tradition, and as soon as his Coronation was over he began preparations for a visit to Ireland, with which he had expressed a good deal of sympathy in his earlier days, and the prospect of making the acquaintance of his Irish subjects was made the more pleasant for him by the fact that Lord and Lady Conyngham lived in Ireland. It is not without interest to compare his visit with the later ones of his niece.

He set out from Carlton House on July 31st, 1821, and travelled to Portsmouth, where he embarked on the royal yacht, the 'Royal George', and cruised leisurely round the coast to Holyhead, where he arrived on August 6th. There the

[1] Up to a few months ago there was a service of Thanksgiving at St Paul's, and Lord Mayoral junketing in the City, when the Queen returned from a visit to the Commonwealth, for all the world as if her life had been in imminent danger from her subjects overseas.

King received a message to say that the Queen had been taken seriously ill with inflammation of the bowels, so he decided to land in Wales, and stay quietly with Lord Anglesey until there was further news. As the Queen grew steadily worse he came to the conclusion that the best thing he could do was to cross over to Ireland, land as unostentatiously as possible, and wait in retirement until the Queen either recovered or died. At this point the weather took a hand in the game, and it became impossible to make the crossing, so that news of the Queen's death reached the King before he sailed. George, to quote Croker's happy phrase, was affected, but not afflicted, though he was heard throughout the greater part of the night pacing up and down the cabin of his yacht.

When the weather improved the King transferred himself to a steamboat, and in due course landed at Howth. His arrival had been meant to be private, but a large crowd collected, and he was loudly cheered as he drove to the Viceregal Lodge attended by a considerable body of nobility and gentry on horseback. When George got out of his carriage, he addressed the assembled crowd in the following words, 'I may not be able to express my feelings as I wish. I have travelled far. I have made a rough sea voyage–besides which particular circumstances have occurred, known to you all, of which it is better at present not to speak. Upon these subjects I leave it to delicate and generous hearts to appreciate my feelings. . . . Rank, station, honour are nothing; but to feel that I live in the hearts of my Irish subjects is to me the most exalted happiness. I must now once more thank you for your kindness and bid you farewell. Go and do by me as I shall do by you–drink my health in a bumper. I shall drink all yours–in a bumper of Irish whiskey punch.' On which Mr Roger Fulford has shrewdly observed, 'It was this gracious, almost brilliant, impromptu speech which paved the King's way to the hearts of the Irish, though stern critics might think that such a very recent widower should not have been talking quite so much about that beaker of whiskey'.[1]

However this may be, the King remained in complete retire-

[1] *George the Fourth*, p. 236.

ment until after the Queen's funeral when, on August 15th, he held a private levee, at which he appeared in deep mourning. Two days later he made his state entry into Dublin, wearing the uniform of a Field-Marshal with a mourning band on his left arm, while in his hat was a large octagonal rosette of full-grown shamrocks. He was received with the greatest enthusiasm all along the route, to which he replied by standing up in his carriage, bowing repeatedly, pointing to the shamrock in his hat, and placing his right hand over his heart. To those round him he said, 'They are a fine, a noble people'.

There was the usual round of official festivities in Dublin, and at the close of them George went to stay with Lord and Lady Conyngham at Slane Castle, where he so greatly enjoyed himself that he jokingly said that he would remain in Ireland and send the Lord-Lieutenant to govern England. During this visit he had some racing at the Curragh, and then embarked for England on September 3rd. On the shore Daniel O'Connell presented him with a laurel crown, and as night fell the Royal yacht stood out from the harbour of Dun Laoghaire (for the next hundred years to be called Kingstown in honour of George IV), with the King reclining on a sofa on the deck while the strains of the band playing 'St Patrick's Day' and 'Garryowen' were borne across the water to those on shore.

This visit was probably the greatest personal triumph ever achieved by an Englishman in Ireland. John William Ward, afterwards fourth Viscount Dudley, might sneer at the King as having behaved like a candidate on an election campaign, but even he was forced to add, 'if the day before he left Ireland, he had stood for Dublin, he might have turned out Shaw or Grattan'. In these circumstances it is probably a pity, from the point of view of Anglo-Irish relations, that George IV never visited the country again, and it is also to be regretted that he did not take O'Connell's advice when the Irish leader advised him to establish a royal residence in Ireland. William IV, it may be observed, did not follow his brother's example, for he never set foot on Irish soil.

The visits of Queen Victoria were very different affairs

from that of her uncle. Her reign was to prove even more revolutionary in Ireland than in England, but it is difficult to resist the conclusion that events might have taken a different course had she not allowed twelve years to go by before she first showed herself to her Irish subjects. She might have built on the foundation laid by George IV, and with the co-operation of Daniel O'Connell the dream of Arthur Griffith might have become a reality; perhaps, however, this would have required a different sort of Sovereign from Queen Victoria, at any rate in her earlier days, and in any case such a solution would have met with the most determined resistance from English politicians of all parties.

In August, 1849, the Queen and Prince Albert paid a state visit to Ireland, and were duly received at Cork, Waterford, Dublin, and Belfast. Queen Victoria at any rate was more than satisfied with her reception, for on August 6th she wrote from the Viceregal Lodge to the King of the Belgians:

> My dearest Uncle
>
> Though this letter will only go to-morrow, I will begin it to-day and tell you that everything has gone off beautifully since we arrived in Ireland, and that our entrance into Dublin was really a magnificent thing. By my letter to Louise you will have heard of our arrival in the Cove of Cork. Our visit to Cork was very successful; the Mayor was knighted on deck (on board the 'Fairy'), like in times of old. Cork is about seventeen miles up the River Lee, which is beautifully wooded and reminds us of Devonshire scenery. We had previously stepped on shore at Cove, a small place, to enable them to call it Queenstown; the enthusiasm is immense, and at Cork there was more firing than I remember since the Rhine.
>
> We left Cork with fair weather, but a head sea and contrary wind which made it rough and me very sick.
>
> 7th. I was unable to continue till now, and have since received your kind letter, for which I return my warmest thanks. We went into Waterford Harbour on Saturday afternoon, which is likewise a fine, large, safe harbour. Albert went up to Waterford in the 'Fairy', but I did not. The next morning we received much the same report of the weather which we had done at Cork, viz., that the weather was fair but the wind contrary. However we went out, as it could not be helped, and we might have remained

there some days for no use. The first three hours were very nasty, but afterwards it cleared and the evening was beautiful. The entrance at seven o'clock into Kingstown Harbour was splendid; we came in with ten steamers, and the whole harbour, wharf, and every surrounding place was covered with thousands and thousands of people, who received us with the greatest enthusiasm. We disembarked yesterday morning at ten o'clock, and took two hours to come here. The most perfect order was maintained in spite of the immense mass of people assembled, and a more good-humoured crowd I never saw, but noisy and excitable beyond belief, talking, jumping, and shrieking instead of cheering. There were numbers of troops out, and it really was a wonderful scene. This is a very pretty place, and the house reminds me of dear Claremont. The view of the Wicklow Mountains from the windows is very beautiful, and the whole park is very extensive and full of very fine trees.

We drove out yesterday afternoon and were followed by jaunting-cars and riders and people running and screaming, which would have amused you. In the evening we had a dinner, and so we have to-night. This morning we visited the Bank, the Model School (where the Protestant and Catholic Archbishops received us), and the College, and this afternoon we went to the Military Hospital. To-morrow we have a Levee, where 1,700 are to be presented, and the next day a Review, and in the evening the Drawing-Room, where 900 ladies are to be presented.

George[1] is here, and has a command here. He rode on one side of our carriage yesterday. You see more ragged and wretched people here than I ever saw anywhere else. *En revanche*, the women are really very handsome–quite in the lowest class–as well at Cork as here; such beautiful black eyes and hair and such fine colours and teeth.

I must now take my leave.

Ever your most affectionate Niece

Victoria R.[2]

In due course the Prince of Wales was stationed at the Curragh, and this brought the Queen and the Prince Consort, as Prince Albert had now become, to Ireland again in 1861. It was a brief visit, and on the Prince Consort's birthday–his last as it was to prove–August 26th, the royal party went to Killarney. Those who were in the West of Ireland at the time have left it on

[1] The Duke of Cambridge.

[2] *Letters of Queen Victoria*, First Series, vol. II, pp. 224–226.

record that the Queen did not meet with anything like so warm a welcome as on her previous visit, and that in particular the stiffness of the Prince Consort rendered him unacceptable in many quarters.

At any rate the relations between the Crown and the Irish people steadily deteriorated, though the faults were by no means always on one side. For example, when the Prince Consort died the Queen presented a statue of him to the city of Dublin, but the Corporation refused to accept it, and sent it back to her; which, politics apart, was a singularly ungracious way to treat a widow in such deep grief that it completely overshadowed her whole life. Then in 1885 the visit of the Prince of Wales was scarcely calculated to improve matters, although at first a certain semblance of loyalty was maintained. The City Council of Dublin flatly refused to take any official part in his reception, and his tour of the South was neither more nor less than a dismal failure: at Mallow ugly incidents were only just avoided, while at Cork the city was hung with black, and coffins were placed in the streets through which the Prince passed. All the same this did not prevent him from becoming a Home Ruler in the following year, and such he remained until the end of his life.

At the Golden Jubilee addresses and telegrams poured in not only from all over the British Empire, but also from abroad; only from Dublin and the South there was nothing. These events not unnaturally did nothing to recommend Ireland to the Queen, though no small measure of responsibility for the estrangement of the Irish people from their Sovereign must rest with those who deliberately went out of their way to identify the Crown with one particular section of opinion in the country.

Paradoxically enough, it was the South African War, concerning which Irish opinion was very divided, that brought this *impasse* to an end. The great qualities displayed by the Irish regiments in the field seem to have convinced the Queen that she had judged her Irish subjects too harshly, and she began a series of attentions which were much appreciated by them:

after one victory, for instance, she sent a telegram of congratulation specially for the Irish troops, and in this way a much more favourable atmosphere was created. In the spring of 1900, the Queen carried the matter a stage further, and paid her third visit to Ireland. In the words of the then Sir Frederick Ponsonby:

> We crossed over from Holyhead in the Royal Yacht 'Victoria and Albert' in April, 1900, and arrived at Kingstown in the morning amidst much booming of guns and hoisting of flags. The Queen landed about eleven, and the procession, consisting of three carriages escorted by the Life Guards, drove off to Dublin. Carington and I rode behind the Queen's carriage, and we went at a slow trot, but it was a long way, and it must have been very trying and hot for the Escort. There were crowds of people practically all the way, but when we got into Dublin the mass of people wedged together in the street and in every window, even on the roofs, was quite remarkable. Although I had seen many visits of this kind, nothing had ever approached the enthusiasm and even frenzy displayed by the people of Dublin. There were, however, two places where I heard ugly sounds like booing, but they only seemed like a sort of bagpipe drone to the highly-pitched note of the cheering. . . .
>
> We settled down at Viceregal Lodge for three weeks while Lord Cadogan with his family and staff went to Dublin Castle. It had been arranged that the Queen should not have functions every day, but lead her ordinary life, merely giving dinner-parties.[1]

The culminating event of the visit was, of course, the formation of the Irish Guards.

Such were the relations between the British Royal Family and the people of Ireland during the second half of the nineteenth century, but the background against which they were set was sombre indeed. The ink had hardly dried upon the Act of Union before the agitation began for 'Repeal', but at first it was little more than an aspiration. Catholic Emancipation had first of all to be achieved, and less than twenty years later there came, as we have seen, the Famine, which paralysed all activity. There was, it is true, Smith O'Brien's rebellion in 1848,

[1] *Recollections of Three Reigns*, p. 63.

but its leader was too honest to be formidable, and his instructions that there was to be no damage to life or property were hardly calculated to appeal to the type of person who makes a successful revolutionary. In fact his feeble attack on the police at Ballingarry, 'in the widow McCormack's potato patch', and his subsequent arrest at Thurles railway station, only served to bring ridicule upon the separatist movement, and it would be no exaggeration to say that in the fifties Ireland was, for one reason or another, materially and morally prostrate.

Such was the situation when Fenianism made its appearance, and it is remarkable in Irish history as being the first movement which was openly and admittedly separatist from its inception, and which never pretended to be anything else. The United Irish Society was at first a purely constitutional body, its objects being Parliamentary Reform and Catholic Emancipation; the Repeal Movement was loyal to the British connection in name, as well as in fact, all the days of its life; and the Young Ireland Party, though its inspiration was that of Wolfe Tone (1763–1798), was not avowedly separatist until 1848 when it came under the influence of John Mitchel (1815–1875). James Stephens, on the other hand, had no other objective than the establishment of an Irish Republic, and his chosen means was revolution. He had no illusions as to the value of constitutional agitation; he neither expected nor looked for justice or redress or consideration from England; and he looked to Ireland herself to recover her liberties by her own strong arm. Such was the strength and weakness of the Fenian position.

John O'Leary[1] in his *Recollections of Fenians and Fenianism* has a good account of the origins of the movement:

> The Famine of '45, in so far as it influenced the '48 movement, and inflamed the minds of men both then and after against England, had, no doubt, some bearing upon Fenianism; and

[1] Born 1830, died 1907. Was Editor of *The Irish People*, and was in 1867 sentenced to twenty years' penal servitude for treason-felony. He served nine years of this sentence, afterwards lived in Paris, and returned to Ireland in 1885. W. B. Yeats wrote of him:

> Romantic Ireland's dead and gone,
> 'Tis with O'Leary in the grave.

certainly the failure of the Tenant-right movement had a very direct bearing upon it. Many men like myself, saw that agitation arise and spread without the faintest belief of any good coming out of it, and were confirmed by its failure in our conviction that legal and constitutional agitation, however efficacious in a free country, was not the means by which an enslaved one could win freedom, or, indeed, much else. But all this was a more or less indirect influence. To my mind Theobold Wolfe Tone and Thomas Davis – the example of the one mainly transmitted to us through the teaching of the other – had much more to do with Fenianism than any famine or failure. . . .

Fenianism is the direct and, I think, inevitable outcome of '48, as '48 was the equally inevitable, if more indirect, outcome of '98, and the immediate origin of the movement is undoubtedly to be found among the '48 refugees in America. The failure of the insurrection of that year naturally scattered the Young Ireland leaders over the globe. Mitchel, Martin, O'Brien, Meagher, M'Manus, and O'Donoghue were transported to Australia, from which place some of them escaped and found their way eventually to the States. Others, and the greater number, including Dillon, O'Gorman, McGee, Doheny, Smyth, and O'Mahony, found their way at once, or nearly so, to America. Dillon, O'Gorman, and others, while retaining their national feelings and aspirations, seem to have had quite enough of the untransacting form of Irish politics, and McGee may be roughly said to have gone over to the side of the enemy. But others among the exiles – notably Doheny and O'Mahony – had in no way lost faith or hope in the old cause, and with them and a few obscurer friends of theirs, Fenianism may fairly be said to have originated. Some time in the year '54, I think, a small body of men was brought together in New York, which called itself, somewhat affectedly, 'The Emmet Monument Association'. This name is easily intelligible to Irishmen, and I may leave Englishmen to find out its meaning from their awakened interest in Irish history. Anyway, the name or the thing matters nothing, as in action they came to nothing. But this association calls for at least mention from me, as it was undoubtedly the precursor of Fenianism. I am not sure whether O'Mahony belonged to this body or not, but certainly Doheny did, and no doubt others who subsequently formed the Fenian Brotherhood. But still we have not got to the *immediate* origin of Fenianism. That, however, was very simple, indeed, as are, I think, most things in this world which come to much.

Some time late in the Autumn of '57 a young man named Owen Considine came over from New York to Dublin, bringing with him a communication for Stephens from certain Nationalists in the former city, among whom were John O'Mahony, Michael Doheny, James Roche, and Oliver Byrne. Considine also brought a private letter from O'Mahony to Stephens. The public, or at least collective, communication expressed confidence in Stephens, and called upon him to put up an organization in Ireland to win her independence. This may be said to be the first step toward the formation of the Irish Revolutionary Brotherhood, popularly known as the Fenian Brotherhood.

Apart from their advocacy of separation the Fenians differed from any other Nationalist movement since 1798 in that their base was outside Ireland, namely in the United States; nor was the movement agrarian in character, and probably for this reason it never succeeded in gaining any strong hold over the peasantry: as for the Roman Catholic Church, its support was neither asked nor given. It is also not uninteresting to note that John O'Mahony was a Protestant, and a graduate of Trinity College, Dublin.

The American Civil War was hardly over before the Fenians succeeded in making their organization felt, and the Government naturally retaliated, for it was generally aware of its opponents' plans since that was the heyday of the informer; accordingly, on the night of September 15th, 1865, the Dublin police raided the offices of *The Irish People*, and arrested O'Donovan Rossa, the proprietor, and the principal members of the staff. James Stephens, the 'head-centre' of the movement in Ireland, was also apprehended at this time, but he managed to escape from jail; the other prisoners were charged with treason-felony, and received long sentences. This move on the part of the Government did not, however, prove decisive, for it was soon discovered that Fenian agents were at work in the counties of Dublin, Cork, Tipperary, and Waterford: there were also reports that attempts were being made to tamper with the British troops, and stores of arms were found in different parts of the country. So alarming, indeed, did the situation appear that the Liberal Lord-Lieutenant, Lord Wodehouse, in February, 1866, demanded the suspension of the Habeas Corpus Act on the ground that Ireland was on the verge of armed rebellion.

The Prime Minister was Earl Russell, who in his earlier days had applauded every revolt against authority on the Continent, but Ireland was another matter being much nearer home than Italy or Hungary, so he at once persuaded his colleagues to comply with the Lord-Lieutenant's request even if it meant inconveniencing the members of the two Houses of Parliament. There was a special meeting of Lords and Commons on Saturday, February 18th, and by evening the necessary legislation had been passed by both Houses. The Queen was at Osborne, and the news of what had been done at Westminster was sent to her by telegraph, whereupon she at once signed a document appointing commissioners to give the Royal assent. The Upper House even met at eleven o'clock that same night, but owing to a goods train blocking the way of the messenger despatched from the Isle of Wight, it was not until Sunday, when both Lords and Commons formally met, that the relevant measure finally became law.

The suspension of the Habeas Corpus Act was followed by a cessation of Fenian activities in Ireland itself, though in the spring of 1866 there was an abortive attempt to invade Canada. In consequence of this delusive lull the British Government, by this time a Conservative one, announced, in the Queen's Speech in February, 1867, a state of tranquillity in Ireland, and it further expressed a hope that administration by the ordinary law might safely be resumed. This promise was not destined to be fulfilled. A few days later a band of several hundred armed men assembled at Cahirciveen in County Kerry, and sacked the coast-guard station at Kells in the same county. Troops were in consequence despatched from Cork, and the Fenians, after capturing some arms, shooting at a mounted policeman, and cutting the Atlantic cable for a few hours, withdrew into the mountains. So ineffectual had this attempt been that the Chief Secretary was able to assure the House of Commons that order had been restored in Co. Kerry.

In respect of Kerry he was right, but on wider grounds his optimism was premature, for at a Fenian meeting in the United States it had been decided to 'carry the war' into England, and the first manifestation of this new policy was at Chester on February 11th, 1867. This was nothing less than a plot to surprise the castle, of which the garrison in those palmy days of peace consisted of a mere three officers and a hundred men, and secure possession of the arms and ammunition stored there. On the morning of the previous day the Home Secretary was informed that a number of doubtful individuals were arriving in Chester; by three o'clock in the afternoon they numbered something like five hundred; and a little later they were seen to be assembling in threatening bodies. A company of the Dorset Regiment was sent from Manchester, and its arrival tended to allay the worst fears of the worthy burghers of Chester, and when morning came the Fenians were found to have melted away. Only a few arrests were made in Chester itself, but sixty-seven men were taken into custody on suspicion as they crossed to Ireland.

Throughout that same year, 1867, there were sporadic disturbances, especially in the neighbourhood of Dublin, Drogheda, and Limerick: telegraph wires were cut, obstructions placed on the railways, and on one occasion communications were severed between Dublin on the one hand and Cork and Limerick on the other. These Fenian activities may appear trivial in retrospect, but they necessitated the despatch of a flying column, consisting of the 4th Dragoons, the 6th Carabineers, and the Northamptonshire Regiment, into the mountainous area on the borders of Cork, Limerick, and Tipperary. The last, however, had by no means been heard of carrying the war into England. Early in September two men suspected of burglary were arrested in Manchester, but further investigation proved that they were Fenians of the name of Deasy and Kelly. Pending a remand the magistrates ordered them to be detained in the city jail, but on the way there the prison van was held up and attacked by a band of forty or fifty men armed with revolvers. They found some difficulty in forcing an entrance into the van, as Sergeant Brett, who was sitting inside, refused to give up the keys: eventually he was killed by a shot through the keyhole, with the result that Deasy and Kelly were released, and even-

British Troops Searching for Fenians in Tipperary, 1867

tually effected their escape to the United States. The upshot was that twenty-six people were arrested, and three of them were hanged. These sentences occasioned further disturbances, and a disorderly mob even forced its way into the Home Office itself. Contemporary opinion was much divided as to the wisdom of inflicting the extreme penalty, for, although murder had been committed, the youth of those responsible, and the courage with which they met their fate, gave a certain romantic interest to men who had ventured their lives to rescue their comrades. Among those who held these views was Swinburne, and the poem which he wrote on the subject had much to do with his failure to be appointed Poet Laureate when Tennyson died, though it is to be noted that he had the support of both the Prince of Wales and Arthur Balfour. In Ireland the 'Manchester Martyrs' are by no means forgotten to-day.

Two months later an attempt was made to rescue two Fenians in Clerkenwell jail by blowing up part of the prison. A barrel of gunpowder was exploded, and destroyed some sixty yards of wall as well as killing twelve people and injuring over a hundred. This was the last serious incident in England, though the murder of a Canadian statesman in Ottawa, and an attempt on the life of the Duke of Edinburgh in New South Wales in the following year, were in some quarters attributed to Fenian agency. Thereafter the movement waned, but not before it had given the British Government a fright such as no Irish agitation had done since 1798, or was to do until 1916, and rightly so according to William O'Brien, who wrote in his *Recollections*:

> It requires little wit to ridicule the Fenian Rising of 1867 as a 'Coroner's Inquest War'. None but the very shallow will make merry over the ridiculous side of a very grave episode in the relations between England and the island which she has spent more than seven centuries in endeavouring to tame. In the harvest of 1865, there were twenty regiments of Militia, and at least eight regiments of regulars, at the call of any daring military spirit who should seize the Pigeon House, Cork, and Clonmel Barracks, where the garrison were sworn friends. There were a hundred thousand–it might be nearer the mark to say two hundred thousand–men in the country panting for the arms that would

A Meath Landowner taking a Walk in his Grounds, 1870

thus have been placed in their hands. The Irish of the English and Scottish cities were ready for anything. The United States were hungering to avenge the depredations of the 'Alabama', and had only just disbanded a hundred thousand Irish veterans of the Civil War, who would have swarmed across the Canadian frontier as joyfully as a bridegroom to his marriage feast. It was the psychological moment at which a soldier of Phil Sheridan's eye and nerve might have at least produced the bloodiest struggle England ever had to make for the subjugation of Ireland. It was a crisis when Napoleon's aphorism, 'In war, men are nothing, a man is everything', was specially to the point. The Fenians had a superabundance of men, but not The Man.

The decline of Fenianism was followed in due course by the appearance of the Home Rule Movement, which in origin was Right Wing, as a more recent generation would have termed it. The leader was Isaac Butt, who had formerly been Daniel O'Connell's chief opponent on the issue of the repeal of the Act of Union, and was for a time a Conservative M.P. and a member of the Carlton Club. Butt announced his political conversion, and in November, 1873, the first Home Rule conference was held under his leadership in Dublin. There was a General Election in 1874, and in the new Parliament he and his colleagues were very vocal on the wrongs of Ireland, but this did not take them very far. Gladstone, who never really understood the Irish, had at any rate disestablished a minority Church, but Disraeli, who understood them very well, did nothing for them at all. In these circumstances it was only natural that some of the more active Home Rulers should begin to clamour for a different policy. Joseph Biggar, M.P. for Cavan, and Charles Stewart Parnell, M.P. for Wicklow, began in 1877 to develop obstructive tactics, and with such success, due largely to a skilful selection of suitable subjects and occasions, that they were constantly involved in scenes of angry disorder. In that year they also acquired an extremely able and resourceful ally in Frank Hugh O'Donnell, the new M.P. for Dungarvan, and they gradually acquired the support of the more enterprising members of the Home Rule group, for it could hardly yet be said to have acquired the status of a party.

By now Butt himself had become old and infirm, and he was horrified at the methods adopted by the younger men. He denounced them in public, and a division soon arose between the opponents and supporters of their obstructive methods. From the beginning there was no doubt to which side the sympathies of the mass of the Irish people inclined, and at a Home Rule conference in Dublin in January, 1878, there was open conflict; with the result that Butt realized for the first time that he no longer commanded the support of the electors, and the point was driven home at the end of the year when a meeting of the Home Rule Confederation of Great Britain formally elected Parnell as its President in his place. Butt immediately offered to resign the party leadership; he was, however, persuaded to continue, but he died in May, 1879. The nominal leadership of the Home Rulers in the House of Commons then devolved upon William Shaw, a cautious member of the older group, but he carried little weight, and in due course he was replaced by the forceful personality of Parnell.

The appearance as the most important figure on the Nationalist stage of a Protestant, a landowner, and an ex-undergraduate of Cambridge University, purely English by descent on his father's side and American on his mother's, coincided with another economic and social crisis of the first magnitude. The late seventies were ruinous to agriculture throughout the British Isles owing to the importation of cheap wheat from the United States, and the harvest of 1879 was the worst in the nineteenth century. If this was bad enough in wealthy England, it spelt disaster in Ireland. The potato crop failed, and the estimated yield for the whole country was barely a third of the average. In consequence the wretched peasants were unable to pay their rent, and having no security of tenure were thrown out upon the roadside with their families. Such were the circumstances in which that leader appeared which Fenianism had so signally failed to provide, and his name was Michael Davitt. Born at Straide in County Mayo in 1846 he was the son of an evicted tenant, and he had worked as a labourer in England, where he had lost his arm in a mill accident. He became an active Fenian, and was for a time in prison. After that he visited America, and then returned to Ireland, where at Irishtown, in County Mayo, he inaugurated the Land League. His own views of the situation as he saw it are by no means without interest in any study of the break-up of the old order in Ireland:

> A bad harvest in 1878, following an indifferent one in 1877, and a marked falling-off in agricultural prices, caused serious apprehension to Irish tenants in the spring of 1879 for their prospects should this condition of things not improve. The importation of food-stuffs from the United States, Canada, and elsewhere was also rapidly increasing in Ireland's only market for her surplus produce, Great Britain, and she was met in this market with meat, grain, butter, and eggs grown upon American or European soil for which little if any rent was paid. The owners of this foreign land were its cultivators. The rent-burden was no obstacle to the full exercise of their energies and enterprise in the industry of their calling. They were secure against every power, caprice, and exaction which discouraged and taxed the labour of the Irish food producer, and this fact brought home to the public mind again, what periods of depression had often done before, the great economic evil which the landlord system was to Ireland, and the intolerable nuisance that lay in the power of a landowner to impose an unfair rent upon a farmer's holding. It was the evidence of a great economic truth tendered by circumstances in support of a movement which the facts of the situation imperatively called for at the time.
>
> The County of Mayo had suffered more from the manifold evils of the landlord system than any other Irish county. It had lost more of its population, had experienced more evictions, had witnessed more 'clearances', possessed a greater number of people on the border-line of starvation, and had more paupers in proportion to the population than any of its sister counties. In a period of thirty years its inhabited dwellings had decreased over 25,000 in number, and yet there had been no corresponding improvement in the condition of the enormously reduced numbers of land-workers who remained. The explanation was this: cattle and not labour were placed on the lands from which the cultivators had been evicted since 1849, while the diminished population were crowded in upon the poorer soil of the county. This, however, was only half the evil. The reclaimed bog-land, or mountain-side, onto which the people who could not emigrate were compelled to migrate, was rack-rented in defiance of all economic or equitable

principles. Without the labour which alone reclaimed such soil and kept it in a state of preservation, it could not produce a shilling of rent per acre. Rent for such land was, therefore, sheer robbery, sanctioned by law, and evictions carried out for arrears of such legal blackmail, in seasons of distress, differed in one sense only from the common crime of house-breaking.

Both Parnell and Davitt were quick to realize that as allies they would be very formidable indeed: the Land League would provide the backing of social and economic grievance, and the Nationalist Party would supply the political machine; in this way was started a movement which was ultimately to achieve the purpose of the Fenians, namely the establishment of an Irish Republic. It is difficult to resist the conclusion that the ineffectiveness in our own time of the Home Rule movements in Scotland and Wales is in no small measure due to the lack of any similar combination.

For the next twelve years Parnell was to be the centre of the Victorian political stage, and in retrospect it is possible to see clearly the effect of the blows which he struck at the fabric of the British Parliamentary System. He was the first effective revolutionary of modern times in the British Isles, and after his incursion into the political arena Parliament was never quite the same again. The tactics of the Irish Nationalists at Westminster revolutionized the procedure of the House of Commons, and they set an example which others in due course were not slow to follow, until that House became the regimented body which it is to-day. Asquith, who knew Parnell well and whose Counsel he was before the Parnell Commission in 1888, found him no easier to understand than the man-in-the-street, and he was genuinely surprised when the Irish leader said that it was a mistake to suppose that Coercion was futile; the Irish would yield to it if it were applied long enough and consistently enough. Yet not long after Parnell's death Asquith wrote:

> Did you know Parnell? I did; that is, at one time I saw a great deal of him in confidential intercourse, and in some critical situations. I was a Parnellite–latterly in a sneaking kind of way –up to the end. With all his limitations, and in spite of the

The Live Shell: 'Which of Them will Throw it Overboard?'

(From *Punch* 188

incredible stupidities both in calculation and in conduct which he from time to time committed, I think he will be reckoned one of the greatest personal forces of this century. There is no English-speaking country in which the course of things has not been for the time, and perhaps permanently, modified by the fact that he existed. Of how many men can that be said?[1]

In Ireland he unloosed forces which in less than a generation transformed out of all recognition a social and political system which had lasted since the Treaty of Limerick. Yet Parnell was only forty-five when he died; had he lived to a normal age he might easily have guided the destinies of his country in the First World War.[2] That Ireland was ever his first thought cannot seriously be doubted even by those who most strongly disagree with his policy, and she probably owes more to him than to any other single individual in all her crowded history.

Yet the Irish are essentially a conservative people, and it is not their fault that they have been driven to acquire revolutionary habits. By instinct an Irishman respects tradition as much as he dislikes authority, and it is the Englishman's insistence upon regarding both with equal affection that has much to do with the lack of understanding between the two races. Furthermore it was at this time, that is to say the closing decades of the nineteenth century, that the Liberal Party under the influence of Gladstone, himself in origin a Tory of the Canning school, began to shake itself free of Whig control, and the Whig magnates thereupon began to secede to the Conservatives. As these magnates were acred up to the eyes with Irish land they swung their new-found Conservative friends in opposition to Irish national aspirations. The negotiations between Lord Carnarvon and Parnell during the first Salisbury administration are still obscure, but they are significant, and they show what might have happened had wiser counsels prevailed. In short, it is surely impossible to resist the conviction that some

[1] *Cf.* Spender, J. A. and Asquith, C.: *Life of Herbert Henry Asquith, Lord Oxford and Asquith*, vol. I, p. 66.

[2] The same observation applies to Lord Randolph Churchill, whose early death may well have deprived us of the spectacle of his son and himself in the same Cabinet.

agreed form of self-government should have been given to Ireland by the Tories, with Liberal support, in the eighties of last century. Joseph Chamberlain was unquestionably sincere in his opposition to Home Rule, but that was not the case with the Whigs; they were thinking in terms of the estates with which William of Orange had rewarded their ancestors two hundred years earlier.

As for Ireland, her representatives in the House of Commons, as the price of Home Rule which they never got until it was too late, were compelled to stultify themselves by voting Liberal for measures in which they did not really believe, until in the end their long-suffering constituents turned to Sinn Fein in despair. Indeed it would be impossible to exaggerate the evils which have been inflicted upon both countries because the heirs of the Cavaliers adopted the policy of the Roundheads.

No account of the influences at work in Victorian Ireland could pretend to be complete without some reference to the Catholic Church. It may be said at once that during the whole period it never lost its hold upon the vast majority of the Irish people, and this hold was possibly stronger when the Queen died than when she came to the throne. Its position was, for historical reasons, peculiar, and has never really been understood by Englishmen whatever their political views, though in reality it is very simple. With the overthrow of the old Celtic order at the beginning of the seventeenth century, and the final exodus of the native aristocracy to France and Spain at the close of the Jacobite War in 1691, Ireland was deprived of her natural leaders, and the clergy stepped into the breach. In the days of the Penal Laws it was the priest who, at the peril of his life, brought the consolations of religion to the people, and who provided the only education they received. A link was thus forged which has never since been broken, and this has put the Church in Ireland in a very different position from that which obtains in any other Catholic country.

In spite of this background it has always been a very conservative force, and during the eighteenth century the connection between the Church in Ireland and the Church in France was very close. Consequently the outbreak of the French Revolution horrified the Irish clergy, who did all they could to prevent the contagion from spreading to their own country. This explains the frigid reception which it more than once gave to nationalist movements until they had proved very clearly that they were not anti-clerical, and it was also the reason why it cold-shouldered the Fenians.

In fine, no part of the Queen's dominions witnessed greater changes during her reign than did what was still the kingdom of Ireland. When she came to the throne it was looking back to the Union, the Penal Laws, and the Treaty of Limerick; when she died it was looking forward, however unwittingly, to the Easter Rising, the establishment of the Republic, and Partition: only the *façade* of the Lord-Lieutenant and Castle government remained, and behind that all was changed.

CHAPTER V

Victorian Scotland

To pass from Victorian Ireland to Victorian Scotland is also to witness a transformation, but one which was of a very different nature and which has very different results. The Ireland of 1837 was almost unrecognizable, save in externals, in the Ireland of 1901, but it had not been industrialized except to some slight extent in Belfast and neighbourhood, but the contrast between Scotland at the Queen's accession and at her death was due to industrialization. At both dates there were two Scotlands: when the Queen came to the throne the division was still the age-old one between Highlands and Lowlands, when she died it was between East and West.

In one respect alone did Scotland remain consistent during the period, and that was in its Radicalism. To the first Parliament of the reign the northern kingdom returned thirty-three Liberals and twenty Conservatives, and only in the last did the pendulum swing to the right with the return of thirty-eight Conservatives and Liberal Unionists as against thirty-four Liberals; this, however, proved to be a mere flash in the pan, for at the General Election of 1906 there were only twelve Conservatives and Liberal Unionists to fifty-eight Liberals. At most of the General Elections between 1837 and 1901 the Liberal strength was double that of the Conservative, and in 1880 the total number of Conservative M.P.s for Scotland sank as low as seven. It is not easy to understand why this should have been the case, but it is difficult to resist the conclusion that it must in no small measure have been due to Gladstone, whose approach to the great problems of the day was calculated to make a special appeal to the Scot. However this may be, constituencies which in the middle of the eighteenth century had been Tory and Jacobite strongholds, and which were to be safe Conservative seats in the middle of the twentieth century, could be relied upon to return a Liberal throughout the Victorian Age.

Behind the Scot's attitude to politics lay his religion. In England, as will be shown on a later page, religion to the ordinary Protestant tended to be a thing apart, and in Ireland it was in the main a cause of division, especially after the bitterness engendered by the Home Rule controversy in the eighties; but in Presbyterianism it permeated the national life.

> Glasgow merchants were rich men in those days but all of them, without exception, lived in fear of what the future might hold. And with reason, for scarcely a month passed in which somebody did not disappear. That process was called 'going down the drain', and the description is apt. Town house and country house, carriage and servants vanished in a night, and the shorn sheep were left to face as best they might a blast the bitterness of which was untempered. Nothing was spared them; if the wretched bankrupt happened to hold office in his Church he was compelled, immediately, to offer his resignation, since default was incompatible with Godliness in its more exalted exercise.
>
> As a rule the family left the neighbourhood, and so were able to join some other, and less important, congregation. These 'mission churches', as they were called, were full of the wreckage of the exchanges. One of them, I remember, was associated with a wealthy congregation over which a famous divine named Dr Edie presided. Dr Edie's church was in Kelvinside, the 'mission church' was hidden in the gloom of Cambridge Street. One Sunday morning a wag pinned the following lines to the rich man's church door:
>
> *This church is not for the poor and needy,*
> *But for the rich and Doctor Edie.*
> *The rich step in and take a seat;*
> *The poor pass on to Cambridge Street.*
>
> There was no appeal. Even the terraces and crescents of the West End were numbered and ticketed so that a man's social status might be accurately and instantly known from his address. The best neighbourhood was that which looks down upon the West End Park. Kelvinside came next with its Atholl Gardens and Windsor

Terrace and Westbourne Gardens. Indeed, the only people who might live in less expensive neighbourhoods without loss of caste, were ministers and doctors.

Ministers formed a class all by themselves, and were a constant source of interest and discussion. Everybody sat 'under' one or other of them, and it was a point of honour to uphold your choice as the finest preacher in the country. The sermons were long and, usually, insufferably tedious. So much so, indeed, that the jokes fired off at Church social gatherings were often, in reality, back-handers at the minister.[1]

To a greater extent even than in contemporary England respectability was the fetish of the day, and by respectability was meant Calvinism. Roman Catholics were beyond the pale, and Episcopalians were regarded with the gravest suspicion. Anyone who visited Scotland even as late as the turn of the century will remember that contemptuous couplet:

Hisky Pisky Amen,
Down on your knees and up again.

On the other hand there was a certain amount of social snobbery attaching to the Episcopal Church, more particularly towards the end of the reign when Englishmen of the upper class began to come North in ever-increasing quantities to indulge in sport in one form or another. They naturally gravitated to the places of worship which most nearly approximated to those to which they were accustomed at home, and there they worshipped alongside the Scottish Episcopalians, who thereupon began to raise their heads for the first time since the fall of the Stuarts. This particular snobbery is by no means extinct even to-day, and there are circles where it is considered to be 'smart' to be an Episcopalian, and to look down upon the Presbyterians in much the same way as the members of the Irish Ascendancy once despised the Catholics.

The theatre was not so much as mentioned in any household with a reputation for Godliness,[2] and Dr. McNair Wilson tells a pathetic story of a doctor's widow, who had been persuaded

1 Wilson, R. McNair: *Doctor's Progress*, pp. 33–39.

2 The author's mother, who was born in Dumfries in 1857, had never been in a theatre until she married in 1880.

against her better judgment to break the rule of a lifetime, and see Wilson Barrett in *The Sign of the Cross*, which was being performed at the old Royalty Theatre in Glasgow. She entered the building with sinking heart and downcast eyes; suddenly she looked up and saw, facing her, in big letters, the direction 'To the Pit'; in an instant she was in the street again, speeding homewards. That old lady must have been akin to the one who rebuked a minister for taking a walk on a Sunday afternoon.

'But,' said the minister, 'we read that Our Lord Himself walked in the cornfields on the Sabbath Day.'

The old woman nodded.

'Aye,' she said, 'we do. And I never thought the more of Him for it.'

In the stricter households no hot meals were prepared on a Sunday, and the sight of smoke coming out of a kitchen chimney on that day was a sure sign that the householder was an Episcopalian. When a pulpit became vacant a scene often ensued which was reminiscent of a Parliamentary election, for the Elders would proceed to invite various ministers to preach, and months might well elapse before one of them obtained a majority of the communicants' votes. On the other hand there can be no question but that the average Presbyterian minister was–and still is–infinitely better educated than his Anglican brother, and only the members of the Orders in the Church of Rome can compare with him in this respect. It has been said that the different approach of the Presbyterian and the Anglican to the problems of eternity is well summed up in the first question of their respective catechisms, for the Presbyterian is asked, 'What is the chief end of man?', while the Anglican gets away with the simple, 'What is your name?'

Dr McNair Wilson has some amusing stories to tell concerning the effect of all this upon the Scottish child in the Victorian Age. His father, it appears, was by no means immune from the business worries mentioned above:

> We asked him once, when his anxiety could not be hidden, what he would like to happen, and he told us–'A rise of 2/- a cwt. in sugar.' That night Willie and Mollie and I added a fervent

> petition to our prayers that the hoped-for rise might take place, and continued to make the same supplication night and morning during several weeks. Judge of our distress when we were told by our mother, to whom we confided the great secret, that things had changed completely, and that what our father now needed was a fall of 2/-. We didn't pray about prices any more after that; indeed we all addressed personal apologies to God.[1]

With this religious background it is hardly surprising that the most important event in Scottish history in the Victorian Age should have been of an ecclesiastical nature, namely the Disruption of 1843.

In the early years of the nineteenth century there were many and various Protestant schools of thought which dissented from the Church of Scotland, such as the Episcopalians and the Cameronians whose separation dated from the Revolution, while there were also four branches of the Secession of 1740 and the Relief Church which originated in 1761. Congregationalists, Baptists, Wesleyans, and some smaller sects, too, had established themselves in the northern kingdom, but the Church of Scotland retained an undoubted predominance. Its discipline had been somewhat relaxed, for successive statutes had removed civil consequences from excommunication and other ecclesiastical sentences, while its jurisdiction had been limited to the ranks of its own members, and even in respect of these there was a certain mitigation of penalties in practice. Nevertheless public confession, rebuke, and restoration were still practised, and fines continued to be inflicted for moral offences. Moreover, as Dr McNair Wilson has borne witness, social, if not civil, coercion was a potent instrument in the hand of the Church for enforcing obedience to its moral and ecclesiastical code.

What may be described as internal Church politics were dominated at this time by the antagonism between Moderates and Evangelists, though these could hardly be described as fundamental, and in the opinion of so considerable an authority as the late Lord Balfour of Burleigh, 'they must be attributed rather to temperament and to policy than to deep-seated principle'.[2]

[1] *Ibid.*, p. 37.

[2] *Presbyterianism in Scotland*, p. 134.

Among the extreme Moderates there might be found ministers who were content to perform their ecclesiastical duties in a perfunctory manner, and who might not unjustly be described as mere 'stipend-lifters'; while at the other extremity were Evangelicals who were fanatical advocates of doctrinal orthodoxy, and were zealots to the verge of antinomianism. Some regarded the Church as little more than a department of the State, while others claimed for it independent powers to which even a mediaeval Pope would hardly have aspired. At the same time there were always plenty of middle-of-the-road men, whom circumstances, rather than deliberate choice, had labelled with a party name, and until a crisis arose which brought feelings to fever-heat even the leaders of the two factions remained on a friendly footing. Such was the case with Principal Robertson and Dr John Erskine, the trusted chiefs of the two schools in earlier days, who became collegiate ministers of Old Greyfriars Church, Edinburgh, where they lived in harmony; indeed, when Robertson died his colleague preached a most appreciative funeral sermon.

Furthermore, the Church was bracing itself up to meet the changing conditions of Scottish life. In 1810 Parliament voted an annual sum of £10,000 to augment the stipends of the worst paid ministers, and later on it built and, somewhat meagrely it is true, endowed forty churches in the more destitute districts of the Highlands. Chapels of ease were erected in growing towns, and in the manufacturing and mining centres of population which the Industrial Revolution had called into existence, Missionary Societies already existed both in Edinburgh and Glasgow, and were working abroad, but in 1829 a further step forward was taken when, under the direction of a Committee of the General Assembly, Alexander Duff was sent to India as the first accredited missionary of the Church of Scotland. Whatever view may be taken of the work of missionaries in foreign lands it will hardly be denied that a desire to proselytize is a sign of vigour in any organization.

Meanwhile the Seceders were becoming a more powerful factor, and were showing a tendency to draw together on the basis of opposition to an Established Church. They abjured for the most part their more extreme Covenanting views, and in the political atmosphere prevalent in the country in the years following the end of the Napoleonic War their democratic opinions found a good deal of favour. In 1820 the Burghers and Anti-Burghers coalesced under the name of the United Secession, and not only did they soon prove themselves to be an earnest and active Church but they became advocates of Disestablishment on the ground of principle. For the first time in the history of Scotland the union of Church and State was seriously challenged.

The Establishment was most vulnerable where Patronage was concerned. This had been abolished at the Revolution, but had been restored by an Act of Parliament during the reign of Anne. The Evangelicals had never ceased to maintain the rights of the people in the choice of their minister, and many even of the Moderates were desirous of seeing more power in the hands of the presbyteries when it came to the rejection of presentees whom they knew to be unacceptable, and therefore unprofitable, to the congregations. Furthermore, the increasing interest and zeal of the people in the work of the Church naturally strengthened their claim to a larger share in the appointment of their own ministers. In theory the position was that each presentee to a parish was supposed to have a 'call' from his parishioners before he could exercise his functions as a minister, and this 'call' had to be signed by a majority of the heritors. A few cases of deadlock had arisen in the eighteenth century, but since 1752 the General Assembly, by a series of decisions, had limited the power of the presbytery to a trial of the life, learning, and doctrine of the patron's presentee, and treated as immaterial the objections of the people, or the slenderness of the 'call'. The year 1834 was destined to witness the beginning of a struggle, chiefly over the question of Patronage, known in Scottish ecclesiastical annals as the Ten Years' Conflict which ended in a secession of such a magnitude and importance as to earn for it the name of the Disruption.

At this point there appeared upon the stage one of the leading figures in the history of nineteenth century Scotland, namely the Rev. Thomas Chalmers. He possessed not only an unrivalled power of organization, but a fiery eloquence akin to that of Wesley, and Jeffrey compared him as an orator with Demosthenes, Cicero, Burke, and Sheridan. He was born in 1780, educated at St Andrews University, and from 1803 to 1815 was minister at Kilmany, Fife. It was at the Tron Church in Glasgow where he laboured from 1815 to 1820, that he first attained national importance. He did not hesitate to bring into his sermons the great civil questions of the day, and he told his congregation, who badly needed the information, some home truths about commercial morality, rents, wages, and the employment of private capital. Pure 'Bible Christianity' was the mainspring of his work, and he even brought this into his teaching of Moral Philosophy. His progress was rapid. In 1813 Chalmers became Professor of Moral Philosophy at St Andrews; five years later he attained the Chair of Theology at Edinburgh; and in 1834, at the age of fifty-three he was Moderator of the General Assembly. In politics he was a Canningite Tory, that is to say he was a supporter of Catholic Emancipation and an opponent of Parliamentary Reform.

With his inspiration the General Assembly in 1834 passed an Act of Calls or Veto Act which declared it to be a fundamental law of the Church that no minister should be intruded on any congregation contrary to the will of the people, and presbyteries were instructed to reject any presentee of whom the majority of male heads of families disapproved. The minority of the Assembly expressed doubts of the compatibility of this measure with the statute law, and especially with the Act of 1712, which had restored patronage; it also objected to the disapproval of a bare majority of the male heads of families being made an absolute bar to the collation of the presentee. All the same the Law Officers of the Crown, together with a number of eminent counsel, held that the Veto Act was in accordance with statute law.

Under the chairmanship of Dr Chalmers, however, the General Assembly did not stop there, for it passed an equally contentious measure known as the Chapel Act. The justification for this was that although something like two hundred of the afore-mentioned chapels of ease had been built their ministers, not being parish ministers, had no seats in the courts of the Church. It was resolved by the Chapel Act to assign districts to these churches as parishes *quoad sacra*, to give them Kirk Sessions and to put their ministers upon the same level as their brethren in powers and privileges: it was claimed that this could be lawfully done in virtue of the sole jurisdiction of the Church and of its inherent freedom in spiritual matters. On the other hand no inconsiderable minority considered legislative enactment by the civil authorities to be also necessary, and even among the Evangelicals support for the Chapel Act was by no means unanimous.

Chalmers held that the measure was legally valid, but his opponents maintained that the General Assembly had no more power to pass the Veto Act without Parliamentary sanction than an English Convocation, had such been sitting, would have had. The legal position, however, had never been clearly stated in Scotland as it had been in England, and since the Revolution the Church in the northern kingdom had at no time acknowledged its subordination to the State. In support of his views Chalmers visited London in 1838, and delivered a series of eloquent lectures against what he described as Erastianism. His audiences were enthralled rather than convinced, and Lockhart was not speaking only for himself when he said that, much as he admired his eloquence, Chalmers was as great a Jesuit as ever walked Spain, and that Cromwell was the only man who knew how to deal with Scottish Presbyterians. In these circumstances it is hardly surprising that from 1834 onwards there should be a series of disputed presentations. The most famous of these was at Auchterarder, and there the dispute dragged on until 1842, when the House of Lords finally gave judgment in favour of the minister, a Mr Young, who had been intruded on the parishioners by the patron, the Earl of Kinnoull, and awarded him heavy damages against the local Presbytery which had refused to institute him. Further evidence

New Year's Eve at the Tron Church, Glasgow

of the mounting crisis had been afforded in the previous year in the parish of Marnock in Strathbogie where the entire congregation had walked out in deep snow while an intruded minister was being instituted in the church.

The law had now been clarified by the House of Lords, and the Veto Act had been found contrary to statute. What would the Church now do? Chalmers himself, in a pamphlet written some time after the Assembly of 1840, said the Veto Act would not have been passed had he and his colleagues foreseen the decision of the Civil Courts that they had thereby infringed civil rights. He added that while they would not have given up the principle of non-intrusion 'they would have devised some other method for carrying the principle into operation'. He made it clear that he was not so extreme as he was represented, and that if it would have brought peace he would have been in favour of the Assembly rescinding the Act, and he went on to say, 'We make no surrender of our spiritual independence by giving up the Veto Law when done by our own act; neither do we propose to surrender the cause of non-intrusion. We only surrender one of the expedients by which we had hoped to have provided for it'; and further on in the same pamphlet he wrote, 'the first thing which, in our estimation, the Church ought to do, is to repeal the Veto Law'.

This was all very well, but Chalmers had raised the wind, and he now had to face the whirlwind. The Evangelicals were roused, and the dominant majority in the General Assembly refused to consent to any line of conduct which could be interpreted as submission to the Civil Courts. Religious enthusiasm and a revival of the old Covenanting spirit was growing among ministers and laymen alike in the Evangelical camp, and they determined to resist what they considered to be an encroachment upon the Crown rights of the Redeemer, the Lord Jesus Christ, the only Head of the Church. Before the House of Lords had given its ruling on the Auchterarder case the General Assembly made a strong Declaration of Spiritual Independence, and of their determination to enforce obedience to their Acts upon all the office-bearers and members of the Church. At the same time it must be noted that the two sections of opinion were not in reality divided by any fundamental principle, and the mover of the Declaration of Spiritual Independence, Dr Buchanan, relied on and quoted the speeches of two of the leading Moderates. He did this with a view to proving how completely they, too, supported the doctrine of the Spiritual Independence of the Church and condemned the view which the Court of Session had expressed, though only by eight votes to five, that by alliance with the State the Church had lost the rights and powers inherent in its Constitution. If further evidence is required on this point it is provided by Dr Hanna, the son-in-law of Chalmers, who wrote in 1861, 'The controversy between us and the Established Church does not touch the doctrine of Christ's Headship as taught in Holy Writ so as to give any grounds for saying that we uphold, and the Established Church denies, that Headship'.

The effect of the House of Lords' judgment was to tie the Church down to the older Moderate position, and to deny any rights to the people at all. This made it impossible for the Church to withdraw the Veto Act, and to fall back on the discretion of presbyteries, which many had hitherto considered ample enough to safeguard the people's interest, and so still more resolute resistance was provoked on the part of the Assembly. It was resolved that henceforth the emoluments of the parish, in obedience to the Civil Law, should go unchallenged to the patron's nominee, but that he could not be admitted to the spiritual office unless in accordance with the law of the Church. This was, in reality, no compromise at all, for the minister could not draw the emoluments until he had been invested with the spiritual office, so that what had been proposed was in the nature of a vicious circle. Accordingly a committee was appointed to consider the situation, and, if necessary, to confer with the Government.

As the late Lord Balfour of Burleigh was to write, 'It was undoubtedly a case for conference. Had the Government been a strong one, or even had it appreciated the gravity of the situation, it could have satisfied by legislation the requirements of the Church, without essential alteration in the terms of the alliance between Church and State'.[1] Unhappily neither of these conditions was fulfilled. The Melbourne administration was tottering to its fall, and refused to undertake any fresh commitments; then occurred the Bedchamber Plot with its various complications described on an earlier page. In short, it was a period of political instability in Whitehall, and no help could be expected from that quarter. Meanwhile in Scotland matters were going from bad to worse, with Strathbogie rather than Auchterarder as the centre of the trouble. The seven members of the presbytery who had accepted the patron's presentee were suspended by the Church, so that their presbyterial functions devolved upon the minority of four. All the same the majority continued to discharge their functions, both in their parishes and as a presbytery, and scandal was presented of two rival presbyteries in the same district in open strife for all the world like a Pope and an Anti-Pope in the Middle Ages. The Duke of Argyll did, indeed, take some ameliorative action by introducing, with the approval of the Assembly, into the House of Lords a Bill which would have substantially legalized the Veto Act, but before it could be passed it was killed by a dissolution of Parliament.

From the General Election there emerged a Conservative administration headed by Sir Robert Peel, who made the offer of a Bill which came nearly to the limits of the Veto Act, but left more power of discretion to the presbytery: this offer was first accepted, and then rejected, by the Non-intrusion Committee of the Assembly. By this time the Evangelicals had got the bit firmly between their teeth, and a resolution was carried to the effect that Patronage was contrary to Scripture, and ought to be abolished. A Claim of Right was passed, in which the independent spiritual jurisdiction of the Church was theologically and historically defined and vindicated, and the recent proceedings of the State condemned as unlawful and unconstitutional. For receiving the Lord's Supper at the hands of the deposed Strathbogie ministers eleven leading men among the

[1] *Presbyterianism in Scotland*, p. 143.

Moderates were suspended from judicial functions for nine months.

The final crisis could clearly not be delayed much longer. On appeal, the House of Lords decided that the members of a presbytery who refused to induct a qualified presentee were liable to pay damages for the pecuniary loss inflicted on him. Such a situation could not last, and a large meeting of Evangelical ministers determined to make final representations to the Government; if these were unsuccessful they would secede. Their resolution was strengthened by a further decision of the Court of Session, which pronounced it unlawful for the General Assembly to admit Chapel ministers to the status of parish ministers. This decision not only nullified the Chapel Act, but it raised the question of the legality of all the proceedings subsequent to that date in the courts in which chapel ministers had sat as members. In this way both the great measures of 1834 were ruled to be *ultra vires*.

Peel now announced that he was not prepared to go any further than he had already offered to go, and he insisted that the Church should recognize the decisions of the Civil Courts. As a last resort a motion was brought forward in the House of Commons for an enquiry into the grievances of the Church of Scotland, but it was rejected by a majority of 211 votes to 76. Religion and Scotland are two subjects which the English M.P. usually finds intolerably boring, and the combination of both was apparently more than he could stand. The Non-intrusionists now prepared for secession, and large sums of money were raised both for building churches and maintaining the ministry.

The final act of the long-drawn out drama took place when the General Assembly met at Holyroodhouse on May 18th, 1843. As the ministers trooped in the portrait of William III slipped from its place on the wall; it was caught and duly rehung, but not before one of those present had observed, 'There goes the Revolution Settlement'. According to custom the retiring Moderator, when the members had assembled after the usual sermon in St Giles's Church, opened the meeting with prayer; but instead of proceeding with the usual business he read a forcible protest against the recent acts of the civil power as contrary to the terms of the union between Church and State, bowed to the Lord High Commissioner, and left the place of meeting, followed by the bulk of the ministers and elders of the Evangelical party. The seceders walked in procession to a hall which had been prepared to receive them, and there formed themselves into the Free Church of Scotland with Chalmers for their Moderator. The long-threatened Disruption was at last an accomplished fact.

Four hundred and fifty ministers seceded, and whatever view may be taken of the actual point at issue there can surely be nothing but praise for these men who put their consciences before any thought of worldly gain. There had been nothing quite like it since the secession of the Non-Jurors from the Church of England at the Revolution. Their sufferings were very real, for unlike their contemporary English brethren few of the Scottish clergy had private means, and most of the protestants went penniless into the world. The nation as a whole was affected as it was not affected by any political issue during the Victorian Age. In some parishes whole congregations deserted the ministers who refused to secede, and in such parishes grass began to grow at the doors of the churches. One such church, Rosehall in Sutherland, fell down on the first Sabbath after the Disruption, but as there were no worshippers there were no casualties. By this time, too, the Scottish Church was strong in the mission-field, and a large majority of the missionaries joined the Free Church.

Then came the partings from the manses, and after that 'the rebuilding of our Zion'. This began at once, and great numbers of the Free Churches were built of wood. 'Weel, Sandy,' was the observation attributed to one 'Established' farmer, 'and how are ye gettin' on wi' your wooden kirks?' 'Fine,' says Sandy, 'and how are ye gettin' on wi' your wooden ministers?' There were some bigoted or curmudgeonly heritors who refused a rood of land on which to build the new churches, but such refusals were on the whole rare. Within thirteen years the Fund for the new Church had reached £160,000 a year, and the stipends of the ministers were steadily raised above the £150 which had at first been thought the possible maximum. 'If there was not another man in Europe but Chalmers who could have raised these funds, there was not another country in the world where they would have been subscribed.'[1]

On the morrow of the Disruption the Church of Scotland lay a seeming wreck, for although only 451 ministers seceded while 752 remained it can hardly be denied that the majority of the most zealous and active among both clergy and laity left the Church in 1843; yet when the lapse of a few years had enabled the situation to be regarded more objectively it was found that the Church, though greatly diminished in strength, was not as moribund as its critics were inclined to believe. It gradually began to recover, and Parliament came to its aid. In the very year of the Disruption a Benefices Act was passed, and this measure entitled Presbyteries to take into consideration the objection of congregations to presentees, while in the following year another Act enabled the Church to set up new parishes *quoad sacra* which had been the object of the Chapel Act.

In the sixties there began a movement for the complete repeal of the Act of 1712, and its protagonists advanced two arguments in their support. The first was that Patronage was from a historical standpoint the cause of much evil, and the second was that its abolition would be a preliminary step towards re-union. In due course the movement was successful, and in 1874 Parliament passed an Act repealing that of 1712, and vesting the right of election to benefices in the regular communicants, along with such adherents as the Church, through its own courts, might decide to admit to the roll in each parish. The optimists felt justified in hoping that this measure might lead to re-union with the Free Church for the demands put forward between 1834 and 1843 had now to a very large extent been met by legislative enactment, but these hopes were not destined to be immediately fulfilled; instead, there arose in certain quarters a fresh demand for the disestablishment and disendowment of the Church of Scotland, inspired to some extent by the fate which had recently befallen the Church of Ireland. The truth

[1] Fletcher, C. R. L.: *Introductory History of England*, vol. V, p. 222.

is that those who left at the Disruption were gradually drawn into closer relations with the older seceders who would have no truck with the State. As has been mentioned the previous century had been fertile in secessions and schisms; there were, indeed, schisms from schisms, Seceders and Relief, Burghers and Anti-Burghers, Old Lights and New Lights—so little had separation from the State made for unity. As has already been noted, with the coming of the nineteenth century centripetal influences began to gain ground, with the result that the United Secession Church came into existence in 1820. Twenty-seven years later a further step was taken when the Relief Church came in, and the name United Presbyterian Church was adopted.

As between the Free Church and the United Presbyterian Church there was this main difference: the latter was opposed to the alliance of Church and State, while the former, although supporting the principle of such an alliance, was dissatisfied with the form of Establishment from which it had seceded. This attitude was difficult either to maintain or justify, so there was a not unnatural trend towards closer relations with the United Presbyterians, and also towards the adoption of a hostile position towards the continuance of the existing relation between Church and State. The situation became for a time very confused, and in 1872 a prospective union broke down owing to the divergent views entertained on this issue. On the other hand as the years went by it became abundantly clear that disestablishment and disendowment commanded very little support in the nation as a whole, and that those who advocated such measures were championing an unpopular cause.

Meanwhile the Church of Scotland had never ceased to desire and work for re-union, and this desire had found particular expression in the negotiations which took place between the Church in the years 1878–79. In 1878 the Established Church issued an invitation 'to frank and friendly conference', and accompanied this with a declaration of willingness to take any steps towards co-operation and union 'consistent with the maintenance and support of an establishment of religion' and 'the sacredness of the ancient endowments'. The United Presbyterian Church replied in the following year that while they regarded it as impossible for them to share the trust reposed in the Church of Scotland, they agreed to 'co-operation' at home, and especially abroad; they further expressed a desire for the creation of some regular channel of communication between the Churches. The reply from the Free Church was equally friendly in tone, and agreed 'to maintain inviolate the principle of a national recognition of religion in accordance with the Confession of Faith'. It went on to make a reference to the documents of 1842 and 1843, and advanced a claim to be regarded as the true representatives of the Church of Scotland on the ground that these documents contained the only principle upon which the Churches would ever be re-united.

If evidence be required of the Victorian Scot's preference for religious rather than political controversy it is to be found in the fact that the Church of Scotland chose that agitated year 1886, when Gladstone introduced the First Home Rule Bill, to renew its invitation to a conference, but the time was not yet ripe, and the overture had no practical result. All the same the centripetal forces were gaining ground in other directions, for in 1876 the Free Church was joined by the bulk of the Cameronians, while in 1900 the Free Church and the United Presbyterian Church became one under the name of the United Free Church. Unfortunately this last transaction was not wholly unanimous, for some thirty ministers of the Free Church stood out, and they and their supporters became known colloquially as the 'Wee Frees'. Cross-actions were brought between the uniting majority and the dissentient minority, for each sought to be declared the rightful holder in trust of the Free Church property.

The Scottish Courts decided in favour of the majority, but on appeal to the House of Lords the decision was reversed. It was held that by passing a certain Declaratory Act in which the doctrine of the Confession had been modified, and by ceasing to maintain the principle of an Established Church, the majority had ceased to represent the Free Church: the ministers and their congregations who held by the ancient standards unmodified were in consequence declared to be the Free Church of Scotland, and entitled to hold its eleven hundred churches and all its property both at home and abroad. As this was manifestly impossible Parliament was called upon to effect a compromise, which was done by the Scottish Churches Act of 1905. This is to anticipate, but after all the controversies of the Queen's reign at the end of it there were two main Presbyterian bodies, the Church of Scotland and the United Free Church, and to one or other of them the vast majority of the nation belonged. At the same time it is to be noted that none of the afore-mentioned controversies was concerned, as were the contemporary controversies in England, with doctrine as such, but rather with problems of Church government.

No apology is required for treating at length these differences in the Presbyterian Church in a book on the Victorian Age. They were, as has already been mentioned, of greater importance to contemporaries than any of the political controversies of the day. They cut across party affiliations and they divided families, and no one who is acquainted with the social background of Victorian Scotland is likely to disagree as to their importance. It is a commonplace in England that the public has a short memory, but that is not true of Ireland or Scotland, and North of the Tweed the differences between Burghers and Anti-Burghers, or between New Lights and Old Lights, were eagerly canvassed long after these Churches as such ceased to exist.

What is not always realized is that the detached air which was adopted by English public opinion towards Scottish religious controversies did not a little to exacerbate feeling in the North against England. 'Our leading public men had displayed an indifference to the tendencies of religious opinion in Scotland, and a scandalous ignorance of her religious affairs, which had alienated from Whigs and Englishmen the confidence and attachment of the population North of the Tweed.'[1] The aloof attitude which the England of those days adopted towards Irish and Scottish problems was to earn her a bitterness in

[1] Trevelyan, Sir G. M.: *Life and Letters of Lord Macaulay*, p. 467.

Dublin and Edinburgh which was to be a cause of not a little embarrassment in the days that lay ahead.

One of those immediately affected was Macaulay, who represented Edinburgh as a Whig. In spite of his Scottish origin he seems to have been regarded North of the Border as an Englishman, and this accentuated his difficulties. In the middle of the nineteenth century Radicalism was stronger in Scotland than in any other part of the United Kingdom, and it was stronger in Edinburgh than in any other town in Scotland, yet Macaulay was a Whig of the Whigs. He was also an Erastian at a time when the relationship of Church and State was being widely canvassed. 'But', wrote his nephew, 'Macaulay might have been as much of a Whig and an Erastian as he chose if he had had in his composition more of the man of the world and less of the man of the study. There was a perceptible want of lightness of touch in his method of doing the ordinary business which falls to the lot of a Member of Parliament.' Lord Cockburn bore testimony to the same effect, for in July, 1846, he is found writing:

> The truth is that Macaulay, with all his admitted knowledge, talent, eloquence, and worth, is not popular. He cares more for his History than for the jobs of his constituents, and answers letters irregularly, and with a brevity deemed contemptuous; and, above all other defects, he suffers severely from the vice of over-talking, and consequently of under-listening. A deputation goes to London to enlighten their representatives. They are full of their own matter, and their chairman has a statement bottled and ripe, which he is anxious to draw and decant; but, instead of being listened to, they no sooner enter the audience chamber than they find themselves all superseded by the restless ability of their eloquent Member, who besides mistaking speaking for hearing, has the indelicate candour not even to profess being struck by the importance of the affair.

Typical of his attitude is a letter he wrote when he was asked to subscribe to a racing cup.

> London, July 14, 1841.
>
> My dear Mr Black
>
> I am much gratified by what you say about the race-cup. I had already written to Craig to say that I should not subscribe,

and I am glad that my determination meets your approbation. In the first place, I am not clear that by giving money for such an object in obedience to such a summons, I should completely change the whole character of my connection with Edinburgh. It has been usual enough for rich families to keep a hold on corrupt boroughs by defraying the expense of public amusements. Sometimes it is a ball; sometimes a regatta. The Derby family used to support the Preston races. The Members for Beverley, I believe, find a bull for their constituents to bait. But these were not the conditions on which I undertook to represent Edinburgh. In return for your generous confidence, I offer Parliamentary service, and nothing else. I am indeed most willing to contribute the little that I can spare to your most useful public charities. But even this I do not consider a matter of contract. Nor should I think it proper that the Town Council should call on me to contribute even to an hospital or a school. But the call that is now made is one so objectionable that, I must plainly say, I would rather take the Chiltern Hundreds than comply with it.

I should feel this if I were a rich man. But I am not rich. I have the means of living very comfortably according to my notions, and I shall still be able to spare something for the common objects of our party, and something for the distressed. But I have nothing to waste on gaieties which can at best be considered harmless. If our friends want a member who will find them in public diversions, they can be at no loss. I know twenty people who, if you will elect them to Parliament, will gladly treat you to a race and a race-ball once a month. But I shall not be very easily induced to believe that Edinburgh is disposed to select her representatives on such a principle.

Ever yours truly
T. B. Macaulay.

If Macaulay treated his Edinburgh constituents with scant ceremony when they came to him he equally displayed little desire to go to them. 'If the people of Edinburgh', he wrote to Mr Napier, 'were not my constituents, there is no place in the island where I should like so much to pass a few weeks: but our relation imposes both such constant exertion and such constant reserve that a trip thither is neither pleasant nor prudent.' And again, 'I hope to be at Edinburgh on August the 19th or 20th. At so dead a time of the year I should think that it might be possible to escape speeches and meetings, particularly as I mean to go quietly, and without sending notice to any of our political managers. It is really very hard that I cannot visit your city as any other gentleman and man of letters can do. My intention is to stay about a fortnight and I should like to go out to you from Edinburgh on Saturday the 20th, and to return on the Monday. I wish to avoid passing a Sunday in the good town, for to whatever church I go, I shall give offence to somebody.'

In these circumstances it was not only the fact that he was an Englishman which told against Macaulay. At the General Election of 1847 'the contest was short, but sharp. For ten days the city was white with broadsides, and the narrow courts off the High Street rang with the dismal strains of innumerable ballad-singers. The opposition was nominally directed against both the sitting Members: but from the first it was evident that all the scurrility was meant exclusively for Macaulay. He came scatheless even out of that ordeal. The vague charge of being too much of an essayist and too little of a politician was the worst that either saint or sinner could find to say of him. The burden of half the election-songs was to the effect that he had written poetry, and that one who knew so much about Ancient Rome could not possibly be the man for Modern Athens.'[1] When the poll was declared Macaulay was out by 377 votes: his nephew did not exaggerate when he described him as 'probably the worst electioneer since Coriolanus'.

It is an interesting speculation why, in view of the prevalent anglophobia in the middle of the nineteenth century, Scotland did not go the way of Ireland. Various answers have been put forward, but surely the attitude of the Royal Family cannot be ignored in this connection. As we have seen, the Queen neglected and disliked Ireland, but she had a deep affection for Scotland, and her feelings were reciprocated by her Scottish subjects, so that for many years she, both personally and as Queen, was the connecting link between the two kingdoms.

As in Ireland, the Queen had to live down, or live up to, the visit of her uncle. The First Gentleman left London on August

[1] Trevelyan, Sir G. M.: *Life and Letters of Lord Macaulay*, pp. 472–473.

10th, 1822, and drove to Greenwich, but he took a route which avoided the City as he wished to mark his disapproval of its attitude during his quarrel with the Queen. The 'Royal George' was on this occasion attached by hawser to the 'Comet' steam packet; and the Lord Mayor's state barge was similarly attached to another steam packet: in this way they went down the Thames until they parted at Sheerness, after which the 'Royal George', still in tow, proceeded up the coast. When the King was off Scarborough the Mayor and Corporation in their robes put off to present a loyal address, but the 'Comet' was going along at such a spanking pace that all they could do was to hand up the address on the end of a long stick.

On August 14th the King anchored off Leith in such torrential rain that he decided not to go ashore until the following day. In the interval Sir Walter Scott came on board and George himself brought him a glass of cherry brandy; Sir Walter drank the King's health, and then took the glass home with him, but in the confusion caused by an unexpected call from George Crabbe, the poet, he forgot all about the glass, and finally sat on it. In any event 'Crabbe's visit was not an outstanding success, because the following morning Scott discovered him talking in polished and animated French to a group of Highland chieftains whom he had mistaken for foreigners'.[1]

George was rowed to the landing-place in the Royal barge on the 15th, and, as in Dublin, he decided to introduce a little local colour into his otherwise formal dress, for he wore the uniform of an Admiral of the Fleet with a gold-laced hat in which were the Cross of St Andrew and a large thistle. He then drove in state to Holyroodhouse amid a wildly enthusiastic crowd, repeating to all within earshot the statement, 'They are a nation of gentlemen'. On the 19th he held a levee at Holyroodhouse, when he wore full Highland uniform, with the Stuart tartan, and flesh-coloured pantaloons under his kilt. One wonders if there was anyone in the Scottish capital that day who remembered a similar occasion seventy-seven years before when the palace of Holyroodhouse was equally brilliantly

[1] Fulford, Roger: *George the Fourth*, p. 246.

illuminated, and was filled with men and women met to do honour to Bonnie Prince Charlie.

At the end of his visit the King dined with the Lord Provost and Corporation of the City, and in reply to the toast of his health he said, 'I am quite unable to express my sense of the gratitude which I owe to the people of this country; but I beg to assure them that I shall ever remember as one of the proudest moments of my life the day I came among them, and the gratifying reception which they gave me. I return you, my Lord Provost, my lords and gentlemen, my warmest thanks for your attention this day; and I can assure you with truth, with earnestness and sincerity that I shall never forget your dutiful attention to me on my visit to Scotland, and particularly the pleasure I have derived from dining in your hall this day.' Just before he left the table he rose and said, 'I have one more toast to give, in which I trust you will join me–Health to the Chieftains and Clans, and God Almighty bless the Lord of Cakes. Drink this three times three, gentlemen'.

The flamboyance which marked so much of the King's visit to Scotland, the fantastic capering in kilts made in London, and the overdone sentimentality of the whole approach to things Gaelic, should not be allowed to engross attention to the exclusion of the importance of the event. With all his faults George IV did take the initiative where relations between the dynasty and Ireland and Scotland were concerned; in the case of Scotland they were followed up by his niece, while in the case of Ireland they were not.

In marked contrast was the scene depicted by Queen Victoria to the King of the Belgians under date of September 10th, 1860, from Balmoral:

> Here we have had a week of very fine weather, but since Saturday it has been extremely cold. We made a most delightful incognito expedition on Tuesday last, 4th, returning on Wednesday, 5th. We drove off from here quite early at eight, for twenty-one miles up to the *Geldie*, a small river–*rode* from here on ponies across the hills to Glen Fishie, a beautiful spot, where the old Duchess of Bedford used to live in a sort of encampment of

wooden huts–on to Loch Inch, a beautiful but not wild lake (another twenty miles), crossed the Spey in a ferry, and posted in very rough vehicles to Grantown, again twenty miles, coming in there at nine.

We passed close by Kinrara where you used to be, but, unfortunately, not by the house. *No one* knew us–anywhere or at the little inn. We went under the names of Lord and Lady Churchill, and Lady Churchill and General Grey who went with us, under the names of Miss Spencer and Dr Grey! Two maids *only* went with us (whom we had sent round with our things) and *no* servants but our two excellent Highlanders, viz. Albert's first stalker or head keeper, and *my own Highland servant* and factotum–*both* excellent, intelligent, devoted people. *Only* when we had *left* was it found out. We posted to Tomantoul, a wretched village–fourteen miles, *in four hours! !* with a pair of wretched tired horses–over a big hilly road. At Tomantoul we again took our ponies and rode by Avon Side, and Glen Avon, also very fine; back to Loch Bulic–eight miles from here–whence we returned home in our carriage. It was a *most delightful* and enjoyable, as well as *beautiful*, expedition. I have been besides on many other ones for the day.

This was all very well, and the Queen can certainly claim to have been the pioneer in opening up the Highlands to the tourist. On the other hand the Royal obsession with Balmoral could prove a serious embarrassment to those who were affected by it. The Queen formed the habit in her later years of staying on there until far on into the autumn, when in the public interest it would have been preferable had she been more accessible in Buckingham Palace or at Windsor: as Disraeli put it in a letter to Bishop Wilberforce, 'carrying on the government of a country six hundred miles from the metropolis doubles the labour'.

A few extracts from Disraeli's letters to his wife will give some idea of the life of the minister in attendance at Balmoral:

Sept. 19, '68.

Arrived here last night, ½ past nine; the household at dinner. The Queen sent a considerate message, that I need not dress, but I thought it best, as I was tired and dusty, not to appear: particularly as I found some important letters from Stanley on my table. They served me a capital little dinner in my room, and I had a very good night . . . I thought it right to appear at breakfast to-day, as I had not presented myself last night.

Lady Churchill in attendance and Miss Lascelles, and Lord Bridport, etc., etc.

Bridport told me that I need not wear frock coats,[1] 'which, as a country gentleman, I know in the country you must abominate'.

Sept. 20.

I write to you whenever I can snatch an opportunity, and they are so frequent here, but so hurried, that I hardly know when I wrote to you last, or what I said. Yesterday, I dined with the Queen, a party of eight. H.M., the Prince and Princess Xtian, Princess Louise, the Duke of Edinburgh, and myself, Lord Bridport and Lady Churchill.

We dined in the Library, a small, square room, with good books–very cosy; like dining with a bachelor in very good rooms in the Albany.

Conversation lively, though not memorable. The Duke of Edinburgh talked much of foreign fruits, and talked well.

Although my diet has been severe, and I have not tasted anything but sherry since we parted, I have suffered much from biliary derangement, which weakens and depresses me. . . . Yesterday morning I went out walking with Lord Bridport, and made a tour of the place: so I quite understand the situation, and general features: I much admire it. Mountains not too high: of graceful outline and well wooded, and sometimes a vast expanse of what they call forest, but which is, in fact, only wild moor, where the red deer congregate. The Duke of Edinbro' came from the Prince of Wales' place with his keepers, and dogs, and guns . . . He wears the tartan and dined in it: and so did Prince Xtian, but it was for the first time; and the Duke told me he was an hour getting it on, and only succeeded in getting it all right by the aid of his wife and his affectionate brother-in-law.

Sept. 21.

The Queen sent for me yesterday afternoon.

Her rooms are upstairs: not on the ground floor. Nothing can be more exquisite, than the view from her windows. An expanse of green and shaven lawn more extensive than that from the terrace of Clifden, and singularly striking in a land of mountains: but H.M. told me, that it was all artificial, and they had levelled

[1] This was something of a concession. The seventh Duke of Northumberland (1846–1918) always insisted on his guests at Alnwick Castle appearing in frock coats at breakfast.

a rugged and undulating soil. In short, our garden at Hughenden on a great scale: except this was a broad, green glade, the flower garden being at the other side of the Castle. I dined with the household, and, between ourselves, was struck, as I have been before, by the contrast between the Queen's somewhat simple, but sufficient, dinner, and the banquet of our humbler friends.

In spite of his kind reception at Balmoral and his evident liking for the place, Disraeli only visited it once again, in 1874, and for the rest of his second administration he prevailed on the Queen to excuse him from taking his turn of ministerial attendance there.[1]

The marriage of Princess Louise to the Marquess of Lorne in 1871 was another very conciliatory move on the part of the Royal Family, though in the Campbell country it was widely regarded as an alliance of equals, and there is nothing inherently improbable in the remark attributed to the old women in Inverary, 'The Queen will be a proud woman now that her daughter is marrying the son of Mac Calein Mor'. What will strike a later generation as more remarkable is the fact that the Marquess of Lorne was an active politician first as a Liberal and then as a Liberal Unionist, and that he represented South Manchester in the House of Commons when in 1900 he succeeded his father as Duke of Argyll.

It has been mentioned on an earlier page that Scotland was transformed during the Victorian Age. When the Queen ascended the throne the population was two-and-a-half millions; when she died it was four-and-a-half millions, and this increase was in the Lowlands, principally on Clydeside. What is significant is that this increase was not by any means wholly natural, for it was to no small extent caused by immigration from Ireland. These immigrants were almost entirely Roman Catholic in religion, so, in view of the rigid Presbyterianism of old Glasgow it may be imagined that their impact was in the nature of a revolution. Yet in 1901 the influences of this movement was only in its infancy, but it had already

[1] Buckle, G. E.: *The Life of Benjamin Disraeli, Earl of Beaconsfield*, vol. V, pp. 52–55.

gone far enough for the more far-sighted to envisage the state of affairs which exists to-day.

If, then, it be asked what were the outward and visible signs of the Victorian Age in Scotland, the answer must be that for the first time in its history the line of division ran between East and West, rather than between North and South, and that this was largely in consequence of the Hibernization of Clydeside. For the rest, Scotland was already well on the way to becoming Anglicized. Its upper classes were increasingly being educated at English schools and universities, and its industries were coming under the control of English capitalism: on the other hand, more Scots than ever were attracted by what Dr Johnson declared to be 'the noblest prospect which a Scotchman ever sees', namely 'the high road that leads him to England'.

CHAPTER VI

Victorian Leisure

In no respect was the Victorian Age more revolutionary than in all that related to leisure and recreation. When it began these were the privileges of the few, but by the end of the nineteenth century they had been widely extended to other classes of the community, though such boons as holidays with pay for the weekly wage-earner still lay in the future. This change was made possible first by the railway and then by the bicycle, and it was regarded with grave misgivings in many quarters; Wellington, for example, declared that he would not be party to any proposal which encouraged the working-classes to roam freely about the country, a remark which is not as foolish as it sounds when the Luddite riots and the lack of an effective police force are taken into account. A great stimulus was given to holiday-making in 1871 by the Act which established Bank Holidays. Indeed, it is remarkable how recent is the now accepted pattern of English life in this respect. In 1837 there was no holiday at Christmas either for rich or poor – on Boxing Day in 1832 the Committee of the Carlton Club met to conduct the Club's business, which is a curious commentary on the habits of the age. Of course in earlier days there had been prolonged celebrations at this season, but like many other old customs they had not survived the advent of Puritanism, and Christmas as the Englishman knows it to-day is largely the creation of the Prince Consort and Charles Dickens. Whether they would not have felt that the festival is now somewhat over-

The Prince Consort's Sitting Room at Balmoral Castle

Victorian Christmas Cards, 1876

done–in short, that it has become a good deal of a racket–is another matter.

Contrary, however, to general belief the Prince Consort was not wholly responsible for the introduction of the Christmas tree into England for that had taken place before his time. Decorated trees were known at Court at the beginning of the century, and Dr John Watkins, in his biography of Queen Charlotte, the wife of George III, records that she spent Christmas Day in 1800 'in a very pleasing manner' at Queen's Lodge, Windsor, which stood opposite the South Terrace of the Castle: he continues, 'Sixty poor families had a substantial dinner given them; and in the evening the children of the principal families in the neighbourhood were invited to an entertainment at the Lodge. Here, among other amusing objects for the gratification of the juvenile visitors, in the middle of the room stood an immense tub with a yewtree placed in it, from the branches of which hung bunches of sweetmeats, almonds, and raisins, in papers, fruits and toys, most tastefully arranged, and the whole illuminated by small wax candles. After the company had walked round and admired the tree, each child obtained a portion of the sweets which it bore, together with a toy, and then all returned home quite delighted.'

There is other evidence, too, which points to Mecklenburg-Strelitz rather than to Coburg as the original home of the Christmas tree. Two years earlier, in 1798, Coleridge had spent Christmas at Ratzeburg, on the borders of Mecklenburg-Strelitz, and had noted the custom of erecting great yew boughs laden with multitudes of little tapers, which were allowed to burn out, so that the twigs and their needles snapped as the flames reached them. Earlier still there is a reference to Christmas trees in the journal of a Mrs Papendiek, whose father had accompanied Queen Charlotte to England in 1761. Mr Papendiek was himself in the Queen's service, and we read that at Christmas, 1789, he 'proposed an illuminated tree, according to the German fashion, but. . . . I thought our children too young to be amused at so much expense and trouble. Mr Papendiek was vexed.'

After that there is no mention of Christmas trees in these

exalted circles–they were hardly calculated to appeal to the First Gentleman–until the reign of William IV when his granddaughter has left it on record that parties were held every Christmas Eve in the Dragon Room at Brighton Pavilion where Queen Adelaide used always 'to prepare an enormous Christmas tree, which was lit up with tapers, while from the boughs were hung gilded fruits–apples, pears, walnuts etc., and innumerable gifts of value for her ladies and for the guests young and old.' By this time the custom had spread to Kensington Palace, for on Christmas Eve, 1832, Princess Victoria wrote in her journal, 'We then went into the drawing-room near the dining-room. After Mamma had rung a bell three times we went in. There were two large round tables on which were placed two trees hung with lights and sugar ornaments. All the presents being placed round the tree. I had one table for myself.'

It would thus appear that in Court circles at any rate the ground had been well prepared for the Christmas tree long before the Prince Consort ever set foot in England, but he lost no time in popularizing it. The first Christmas after their marriage he and the Queen spent at Windsor when, to quote his biographer, Sir Theodore Martin, 'he clung to the kindly custom of his native country, which makes it a day for the interchange of gifts, as marks of affection and good will. The Queen fully shared his feelings in this respect, and the same usage was then introduced into their home, and was ever afterwards continued. Christmas trees were set up in the Queen's and the Prince's rooms, beside which were placed the gifts with which each took pleasure in surprising the other.'

By 1847 this was an established custom, and at Christmas of that year the Hon. Eleanor Stanley, a Maid of Honour, gave her mother an account of the scene in the Oak Room on Christmas Eve when the Ladies in Waiting received their gifts. The Queen and the Prince stood by a large table, which was covered with a white cloth, and in the middle of it was a decorated fir tree surrounded with presents. The royal children, like the Ladies in Waiting, shared a tree, but the Queen, Prince Albert, and the Duchess of Kent had one each. After the distribution of the presents the candles were put out, and were relit at dusk on Christmas Day. In the dining-room, too, there were three small trees which were lighted when dessert was served, and all the trees, both in the drawing-room and in the dining-room, were illuminated again on New Year's Day and Twelfth Night. Gingerbread, it may be added, was invariably used for decoration.

The Prince Consort was not the man to do anything by halves, and having established the Christmas tree at Court he used his influence to spread the custom elsewhere; he presented trees to barracks and schools where large children's parties took place, and he encouraged the other members of the Royal Family to do the same. Before his death they had become a familiar and indispensable item in English Christmas celebrations, and the Queen was fully justified in writing to Major (later Sir) Howard Elphinstone on January 16th, 1865, that 'she rejoices to think that the Prince and herself are the source of Christmas trees being so generally adopted in this country'.

The Christmas card made its appearance about the same time, but it was far from being the elaborate affair that it has now become; it cost a penny to buy, and half that amount to post, so that for a sovereign it was possible for the ordinary person to send cards to all his friends. Neither the Christmas tree nor the Christmas card, it may be noted, made any headway in Scotland, where the festival was ignored in strict Presbyterian circles, and the shops in the Scottish cities were open on Christmas Day down to the Queen's death.

As far as travel and an admiration for the beauties of nature are concerned, they were the products of increased security, and the Romantic Movement. The joys of a holiday by the sea could hardly be appreciated to the full when there was considerable danger of being carried off by pirates and ending up in the slave-market at Algiers, while the beauties of mountain and forest were marred by the thought that both were infested by brigands. 'Caledonia, stern and wild' became a magnet for the Victorian holiday-maker once the Queen had established herself at Balmoral, but to his grandfather it represented an unknown and savage land whence had issued that Jacobite army which reached Derby, and came within an ace of returning Her Majesty's forebear to his native Hanover. Internal security made travel, at any rate in the British Isles, a safe proposition, while the Romantic Movement rendered it fashionable, if not obligatory, to go into rhapsodies over waterfalls, sylvan glades, and, above all, ruins of every kind and description: indeed, such was the demand for ruins that new ones were constructed up and down the country. In due course there came into existence that typically Victorian institution, the picnic. Convention forbade a young man and a young woman who had any pretensions to gentility or respectability from being left alone together unless they were engaged, and not always then, but a picnic in a ruined abbey provided many opportunities for the Alberts and Ermyntrudes of the day to become more closely acquainted with one another.

Travel had, indeed, been becoming quicker and easier for some years before the introduction of the railways owing to the great improvement in the roads, for in the earlier part of the previous century nobody would have thought of travelling for pleasure. The situation was well summed up by a writer in *The Gentleman's Magazine*, 'A rich citizen of London has perhaps some very valuable relations or friends in the West; he thinks no more of visiting them than of travelling the deserts of Nubia, which might as well be in the moon, or in Limbo Patrum, considering them as a sort of separate being'.[1] On at least one occasion the mail from London to Edinburgh contained but a single letter. It was not until the reign of George III that there was much improvement in the method of conveyance, and those who could afford to do so either rode on horseback or travelled in their own carriages. In 1784, however, the coaches began to carry the mails, and five years later they were provided with springs, of which they had previously been innocent. The next step was the introduction of lighter vehicles; and by the end of the eighteenth century it was possible, thanks also to the improvement in the roads, to get from London to Brighton in

[1] Vol. XXII, p. 553.

eight hours at the cost of some fifteen shillings for a single fare. Before George IV was dead, over three hundred coaches used to pass Hyde Park daily. The gradual change in the speed of travelling, even by coach, can be gauged from the fact that in 1750 it took three days to go from London to Bath; in 1776 Dr Johnson started at 11.0 a.m., and arrived the next day at 7.0 p.m.; while in 1827 Dickens made his hero leave at 7.0 a.m., and arrive at 7.30 p.m. Fourteen years later it was possible to do the journey by train in a few hours.

Until the French Revolution travel abroad had, at any rate since the close of the Middle Ages, been the preserve of the rich save for the occasional political exile. The conclusion of the Treaty of Amiens in 1802 witnessed the descent of a swarm of English visitors upon France for much the same reason as their descendants go to Russia to-day whenever they get the chance, namely because it 'is the thing to do'; in this particular instance quite a number of them paid for their curiosity by internment until the end of the war which soon broke out again. With the exile of Napoleon to St Helena and the signature of the Treaty of Vienna travel, in what may be termed its modern form, really began. The middle-classes began to visit the Continent, in particular France, Italy, and the Rhineland, and the foreigner soon had it borne in upon him that a travelling Englishman was no longer necessarily '*un milord anglais*'. Certainly a perusal of the phrase-books and guides published in the latter half of the nineteenth century gives a most unflattering picture of the ordinary English tourist of that day, and it is to be feared that the female of the species was even more deadly than the male. Even a man of the stamp of Walter Bagehot could write home from Paris, 'It is a bad habit to run in a Revolution, somebody may think you are the "other side" and shoot at you, but if you go calmly and look English there is no particular danger.'

The situation was, of course, very different from what it has now become with tourism as one of the major industries of the modern world, and examples of the vast literature it has created stare at us from the counters and windows of every bookseller.

Volumes with such titles as *What to Eat in Patagonia*, *How to Make Yourself Understood in Ruritania*, and *Frolicking with Fakirs in Fez*, are legion, and the tourist of to-day has only himself to blame if he does not go abroad prepared for every emergency, social, culinary, or linguistic. The Victorian traveller, however, was by no means so well catered for, and the literature upon which he had to rely was characteristic of a movement still in its infancy. Yet presumably those responsible for it knew the public to which they were appealing, and in consequence what they wrote throws a good deal of light upon the manners, habits, and outlook of the travelling Victorian, or at any rate upon his wants as the authors in question presumed them to be.

These Victorian travellers certainly seem to have had no hesitation in demanding what they wanted. For example, among the useful phrases suggested for a visit to a café in the Ottoman Empire in 1880 are included the following:–

'Waiter, give me some ale.'

'And you, Gentleman, will you have some too?'

'No; give me some steaming hot punch.'

A conversation which surely reflects somewhat adversely upon both the manners and the customs of the contemporary tourist; yet how easy it is to imagine the scene with the Victorian in his deer-stalker and ulster determined not to depart from the habits of a lifetime merely because he was abroad.

For the few who ventured as far as Russia there was special advice. The opening phrase in a section entitled General Conversation was, 'Alas, alas, my postilion has been struck by lightning', while equally useful was, 'Oh, Lordy, we are beset upon by wolves. Some fine fellow do please dispel the noisy brutes!'

The Victorian traveller would appear to have been none too easy to please once he had crossed the Channel, as this suggested dialogue would seem to infer:–

'What is the price of this room?'

'Two shillings a day, service included.'

'Have you no better one for that price? It does not suit me; it is too dear.'

This conjures up visions of the legendary English old lady who boasted that she had travelled all over Italy with only two words, '*Quanto?*' and '*Troppo*'. One can imagine her, possibly rather gaunt and ever suspicious of being cheated; mindful of the repeated warnings she had received about the doubtful honesty of foreigners and of the 'tricks' they would be up to; pointing an authoritative forefinger at any article she wanted as she uttered the first part of her somewhat limited vocabulary; and then, almost immediately, perhaps even before she received an answer or thoroughly understood it, saying '*troppo*' in the firm tone of one determined to be ever on the defensive.

Occasionally, however, a milder note is struck, and phrases are suggested which look forward to an age of austerity and of currency restrictions, as for example:

'Let us go down this street: there are some fine shops.'

'Have you any money?'

'No, I forgot my purse at home.'

'I have not any either.'

'Then we cannot buy anything to-day.'

That has a real mid-twentieth century ring.

The compilers of these books appear to have assumed without question that their readers would be spoiling for a row from the moment that they entered their hotel, and that even the scantiest vocabulary must contain a minimum number of appropriate phrases of protest. 'This room is far too small', or it is 'far too expensive', or 'it has no view', are expressions of annoyance that occur with almost monotonous regularity. That the customer was always right seems to have been taken for granted.

As for the Victorian traveller's tastes at table a Russian guidebook contains some information for those who might be called upon to wait on him, and they are advised that 'the soups provided in English restaurants and hotels are generally of a greasy nature and highly seasoned. Those mostly in use are ox-tail soup, mock-turtle soup, and mulligatawny soup. Others of a milder character are chicken broth and mutton broth.' In this respect the Victorian Age would seem to have set a precedent which subsequent generations were not slow to follow.

The dominant position of Great Britain in the world is implicit in all the tourist literature of the period, and there are repeated phrases such as 'I want to see the British consul', which show pretty clearly how the wind was blowing. The impression one gets is that if the right rooms were not immediately forthcoming at an acceptable price, or if the laundry failed to return in time, recourse would be had to the British consul without any undue delay, and that if speedy redress were not obtained Lord Palmerston would send a gunboat. Behind–and not very far behind–the British tourist was the British Navy. That the aforesaid tourist could ever be wrong was, as we have seen, generally ruled out from the start, but sometimes the phrase-books admit a few lingering doubts as to his honesty on all occasions. The scene is laid in a Russian customs-house:

'You have here a new lady's dress, with costly laces, too.'

'Is this prohibited?'

'Not at all, but such goods cannot pass free of duty. You must pay the duty and the fine.'

'That's very annoying. I did not know.'

'A new lady's costume in a gentleman's trunk is not a necessary article, nor are such fine laces necessary for you.'

The politics of the countries visited were apparently beneath the English tourist's notice, for it was very rarely considered necessary to equip him with the vocabulary essential to discuss them. There were, however, exceptions, and in a book entitled *Practical Spanish*, published towards the end of the Victorian Age, he is provided with such useful phrases as 'The Russian ambassador, after a conference with the Turkish Minister for Foreign Affairs, has presented a note on the question of the indemnity for the murder of the Vice-Consul'; or 'The representatives of Great Britain, Germany, the United States, Austria-Hungary, and Belgium declare that they are authorized to sign and transmit to the Chinese court the proposals adopted by the Diplomatic Corps as a basis for the negotiations'. The Victorian traveller must have found this sort of information uncommonly helpful when he wanted to order a glass of sherry in a Madrid café. Even the great Herr Baedeker himself had some remarkably odd ideas as to the words which the English tourist might find of service, for in his guide to Austria-Hungary he includes among 'Words of frequent occurrence' in Hungary a cow-herd, a book of complaints, and a justice of the peace.

Sport and games had not in the nineteenth century attained the proportions which they were later to assume, so it is not surprising that there is little reference to them in tourist literature. In one German phrase-book of somewhat later date, however, there is a page devoted to light conversation at a football match between Prussia and Bavaria, and on it is to be found the remark, 'Hurrah! The Prussian swine are getting the worst of it'. Significantly enough, the next section deals with phrases suitable for a patient in a hospital.

In more recent times a great deal has been written about the curious habits of the American tourist, but one attribute can be granted him without fear of contradiction, and that is his general, if pathetic, desire to be liked when he goes abroad. His English counterpart in Victorian times was subject to no such weakness, and he was sublimely indifferent to what the local inhabitants thought about him. Yet, with all his consciousness of being a very superior person, he had his lighter moments.

'And that lady, do you know her?'

'Certainly, she is a friend of ours.'

'Is she married?'

'No, the gentleman accompanying her is her brother.'

'I should like to make her acquaintance. Can you introduce me to her?'

In this instance, however, the course of true love was not destined to run smooth, for a sentence or two further on it transpires that the lady was leaving on the following day for 'her summer resort', and urgent enquiry elicited the fact that she would not be back until the end of October. 'Then the thing is impossible' were the words put into the mouth of her English admirer, who would presumably be back in his counting-house by the date in question.

The portrait of the Victorian tourist that emerges from these old guide- and phrase-books is that of a strong individualist. He would have been most unlikely to have fallen for the bulk travel of to-day, though, of course, to go abroad with the normal family of those times was in itself bulk travel of a sort. Nor would he have taken at all kindly to the idea that he was an unofficial ambassador, as is the conception in some circles at the present time. He almost certainly held the view that 'niggers begin at Calais', and for all Continental nations, with the possible exception of the Germans, he had the most profound contempt. England was the greatest, the richest, and the most progressive country in the world. She had defeated Napoleon, who had defeated everybody else, so any subject of Queen Victoria was entitled to put his weight about when he crossed the Channel, and he wanted the best that money could buy.

At the same time he was far from mean, and if he got the service he demanded, which included a certain amount of servility, he was quite prepared to tip well, which, to judge from all reports, is not always the case with his American successor. Generally he was a typical product of the Industrial Revolution, and he was not capable of appreciating the culture of the lands he visited as had been his aristocratic predecessor of the eighteenth century. He went abroad, not because he particularly enjoyed it, but because it was the thing to do. When he came home he brought with him as trophies such articles as cuckoo-clocks, models of the Leaning Tower of Pisa or of Swiss chalets, and glass paper-weights through which could be seen a coloured picture of some building of architectural interest: many of these trophies are still to be found in English homes. While he was abroad, whether he was sailing up the Rhine in a steamer or gliding in a gondola along the canals of Venice, the Victorian traveller never forgot that he was an Englishman, and he expected all foreigners to conform to his ways. We shall not look upon his like again–which is probably just as well.

It is an easy and natural step from the way in which the Victorian behaved abroad to his taste in drink and food when he was at home: here, too, the reign was marked by many changes.

The late Sir Richard Lodge, sometime President of the Royal

Historical Society, used to say that when he was Professor of Modern History at Glasgow in the nineties of last century it was in Scotland generally possible to tell a host's politics from the wine he gave his guests to drink after dinner: if he was a Liberal he would provide Port, but if he was a Tory he would produce Claret. In this connection it must, of course, be remembered that there was always more Claret than Port drunk in Scotland; the same is true of Ireland, and to-day it is possible to get good Claret, if one knows where to find it, in Cork, Limerick, and Galway. It is easier, perhaps, than in Dublin, which has always been very much under the shadow of England, while the ports of the South and West have a centuries' old connection with France. How close was this connection can be gauged from a letter written from Bordeaux on July 9th, 1720, by the Marshal Duke of Berwick to his son the Duke of Liria, in which he says, 'If you really are going to Ireland, you can return here by sea. Boats come daily from Cork, especially in October.' Often, no doubt, these vessels went out laden with wine from Bordeaux and returned with recruits for the Irish Brigade which was serving under the Lilies of the French King. For the vast majority of Irishmen Paris, not Dublin, was the capital of Ireland in the eighteenth century, and it is therefore not surprising that they should have shown a preference for the wines of France even throughout the Victorian Age.

In the Highlands of Scotland there was also a close connection with France during the first half of the eighteenth century, and it is not too much to say that one of the ways in which the memory of the 'auld alliance' was kept alive was by the drinking of Claret. Edward King in his *Munimenta Antiqua* has left it on record that at Castle Dounie the eleventh Lord Lovat was in the habit of regaling his more distinguished guests with Claret and French cooking, and there is no reason to suppose that he was in that respect at any rate exceptional among the Highland chieftains of the day. It was the same with Brandy, for the ease with which Bonnie Prince Charlie was able to secure it in the most remote districts during his wanderings after Culloden proves that it must have been imported upon a considerable scale to be obtainable in the wilds of the Western Highlands and in the Isles.

Ireland, that is to say the Celtic Ireland, not Dublin of the Ascendancy, was Jacobite, and so were the Scottish Highlands: in these circumstances it is surely not fanciful to see a connection between the political views they professed and the wine which they drank. France was the country in which so many of their fellow-countrymen were exiles, and Bordeaux was in France. Port came in with the Whigs, and, like their principles, its flavour appealed to only a limited circle. So the tradition lingered on until Sir Richard Lodge found it still existing in Victorian Glasgow, and it is not wholly extinct even to-day.

Drinking played no small part in the lives of all classes in the Victorian Age, and such being the case it is well to examine the origin of this state of affairs, more particularly in view of the fact that English politicians, notably Gladstone, have more than once influenced the English palate.

There is evidence that wine was made in Britain in Roman times, possibly from grapes grown on the slopes of Purley and Caterham in Surrey. It was probably not a very good wine, just a *vin ordinaire*, and the richer members of the community would import something much better from Italy or Gaul. This cultivation of the grape continued right down to the Norman regime and even later, for the records of the expenses of Warwick Castle mention payments to women for several days in the year for gathering the grapes in the vineyard at the castle, and the *Vinum de Ledebure*, or Ledbury, had its reputation in mediaeval days. Then there was the native Mead, which had enjoyed great popularity ever since Anglo-Saxon times, if not from a still earlier date. What killed the industry seems to have been the closer association with the Continent which was established in the eleventh and twelfth centuries.

First of all there was the importation of German wines, for it was then that Hock made its first appearance on the English market, and the suggestion has been made that the name was derived from the village of Hockheim, which is situated on the right bank of the River Main close to its confluence with the Rhine, probably because it was easier than most foreign words for English people to pronounce. However that may be, the generic term for German wines in the Middle Ages was Rhenish, and in Norman and Plantagenet times they were drunk in considerable quantity. In these circumstances it was naturally a matter of great concern to the consumer when there was any interruption in the supply of Rhenish. Indeed, on one occasion Alderman Sir Henry Picard, Master of the Vintners Company, fitted out some ships at his own expense, and cleared the North Sea of the pirates who were interfering with the wine trade. So powerful were the importers of wine in those days that in 1363, when Edward III dined in the Vintners' Hall, he brought with him no fewer than four other Kings, namely John II of France, who had been captured three years before at Poitiers; David II of Scotland, son of the victor of Bannockburn; Waldemar IV of Denmark, one of that country's greatest rulers; and Peter of Cyprus, who hoped for English aid to recover the kingdom of Jerusalem. There is, it may be added, to this day a tablet in the Vintners' Hall to mark the event.

Then, secondly, there was the competition of French wines, for under the Plantagenets large areas of South-West France acknowledged the King of England, and Bordeaux itself was in English hands from 1152 to 1453. So it is no exaggeration to say that the production of wine in England was killed by a policy which had for its basis the maintenance of a strong foothold at the mouth of the Garonne and friendship with the German princes as a counterpoise to the dominance of France.

What the English producer had had to face by way of competition before he was finally forced out of business can be estimated from some figures quoted by Lieut-Colonel G. R. Gayre in a recent work.[1] 'We find', he says, 'that in the thirteenth century Gascon, Auxerre, France, and Moselle wines were coming in at a rate of between ¾d. and 3½d. a gallon. By the fourteenth century Gascon wine (which was 90 per cent of our imports) was priced at 3½d. a gallon, although in London

[1] *Wassail! In Mazers of Mead*, p. 101.

in 1388 it went as high as $4\frac{1}{2}$d. Rhine wine at the same time cost from 6d. to 1s. 6d.' In comparison, Colonel Gayre goes on to say, Mead could hardly have been sold for less than 11d. a gallon, and was probably nearer 1s. 6d. For the next two or three hundred years there were no notable changes in the drinking habits of the English people, and home-brewed ale and light wines formed their staple drink. Towards the end of the seventeenth century, however, politics once more took a hand, and a transformation in taste occurred of which the effects can be traced down to the present day. The Revolution of 1688, by expelling the main line of the House of Stuart, severed the link which had for so long connected England and France; and the resulting rivalry between the two countries was soon carried into the economic field, with consequences which were to prove disastrous to the English palate.

In 1703 there was concluded the Methuen Treaty with Portugal, and from that date may be traced the rise of Port-drinking in England, which in due course was to result in the victory of Port over Claret, and in the establishment of gout as a national infirmity. Between 1675 and 1688 England had imported from France a yearly average of about 15,000 tuns of wine as compared with a mere 300 tuns from Portugal, but when, after 1688, the French export was stopped by war the Portuguese imports rose to an annual figure of 9,459. The writing was already on the wall. In 1702, after five years of peace, the War of the Spanish Succession began, and the wine trade between France and England was again interrupted; then, in the following year, came the Methuen Treaty.

Its object was two-fold–to give England a monopoly for her woollen goods in the Portuguese markets and to injure France by granting preferential duties to Portuguese wines, which were to be admitted at a third less duty than their French rivals. The treaty suited the governing classes of both countries. The great landowners of Portugal foresaw a rise in the price of their wines; the great landowners in England increased profits from their wool; the merchants an active exchange; and the shippers profitable freights. So Portugal proceeded to join England, Austria, and the Dutch in the war against France and Spain; her soldiers in due course marched to their downfall at the battle of Almansa; and the death-knell of light wines in England was sounded. Between 1704 and 1712 the importation of Port rose to a total of 118,908 tuns, and a new habit had been acquired. Incidentally, the Methuen Treaty also dealt a heavy blow at the German wines, though the effect was not so immediately felt, for the importation of them fell from over 250,000 gallons in 1700 to less than 28,000 in 1824. All the same, Claret fought a gallant, if losing, battle with Port throughout the whole of the eighteenth century, and, as we have seen, it held its ground in Ireland and Scotland. It should, however, be noted that the two-and three-bottle men of those days drank a wood, not a vintage, Port, and they drank it from smaller bottles than are used to-day. Furthermore, even the connoisseur would appear to have had a sweeter tooth than his modern descendants, though this may have been due to the difficulty of procuring sugar, for there was to be a definite demand for the sweeter wines during the Second World War when sugar was again scarce.

The difference between French and Portuguese wines may be held to be a mere question of taste, but the same age that witnessed the triumph of Port over Claret also saw the beginning of an orgy of spirit-drinking, the deleterious effects of which are indisputable, and which lasted well on into the Victorian Age which was the heyday of the gin palace. Dutch William brought with him the coarse habit of drinking that particular beverage, and it spread with lightning rapidity among the lower classes. Gin became so cheap that a tavern in Southwark could put up a notice, 'Drunk for 1d., Dead drunk for 2d. Clean straw for nothing'. So great had the evil grown that by 1751 Carlyn Morris was writing in his *Observations on the past Growth and present State of London*, 'The diminution of births set out from the time that the consumption of these liquors by the common people has become enormous. . . . As this consumption hath been continually increasing since that time, the amount of the births hath been continually diminishing. . . . Can it be necessary to add to this shocking loss . . . the sickly state of such infants as are born, who with difficulty pass through the first stages of life, and live very few of them to years of manhood? . . . Enquire from the several hospitals in this City, whether any increase of patients and of what sort, are daily brought under their care? They will declare, increasing multitudes of dropsical and consumptive people arising from the effects of spirituous liquors.'

While the monarchy still stood with its powers unimpaired such a state of affairs would have been unthinkable, for the distillers of London had been incorporated by Charles I and had been given a right of search within a radius of twenty-one miles. The distilling trade, however, was regarded as the great support of the landed interest, which now controlled the country's destinies, so the charter was over-ridden; and to protect distillers from actions brought against them by the Distillers Company they were also freed from the statutory obligation to serve a seven years' apprenticeship. Anyone was free to distil on giving notice to the Commissioners of Excise and paying the low excise duty, and anyone was free to retail spirits without the justices' licence required from alehouse-keepers. So large vested interests were created, and Lord Harvey (or rather Samuel Johnson) could say in 1743 'that the great fortunes recently made were to him a convincing proof that the trade of distilling was the most profitable of any now exercised in the kingdom except that of being broker to a Prime Minister'. Against the vested interests the Whig oligarchy was impotent even had it wished to take action, and there is not the least evidence that it had any such desire. It is possible to hold one of several opinions concerning the political consequences of the Revolution of 1688, but there can be no denying the fact that it made drastic changes in the drinking habits of the English.

Four years after the conclusion of the Methuen Treaty came the Union of England and Scotland, and the introduction of Port into the northern kingdom: the two events were commemorated by a contemporary in the following lines:

Cricket at Lord's, 1850

Football at Rugby, 1870

Firm and erect the Caledonian stood,
Old was his mutton, and his Claret good.
'Let him drink Port!' the English statesman cried:
He drank the poison and his spirit died.

For the rest of the eighteenth century the taste for Port continued to increase, and in 1783 we find the Younger Pitt complaining that in Rheims–of all places–he could not get any wine that was even tolerable. Yet he was by no means insensible to the appeal of the French vineyards, for when he concluded his commercial treaty with France three years later it was agreed that a most-favoured-nation clause should be inserted by which the duties on French wines should be reduced to the level of those imposed upon the wines of Portugal. In spite, too, of Pitt's apparent distaste for it, Champagne was beginning to acquire some popularity in England, though Monsieur André Simon holds that it had been drunk in the days of Charles I, who 'tasted sparkling Champagne before anybody had the chance of doing so in France. . . . It was shipped in casks not long after the vintage; it was bottled on arrival, corked down, and drunk in a semi-sparkling condition.' What might have been the effect of Pitt's reversal of the policy which had dictated the Methuen Treaty, and whether Claret might have regained the ground it had lost, is impossible to say, for hostilities supervened once more, and for the next twenty-two years France and Britain were at war; with the result that to all intents and purposes a whole generation grew up knowing little or nothing of French wines; nor was this all, for the men who served in the Peninsula became more than ever addicted to the products of Spain and Portugal, and their preferences remained unchanged when they returned home.

This apparent digression has been rendered necessary in order to describe the background of the Victorian Age in the matter of drink, and during the reigns of George IV and William IV, as well as during the earlier part of the reign of their successor, there was little alteration in the pattern of English drinking. William IV was fully in the Hanoverian tradition when he sent his ministers an invitation to dinner accompanied by the proviso that he expected each of them to drink two bottles of wine. The number of people who habitually drank wine with their meals was, as it still is, comparatively limited, but there was a widespread demand for a glass or two of Port after a meal; while when they wished to ring a change the early Victorians had a great variety of dark and rich after-dinner Sherries from which to choose, and there was, of course, always Madeira. Claret was almost completely out of fashion. The revolution in drinking habits may be said to have begun in 1860 with Gladstone's famous Budget in which he drastically reduced the duties on foreign wines, and in consequence there was soon a modification in the popular taste.

The chief, and immediate, beneficiary was Champagne, on which the duty was now a mere 5d. a bottle. The age, too, was becoming democratic, and Champagne, with its gas and glitter, is pre-eminently the wine of democracy and the democratic politician. What had, among other things, hitherto militated against any extensive consumption of Champagne in England was that it was sweet, and the Englishman's palate in those days would appear not to have been as sweet as that of his Continental neighbours. Canning was an exception, for on being asked his opinion of a bottle of dry Champagne, he declared, 'The man who says that he likes dry Champagne will say anything'. In the sixties a drier Champagne than heretofore began to find its way on to English dinner-tables, and the success of the wine was assured. From then until the outbreak of the First World War it was the fashion, and the Naughty Nineties and the Edwardian Era would have been unthinkable without 'bubbly' as it was affectionately termed.

The year 1878 seemed to many to mark the heyday of the Victorian Age, and not for wine alone:

A year there was of glory,
Of promise false and fair,
When Downing Street was Tory,
And England foiled the Bear;
When all the wine succeeded
From Douro to Moselle,

And all the papers needed
The wares I had to sell;
When, friends with love and leisure,
Youth not yet left behind,
I worked or played at pleasure,
Found god–and goddess–kind;
Played my last rubber cosy,
Took my last miss at loo,
When all my world was rosy,
But when I knew not–You!

There was another aspect of the Victorian revolution in drinking habits, and it related to the consumption of spirits. For very many years the only spirits drunk in England were Brandy by the upper classes and Gin by the lower; both Scotch Whisky and Irish Whiskey were unknown, and when the novelist wanted to portray his villain as drinking himself to death it was to Brandy that he sent him. 'Scatcherd has been drunk this week past', Trollope wrote of Sir Roger in *Dr Thorne:* 'I am told that he has taken over three gallons of Brandy.' Yet by the end of the century Scotch and Irish had displaced Brandy save as a post-prandial liqueur, and it was exceedingly rare to hear anyone, who was not a sea-sick passenger, call for a Brandy with either water or soda.

During the Victorian Age the *apéritif* of more recent times was unknown, Sherry was either consumed with a biscuit in the middle of the morning, or it was drunk with the soup. Even as early as the Peninsular War the tolerant Sir George Bell comments most adversely upon the conduct of an officer who came into the Mess of the Border Regiment and proceeded to help himself to Sherry before the meal was served. Queen Victoria had been for some years in her grave before the practice became common of drinking a glass or two of Sherry before going in to lunch or dinner.

If, however, the Victorian Age effected some revolutionary changes in drinking habits, this was nothing to its achievements in the field of smoking. When the Queen came to the throne the custom of taking snuff was still unchallenged, and the habit was indulged in by women just as much as by men. Queen

Charlotte in particular was a great snuff-taker, and Captain Gronow records how he saw her on the terrace at Windsor using her snuff-box very liberally indeed. George IV followed his mother's example in having a snuff-box, but it was more for show than for use: he made a great parade of taking snuff, and conveyed it to his nose with a great deal of circumstance, but he never allowed any to enter his nostrils. Everyone carried a snuff-box, and intimate friends would offer one another a pinch, but the importunate were often refused. On one occasion Beau Brummell, who prided himself on the quality of his snuff, was very rude to the Bishop of Winchester, when they were dining together at the Pavilion at Brighton as guests of the Regent. The Bishop, uninvited, took a pinch from Brummell's box, which lay within easy reach, whereupon the Beau told a servant to empty the rest of the snuff into the fire. The Regent was very angry, and severely reprimanded Brummell: indeed, some authorities hold that this incident was the first cause of difference between them.

The Beau opened his snuff-box with a particular grace, and with one hand only, the left. The favourite snuff in the early part of the nineteenth century was that sold by Messrs Fribourg and Tryer, and the best was known as the 'veritable Martinique'. When a hogshead of this precious stuff arrived it was solemnly opened in the shop, and submitted to the judgment of some great authority. On one occasion Brummell was performing this function, and, after taking a few pinches, he condemned the snuff unhesitatingly: 'It is not at all the sort of thing,' he said, 'that any man with the slightest pretension to correct taste could possibly patronize.' At this observation the importers were in despair, for the adverse opinion would soon spread, and the stock of snuff would remain on their hands. There was nothing for it but to conciliate the Beau, which was not difficult, as he was extremely venal. After, therefore, being diplomatically approached, he informed Messrs Fribourg and Tryer, 'By some oversight I did not put my name down on your Martinique list and so I obtained none of this, which as a matter of fact I do not dislike. Since the hogshead has been condemned you will not object to me having three jars full of it. You may mention the fact, and when once known I think there is little doubt there will be a speedy demand for the remainder.' The hint was taken; it was given out that Brummell had paid for three jars; and in a few days the whole consignment was sold.

It is not generally realized how slowly the use of tobacco made its way in society, and as late as 1850 Gronow could write, 'Nowadays snuff-boxes are on the tables of great people and at messes'. There was a complete absence of any provision for smoking in club accommodation, and either there was no smoking-room at all or there were the most meagre arrangements for those who wished to smoke. A smoking-room was not provided at the Athenæum for some time after its foundation, nor was any such place included in the first plan of the Reform Club. There was no provision for it in the original Oriental, and permission to smoke within its walls was not given for some forty years, although a constant bone of contention between opposing factors all that time. The persistent resistance of the non-smokers to any improvement in the smoke-room of the Alfred is said to have been a contributory cause[1] to the demise of that club in 1855, for it was perfectly solvent.

Queen Victoria entertained an aversion to smoking in any form which was as pronounced as that of her ancestor, James I, in his *Counterblasts against Tobacco*. He denounced the habit as 'a custome lothsome to the eye, hatefull to the nose, harmefull to the braine, dangerous to the lungs, and in the blacke stinking fume thereof, nearest resembling the horrible Stigian smoke of the pit that is bottomless'. Queen Victoria would certainly have agreed with this denunciation, though she might have expressed herself differently. She even objected to reading letters written by anyone who had smoked when writing them, and on one occasion Frederick Ponsonby received a message from her asking him not to smoke when decyphering telegrams because the official box in which he sent her the decoded document smelt

[1] Another is said to have been its dullness, for Lord Alvanley remarked one day at White's, 'I stood it as long as I could, but when the seventeenth bishop was proposed I gave in; I really could not enter the place without being put in mind of my catechism'.

strongly of tobacco. Whether or not it was due to this Royal disapproval, the practice of smoking was of slow growth. The clergy as a whole made no secret of their condemnation of it; it was not considered good form to smoke in the streets; and a cigar was not tolerated in the presence of ladies. Smoking was not permitted in regimental messes or barracks until 1856, nor was it allowed in the waiting-rooms or on the platforms of railway-stations.

Agitation for permission to smoke began in the West End clubs as early as the thirties, but the demand came from a minority which was constantly out-voted, and it was not until 1845 that White's placed a room at the disposal of smokers. The habit, however, was much more prevalent on the Continent, and the first great impetus to the spread of smoking was the Great Exhibition of 1851; this event brought a large number of foreign visitors to London, and they were constantly to be seen smoking in the streets and other public places. The Carlton was distinctly progressive in this matter, and as early as 1836 the committee 'directed a notice to be put in the morning-room that there being a smoking-room, smoking could not be allowed in any other apartment', while by the middle fifties it was also permitted in one of the billiard-rooms. White's would seem to have repented of the concession it had made, for in 1866 there was a particularly fierce battle over a resolution to allow smoking in the drawing-room: old members who had not been seen in the club for years were dragged up to London to vote against the revolutionary measure, which was in consequence lost by a considerable majority.

Unfortunately for White's this decision came at a moment when the Prince of Wales was beginning to take his place as the leading figure in London life, and he was a confirmed smoker. He had signified his intention of becoming a member of White's and of making it his principal club, but in view of this adverse decision he reconsidered his intention, and encouraged the foundation of the Marlborough, which enjoyed his patronage and support to the end of his life, not least because smoking was permitted in every part of the house except the coffee-room.

When one passes from where the Victorians did or did not smoke to what they smoked it is to discover that revolutionary changes took place during the reign, for one of the consequences of the Crimean War was the production of the cigarette commercially, for the first factory was set up in 1857. The cigarettes of those days were twice as thick and half as long again as their successors to-day, and they had a straw or cane mouthpiece. Many people, of course, preferred to roll their own. All the same, even so late as 1900 less than one eighth of the tobacco sold was in cigarettes, while pipe tobaccos were at their peak of consumption; and it was not until after the First World War that the cigarette sales went ahead of those of pipe tobaccos. Cigars were more of a habit than they have since become, and they were all the rage in the numerous dives or 'divans'. Typical of the attitude towards them is the alleged conversation between a smoker and a poet:

'Did you like Venice?' asked the poet.

'I didn't like Venice,' came the reply.

'Why not, Sir?'

'They had no good cigars there, and I left the place in disgust.'

In one respect most West End clubs were extremely conservative throughout the Victorian Age, and that is where the admission of visitors was concerned. The Guards', then, of course, situated in Pall Mall, as late as 1901 refused to allow strangers to enter its doors, while although the Carlton would permit them to pass the threshold they could go no further than the great hall: the Athenæum allotted a small chamber near the entrance where members might give interviews to passing friends and callers. The Travellers' permitted strangers to dine, but not during the Parliamentary Session, while the Oxford and Cambridge allowed six members to entertain two guests apiece upon giving sufficient notice. Only the Garrick was more hospitable, for there a member might introduce three friends to the Strangers' coffee-room for dinner, or two for luncheon or supper, but not more than five times a year; even more liberal rules applied with regard to supper on Saturday night.

Until long after the Queen's death it was in all clubs with the exception of Pratt's essential to dress for dinner, and only in the matter of wearing hats on the premises was there any latitude: in some clubs it was considered bad taste to keep them on indoors while in others it was the traditional custom to keep them on at all times and in all parts of the house. Generally, the hat was deposited under a man's chair at meals, and in the library, when used as a dormitory, it found a place on the mantelpiece. The Oriental and the St James's frowned on the wearing of hats at dinner, though it was permitted at breakfast and lunch.

The London clubman of Victorian times did not keep very early hours. Few clubs opened their doors before 9.0 a.m., or perhaps 8.30 a.m. in the summer, and by that time the housemaids, who lived on the premises, would have completed their cleaning. Breakfast would have been ordered overnight, but it was not greatly patronized. Lunch, like smoking, made its appearance slowly, and it is not until 1856 that it is mentioned in the minutes of the Carlton, when it was decided that luncheons could not be served after 4.0. p.m. This, incidentally, brought a protest from the Marquess of Salisbury and Lord Dynevor, who wanted the hour put forward until five o'clock. By the end of the nineteenth century luncheon had firmly established itself, and was generally taken between 1.30 and 3.0. Afternoon tea, too, was unknown to the earlier Victorians who consoled themselves with Sherry and Bitters at that hour. The time of, and the attendance at, dinner varied, but it tended to grow later with the passage of the years than six or six-thirty which it had been in the fifties, though people dined early by modern West End standards until the accession of King Edward VII, and this was particularly the case, it may be added, in the provinces. Supper was very much in fashion throughout the period, and this tended to cause clubs to keep open until three or four in the morning: on one occasion some members of a West End club sat up until daylight in order to swim a match in the Serpentine.

What of the outlook and habits of those who belonged to

these clubs? The late Viscount Mersey of Toxteth wrote a description of his life as an officer in the Grenadier Guards in the nineties:

> Our daily life in London was pleasant though rather idle. When not on guard we were usually clear of duty by ten o'clock in the morning, and one then either rode in Hyde Park, played racquets at Prince's, or strolled along Piccadilly in a tall hat and a frock coat meeting one's friends, and a tame goat which used to perambulate the pavement from Park Lane to Devonshire House. We drove about in hansom cabs, and very smart many of them were, with the driver in a double-breasted yellow greatcoat with a buttonhole and a shiny top hat, a bow on his whip, a tasselled white linen cover over the roof, and the harness glittering and jingling with polished bells. . . .
>
> There was a good deal of lunching out—2.0 p.m. was the ordinary hour, and the amount of food consumed was considerable; claret and brandy-and-soda being more general drinks than the present barley-water or whisky. In the evening we dined at a club, Brown's Hotel, the Café Royal, or the newly opened Savoy where Monsieur Ritz was the head waiter. Ladies never came to these places. One paid 10s. 6d. for a bottle of Champagne, 1880 or 1884, and the same amount for a stall at the theatre. . . .
>
> After dinner we would go on to the Gaiety, the Empire, or the Alhambra, to see Fred Leslie, Nellie Farren, or Arthur Roberts, the best comedians that I have ever known. They began the happy sequence of comic operas, 'Little Jack Sheppard', 'Ruy Blas or the Blasé Roué', 'Faust up to Date', 'Carmen up too Late', 'The Geisha', and the long line of 'Gaiety', 'Shop', 'School', 'Country', 'Runaway', 'Circus', 'Quaker', and other 'Girls', which for years succeeded each other with such phenomenal success under the direction of George Edwardes, that prince of theatrical managers. At the Lyric and Daly's there were similar attractions graced by Mary Yohé, Letty Lind, Edmund Payne, and George Grossmith. . . .
>
> The stalls at a popular theatre were then a bright, gay, and exhilarating sight. All the men and women were in evening clothes, and one knew many of them: nobody ate chocolates during the performance, and smoking was not allowed. We always wore tail coats; short jackets were unknown. At the Opera, the ladies were in *grande tenue* with their diamonds, Mrs Sam Lewis being a prominent figure. The Prince of Wales was often present in the long omnibus box on the ground tier. Outside the Opera stood two Guards sentries, while rows of footmen in long coats

waited to call up the carriages which had put up during the performance in some neighbouring livery stable.[1]

At the other end of the social scale there was, until 1866, the excitement to be obtained from a public hanging. One example will suffice to illustrate this aspect of the Victorian Age, and its scene is laid in Horsham on the day after Good Friday, Saturday, April 6th, 1844, when John Lawrence was hanged there for the murder of the Chief Constable of Brighton, one Henry Solomon. It was, incidentally, the last execution to take place in Horsham, for the gaol there was demolished in the following year.

Lawrence was a young ne'er-do-well of twenty-three from Tunbridge Wells, where he had been a pot-boy at the 'Camden', and he had been living with a prostitute known as 'Hastings Bet': on the afternoon of the murder the couple had a quarrel in which the woman was beaten and kicked after Lawrence discovered that she had pawned his clothes. He then went on a bout of drinking at the 'Globe' in Edward Street, after which he proceeded to steal a large roll of felt carpet from outside the premises of a draper in St James's Street. Presumably his intention was to pawn the carpet for the purpose of redeeming his clothes, and it is not without interest to note that when the case came before the magistrates the chairman of the Bench reprimanded the shopkeeper, Caleb Collins, for leaving carpets outside his shop, and described it as 'a very improper practice'.

Carpets are not the easiest things to get away with successfully, and in any case Lawrence seems to have been a bungler as well as a blackguard. He was duly arrested and taken to the police station, then as now in the Town Hall; on his arrival he asked for a knife with which to kill himself, at the same time declaring, 'I am tired of life'. The Chief Constable calmed him down, and was sitting at his desk waiting with two or three other police officers for the arrival of Collins, when Lawrence suddenly grabbed a poker from the fireplace, and struck the unfortunate Solomon such a blow with it on the right side of his head as to kill him: to the other policeman in the room he

[1] *A Picture of Life*, 1872–1940, pp. 44–46.

exclaimed, 'I hope I have killed him so that I may be hung'. The records, it may be added, show that the Chief Constable, a man of forty-three with a wife and nine children, had served for twenty-three years in the Brighton police force, and was widely respected as 'a most courageous, intelligent, active, and humane officer'. Indeed, he had done so little to provoke Lawrence that it was suggested at the trial that the only reason why he lost his life was that he alone in the office had no helmet on his head, and so was the easiest person to murder.

However this may be, Lawrence duly appeared at the Sussex Assizes before Chief Justice Denman, when counsel for the defence pleaded that the blow had been struck 'solely that he himself might be hanged'. The judge held that 'a wish to destroy oneself is not a proof of the deprivation of reason', and the jury took only twelve minutes to find Lawrence guilty of murder. The murderer, who had been educated at a school run by the Countess of Huntingdon's Connexion, spent his last days 'praying, reading, and humming the hymns the chaplain of the gaol had taught him'.

The Saturday morning on which he was hanged was also the day of the Horsham Lamb Fair, and the town was crowded with cattle, sheep, horses, and vehicles, besides the mere spectators of the execution. The fact that the murdered man had been Chief Constable of Brighton naturally attracted great attention in that town from which many costermongers came to Horsham to sell gingerbreads and oranges. The public-houses did a roaring trade, and one landlord was heard to express the wish that 'a man might be hung in Horsham every day'. Yet when Lawrence was turned off an eye-witness reported that the crowds 'exhibited the greatest decorum, and at the last moment the slightest whisper might have been heard'.

It would, however, seem that by this time public executions had ceased to attract the upper classes–perhaps that is why they were abolished with so little opposition–for gone were the days when George Selwyn rarely missed a spectacle of this nature. On this occasion 'many of the respectable inhabitants left the town', and the Rev Jarvis Kenrick, the curate of Horsham, urged those who remained to avoid the scene of execution, expressing his 'extreme regret that the eve of the principal Festival of the Church should have been selected for the hanging of a murderer'. Nor did he content himself with words alone, for he persuaded the schoolmasters in the town to march their pupils to Denne Park to keep them out of the way, but all the same a great many children were present when the town was 'inundated with the lower orders, principally from Brighton'. This particular Victorian recreation came to an end, as we have seen, in 1866, and the best part of a century was to elapse before the cinema and television once again enabled the British people to get the same sort of thrill that their ancestors had obtained from a public hanging–in the interval they had to be content to read about such matters.

At the same time it must be remembered that in the earlier years of the reign organized sport as we know it to-day was in its infancy. In former days football in particular had been severely frowned upon by authority, and James III of Scotland had in 1447 ordered that 'football and golfe be utterly cryed down and not to be used'. Charles II was an exception to this rule as to so many others, and in 1681 he organized a football match between his household and that of the Duke of Albemarle. In the earlier part of the nineteenth century, however, it was not so much official disapproval that prevented the playing of the game as the fact that there was no half-day on Saturday, while to have played on Sunday would have been to awake an outcry about the desecration of the Sabbath from all who had no wish themselves to indulge in the game. So it was not until 1863 that the Football Association came into being, but after that events began to move rapidly, for the English Cup was instituted in 1871, while the English League dates from 1888. Curiously enough, the birth of the Rugby Union was in the same year as that of the English Cup. The latter part of the Queen's reign thus witnessed the development of organized sport, though attendances at matches were far from being on the scale which is now the case. On the other hand Lawn Tennis, at any rate in its modern form, was still in its infancy when the Queen died, though the British Championship was first contested in 1877 when the Men's Singles were won by S. W. Gore.

It was quite otherwise with cricket which was flourishing in 1837, and was even more flourishing in 1901. The M.C.C. had been in existence since 1787, and had been settled at St John's Wood since 1814, while the first Test Match was played in 1880. Perhaps the most remarkable year in the cricket history of the nineteenth century was 1896, which is often claimed to mark the end of an epoch, for it was the last year in which the rubber in England consisted of only three Tests, and it was the last time that W. G. Grace played in a Test Match at Lord's.

The setting was somewhat different from what it is to-day. The two most famous buildings, that is to say the Pavilion and the Tavern, stood very much as at present, but in front of the Tavern and the members' luncheon room were ranged coaches and a wagonette or two, while behind the Tavern, where now is the Mound stand, lay the Tennis Court, in the wall of which was the clock that now adorns the Nursery Clock Tower. The Nursery garden at the end furthest from the Pavilion had been bought and made into a practice ground in the centenary year of 1887, but there was no Nursery stand. Indeed by modern standards the public accommodation left a good deal to be desired, for apart from the old Grand Stand–on the site of the present one–it consisted mostly of wooden benches, so that the spectators had either to squat on the turf, or to stand, seizing what vantage-point they could on the open ground beyond the ropes. There was an enclosure for members' friends, which was patronized by Society, for that is the scene of the well-known picture, painted a little earlier, that now hangs in the Memorial Gallery. This shows the Prince of Wales, Lily Langtry, and Lady de Grey, as a recent writer has put it, 'Taking the most desultory interest in what appears an astonishing effort at a catch in the deep field by Bonnor, the Australian, what time one lady, seemingly transported by her proximity to the Royal personage, sits literally on air, and Lord Harris surveys nothing with a look of inscrutable *hauteur*'.

The Tavern seems to have been more indulgent to its patrons' thirsts than is now always the case, for there were potmen wandering about among the crowd, but as a whole the ground wore an air of what has come to be known as Victorian propriety–'the quiet and decorum of Lord's ground', as Wisden describes it, was much in evidence.

The match which began on the morning of June 22nd, 1896, certainly witnessed Victorian cricket at its best, and something like thirty thousand people swarmed in through the gates; in these circumstances it is not surprising to hear that 'the field of play was seriously encroached upon'. There was plenty of excitement, for the two great Surrey bowlers, Richardson and Lohmann, had Australia all out for 53 before lunch. It was then that according to Sir Pelham Warner occurred one of the great cricketing feats of all time, namely that the first ball of the England innings, bowled by Ernest Jones, went through W. G.'s beard. As in the case of so many legendary events there is a conflict of evidence, for the late C. B. Fry always maintained that it was at Sheffield Park, earlier in the tour, that the incident took place. Fry, who was playing in the match, went even further, and averred that he heard the following conversation:

'Where the hell are you bowling, Jonah?'

'Sorry, Doctor, she slipped.'

Anyhow, Grace was not unduly perturbed, for he started off the England innings with a score of 66, but there were several ups and downs after that before England finally won by six wickets. The behaviour of the crowd seems to have got steadily worse as the game progressed, and *The Times* observed that Lord's 'has scarcely ever before been the scene of so much noisiness and rowdyism', while Lord Harris, in *A Few Short Runs*, wrote, 'It was a dreadful sight for those who love the strictness of first-class cricket as played at Lord's'. It required the experience of two World Wars to discipline an English crowd.

Few men have had so much influence on sport as Grace, and none has had greater, for it is no exaggeration to say that he revolutionized cricket in the Victorian Age. He found it a

The Sultan of Zanzibar at Ascot, June, 1875

country pastime, and he left it a national institution. The Prince of Wales apart, he was the best-known man in England with his beard and cut-away coat, the blackthorn stick and twinkling eye, his mind an engaging blend of simplicity and shrewdness. A former Bishop of Hereford said of him, 'Had Grace been born in ancient Greece the *Iliad* would have been a different book. Had he lived in the Middle Ages he would have been a Crusader, and would now have been lying with his legs crossed in some ancient abbey, having founded a great family. As he was born when the world was older he was the best known of all Englishmen, and the King of that English game least spoilt by any form of "vice" '. Grace died in 1915 at the relatively early age of sixty-seven. He disliked the Zeppelin raids, and when he was dying Shrimp Leveson-Gower went to see him, and asked, 'How can you mind the Zepps, W. G., you who have played all the fastest bowlers of your time?' He simply replied, 'Ah, but I could see those beggars. I can't see these'.

Throughout the reign the Turf played a prominent part in the sporting life of the country, and, although frowned upon by the Queen, its tone was a great deal higher than it had been at the end of the previous century. Much of this was due to three men, that is to say Sir Charles Bunbury, Lord George Bentinck, and Admiral Rous. It was adorned by some very eccentric characters. One was the fifth Earl of Glasgow, who was described as 'a wiry, wizened, tough-looking little fellow, perpetually scratching the back of his neck'. On one occasion at Doncaster he set fire to the bed-clothes of a club steward to remind him to bring the drink which he had ordered, but which the man had forgotten before going to bed. All the same, the noble earl seems to have had some redeeming features, which is more than can be said for Lord Barrymore, who offered to eat a live cat for a bet, or the Marquess of Hastings, who was so drunk the night before he won the Cesarewitch that he could not remember the next day the bets which he had made, while those with whom he had betted were certainly in no mood to refresh his memory. This particular nobleman died, completely ruined, at twenty-six, and 'was for years held up as a dreadful warning to young men who showed an inclination towards the Turf'.

Among the wits of the racing world was undoubtedly Lord Marcus Beresford, who managed the stable of the Prince of Wales, for when a rather 'warm' owner told him that he had

The Baked Potato Man, 1851

named a horse of his 'False Tooth' Lord Marcus replied, 'Excellent; that's one at any rate that you won't be able to stop.'

Even before the Victorian Age was over sport was beginning to show the shape of things to come, for in 1899 the Grand National was 'bioscoped', and shown at the Palace Theatre in London the same day.

Two operators took the necessary apparatus to Aintree in a railway van, and arranged with a man who said he had the fastest horse in Liverpool to drive them back to catch the train at Lime Street. The London and North-Western Railway Company had agreed to put on a special car, arranged as a dark room, in which was the developing paraphernalia, and as a concession promised that if necessary the train would be delayed for ten minutes. The race started at 3.35, and as soon as they had taken the picture the camera-men bolted across the course to the place where the fast horse and trap were waiting for them, the driver having a white handkerchief round his arm for identification purposes. They had twenty minutes in which to do the five miles to Lime Street, but they got there at 4.7, so the train was only delayed by two minutes. The film was developed on the journey, put on a big wooden drum, and constantly turned to dry. At Euston the train was met by a furniture-van, and the drum, not yet dry, was lifted into it. Finally, the film was got into the printing-machine, the positive printed from the negative, developed, and dried: at eleven o'clock that night the patrons of the Palace Theatre were watching the Grand National run that afternoon.

CHAPTER VII

Victorian Women

In no respect was the Victorian Age more markedly different from the periods which preceded and succeeded it than in its attitude towards women. The Lady Nithsdales and the Flora MacDonalds of an earlier day join hands across it with the women of the two World Wars, but they would all be hard put to it to find anything in common with the Victorian woman of the upper, or upper-middle, class. The bustling dames of the age of Chaucer, of Elizabeth I, and of the Civil War had long since passed away. In their time spinning and weaving, the care of dairies, and the management of large estates while husbands were away at the wars, at the Court, or concerned with their judicial duties, had been the responsibility of ladies in the manor-houses up and down the country, and the direction of large numbers of servants and retainers, combined with the entertainment of distinguished visitors, had called forth executive powers of no mean order. The change commenced with the Restoration when the women of the upper classes began to be attracted to Court, but it only affected a very narrow circle at first, for until the end of the century there were plenty of forceful ladies who were never at a loss to express their views even to the highest in the land, and wits like Charles II himself, or bullying counsel like Jeffreys, by no means always came off best when they crossed swords with them.

Even until well on in the eighteenth century women of the upper classes were still personally interested in the management of their estates, as the case of Mrs Montague abundantly proves. She was a well-known figure in London society with a husband who was a colliery owner in the North of England, and from the time of her marriage she seems to have been concerned in his business affairs. In 1766, for instance, she is found writing to a friend, 'I am still in the northern regions, but I hope in a fortnight to return to London . . . Business has taken up much of my time, and as we have had farms to let against next May-day, and I was willing to see the new colliery begin to trade to London before I left the country, I had the prudence to get the better of my taste for society. I had this day the pleasure of a letter from Billingsgate (a polite part of the world for a lady to correspond with) that the first ships which were then arrived were much approved. At Lynne they have also succeeded, and these are the two great-coal-markets. So now, as soon as I can get the ends and the bottoms of our business wound up, I shall set out for Hill Street.'

A few years later she is found writing at New Year: 'I have almost put my eyes out with accounts, of which our steward brings a plentiful quantity at this time of year. He is a very diligent person, and expects that I will apply many hours in the day. Our affairs go on very prosperously, and in great order, so that I have as little trouble as is possible in a case where so many large accounts are to be look'd over.' After her husband's death in 1775 her responsibilities were naturally vastly increased. Her letters show her visiting agricultural tenants, rejoicing at the improvement of her property as a result of good cultivation, and displaying a maternal interest in those working in the collieries. 'Some have more children', she wrote, 'than their labour will clothe, and on such I shall bestow some apparel. Some benefits of this sort, and a general kind behaviour, gives to the coalowner, as well as to them, a good deal of advantage. Our pitmen are afraid of being turned off, and that fear keeps an order and regularity amongst them that is very uncommon.' The coal trade and all her concerns were in a thriving way, and if this happy state of affairs continued, she promised 'to establish a spinning, knitting, and sewing school for ye girls'. All the same such a preoccupation with industrial affairs had become rare among women of the upper classes by the reign of George III, and Mrs Montague alluded to herself as 'a countrywoman of the last century'.[1]

The improvement in the means of travel as the eighteenth century progressed encouraged the countrywomen to imitate the aristocracy, and they formed the habit of congregating at Bath, Cheltenham, and Tunbridge Wells, or of accompanying their husbands to London. Mechanical inventions also played their part in the production of the idle woman, for the use of machinery for making textiles took away her occupation at the spinning-wheel, while the invention of the sewing-machine also gave her a great deal more spare time. Nor was this all for marriage was now postponed from the age of fourteen or fifteen to twenty or twenty-one, which meant that girls were kept hanging about at home for a period of years after they left school, while if they never married there were no longer nunneries to which they could retire. Snobbery also played its part, for the Industrial Revolution increased both the population and the wealth of the country, and it became the sign of a man's importance that he kept his women-folk in idleness; that they were not compelled to work was the outward and visible sign of the success of their husbands and fathers. The example spread through the middle-class, until work for women became a misfortune and a disgrace. Only financial ruin sent a girl out of her home to seek employment, in which event she was pitied by others and she pitied herself.

This had, as has been mentioned, not always been the case, and women's industrial work in the previous century was by no means limited to the textile and smaller domestic industries. In addition there were numerous crafts and trades in which they were engaged, either on their own account or as married women assisting their husbands. It was still the age of small scale businesses, and in many trades the skilled worker was both craftsman and merchant, producing goods at home and selling direct to the consumer; such workers, both men and women, formed a considerable section of the shopkeeping classes. Where the work-

[1] Doran, J.: *A Lady of the Last Century*, pp. 139–140, 184–185, and 199–202.

shop was attached to the home it was customary for the whole family to work together in the craft. Goldsmiths' daughters, for example, were frequently expert in designing and chasing, while furniture makers, stone masons, and engravers brought up their daughters to assist them in carving, sculpture, drawing, and graving. The craftsman's wife was not infrequently so familiar with her husband's business as to be 'mistress of the managing part of it', and she could therefore carry on in his absence or after his death. Marriage was, in fact, a business partnership.

Nor did women hesitate to call attention to their activities. In the *Newcastle Courant* of February 13th, 1779, there appeared the following notice:

> M. Hawthorn, Widow of the late John Hawthorn, Watchmaker of this town, tends her grateful thanks to the friends of her late husband; and begs to acquaint them and the public, that she will carry on the said Business (having engaged able workmen therein) and hopes for the continuance of their favours, which she will at all times studiously endeavour to merit.
>
> Jewelry, Trinkets, Watches, Music and Musical Instruments.

Jane Jones was even more enterprising in her appeal:

This, Ladies, is to let you know,
Jane Jones, from Crompton Street, Soho,
Who quondom kept the Star and Fan
Near to the Church of good St. Ann,
Of Fans the Mounter and the Maker,
Is lately moved to Long Acre;
To make direction still more plain,
Within few doors of Drury Lane;
Where Fans of diff'rent Sorts conduce
To suit each Taste and ev'ry use:
Fans fit for Gayety and Airs,
And decent Mounts to use at Pray'rs;
Designs expressing ev'ry Passion,
Painted well, and quite in Fashion.
She mends of damag'd Sticks the Flaws;
For Needlework neat Patterns draws,
Note *At the same shop are Plays, new Pamphlets, sold,*
And likewise Prints, some modern, others old.

During the period of the Industrial Revolution the tendency was for women's activity in the business sphere to decrease except in the trades conducted chiefly by women. This was due firstly to social changes following on the increase in wealth, and secondly to the reorganization demanded by the new commercial and industrial conditions. When the home became separated from the business premises women ceased to take their old interest in their husbands' affairs, and so lost the experience which they would otherwise have gained; moreover, the development of large scale business, combined with the need for greater capital, made it increasingly difficult for women, even in their own trades, to set up in business on their own account.

It is only necessary to contrast the vigorous life of the seventeenth and eighteenth century business woman, travelling about the country in her own interests, with the sheltered existence of her Victorian descendant, to realize how much the latter had lost in initiative and independence by being protected from all real contact with life.

Few aspects of modern society are as well documented as the middle-class woman of the nineteenth century, with whom contemporary fiction so largely dealt. The Victorian heroine was an almost standardized product, and her functions were courtship and marriage. Novels like *Vanity Fair* began with the day a girl left school and they generally ended with her wedding. From infancy all girls who were born above the level of poverty had the dream of a successful marriage before their eyes, for by that alone was it possible for a woman to rise in the world. Ethel Newcome, the daughter of a manufacturer descended from a weaver, married Lord Farintosh, and so entered the charmed circle of the aristocracy, and even Rosamond Vincy, whose father was a provincial silk manufacturer and whose mother was a vulgarian, was not considered to have done too badly in marrying a doctor who was cousin to a lord. One reason for this cultivation of the aristocracy of course was that it was more stable in the Victorian Age than it had ever been before or was ever to be again. In an earlier day one political miscalculation and a noble lord found himself on the scaffold or living in poverty in a French garret, while in the twentieth century the revolutions of fortune were to be equally sudden though for economic, rather than for political, reasons; but the Victorian girl who married a peer could be reasonably certain, unless her husband was a drunkard or a wastrel, of an easy life.

'To get ready for the marriage market a girl was trained like a race-horse. Her education consisted of showy accomplishments designed to ensnare young men. The three R's of this deadly equipment were music, drawing, and French administered by a governess at home, or, for girls below the aristocratic and the higher professional ranks, by mistresses in an inferior boarding-school.'[1] Miss Pinkerton's academy as described in *Vanity Fair* was probably typical of the more ambitious girls' school. Amelia Sedley for six years studied music, drawing, orthography, every variety of needlework–in all of which, according to Miss Pinkerton's testimonial she 'realized her friends' fondest wishes'–and geography, which she apparently less completely mastered. Formal walks, stigmatized by Alfred Garth in *Middlemarch* as 'such a set of nincompoops, like Mrs Ballard's pupils, walking two and two', gave the only outdoor relief from the prison of the schoolroom.

The artificiality in the relations of the sexes where the upper and middle classes were concerned outlasted the Victorian Age, for it continued to exist to no inconsiderable extent until the outbreak of the First World War. If a woman went in a hansom alone with a man who was neither her father nor her husband, nor old enough to be her grandfather, her reputation was irretrievably lost. The ruling convention was directed against unmarried men and women ever being alone together unless they were engaged, and not always then, for it would appear to have been tacitly assumed that on the slightest provocation the Victorian male would take advantage of the Victorian female, who would then suffer the fate described by contemporaries as 'worse than death'. If an engagement was broken off the girl suffered in consequence, while divorce was never mentioned in polite society.

[1] Neff, W. F.: *Victorian Working Women*, p. 190.

Fashions for April, 1849

The effect of these taboos was to drive the young man of the classes in question to somewhat sordid intrigues in other quarters. Readers of *Mary Barton* and *The Newcomes* will remember how young Carson and Barnes Newcome treated the girls of a lower social status than their own. Youths in their teens were apt to take rank among their fellows according to their alleged triumphs over what were generally termed 'scivvies' or shop-girls, and such conditions were not good for either party, while in the presence of women of their own rank in life they were too often diffident and tongue-tied. It would be rash to dogmatize in these matters, but it is difficult to resist the conclusion that the Victorian segregation of the sexes in what was then termed 'polite society' occasioned just as many *liaisons* of one sort and another as have marked more recent generations, even if not so much was said about them.

As the Industrial Revolution developed it became the respectable thing for middle-class households, as well as for the aristocracy, to have a governess, and in the Victorian Age she became a firmly established institution. Her importance is proved both by the census figures, and by her frequent appearance as a heroine or in some minor capacity in the novels of the period. In the census of 1851 over twenty-one thousand women appeared as governesses, and the field of their employment was rapidly spreading. Mark Pattison, giving evidence before the Schools Inquiry Commission fourteen years later, explained that the daughters of the aristocracy, the upper middle-class, professional men, and the clergy were educated mainly by governesses, but those of the middle-class proper received their tuition in boarding-schools: other witnesses of broader experience reported that the fashion of educating girls at home had spread downward in the social scale, and that owing to the inadequacy of suitable schools farmers and tradesmen had governesses.

By tradition the governess was supposed to be a girl of gentle birth, but such was by no means always the case. Esther Lyon in *Felix Holt* came from the household of a Dissenting minister, while Becky Sharp's father was a Bohemian artist, and a writer in the *Quarterly* said, 'Farmers and tradespeople are now educating their daughters for governesses as a mode of advancing them a step in life, and thus a number of underbred young women have crept into the profession who have brought down the value of salaries and interfered with the rights of those whose birth and misfortunes leave them no other refuge'. However this may be, governesses were not rated high. The friends of Janet in *Scenes of Clerical Life* excused her marriage to a drunken scoundrel on the ground that she 'had nothing to look to but being a governess'. Mrs Vincy in *Middlemarch* referred to Mary Garth as 'a dreadful plain girl–more fit for a governess', while Rosamond Vincy thought of the family governess as 'brown, dull, and resigned, and altogether, as Miss Vincy often said, just the sort of person for a governess'.

In these circumstances it is in no way surprising that they were badly paid; the usual annual salary seems to have been about thirty-five pounds, though wages as low as twelve were far from unknown: these figures can be compared with the fifty-five pounds paid to a housekeeper in a West End club. So low was their standing in the world at large that a circulating library in a London suburb had a rule that no person engaged in education should be admitted as a subscriber. Servants were generally insolent towards them, and the lady's-maid in particular considered herself superior. Mrs Blenkinsop in *Vanity Fair* expressed the views of the average servants' hall when she said, 'I don't trust them governesses, Pinner. They give themselves the hairs and hupstarts of ladies, and their wages is no better than you nor me.'

A study of the daily life of these young women shows it to have been one of great loneliness, and their isolation was increased by the general reluctance of their employers to allow them visitors. Of such isolation Thackeray wrote, 'She sits alone in the school-room, high, high up in that lone house, when the little ones are long since asleep, before her dismal little tea-tray, and her little desk, containing her mother's letters and her momentoes of home'. Petty discrimination and tyranny on the part of their mistresses was the rule rather than the exception, and Charlotte

Brontë bitterly resented the attitude of the women who employed her: of one she wrote, 'I have never had five minutes' conversation with her since I came, except while she was scolding me'. She related an incident to Mrs Gaskell which well illustrated the snobbery of the day. The small boy of the family had thrown a stone at her, but she concealed the offence, and in gratitude the child said in front of its mother, 'I love 'ou, Miss Brontë'. Whereupon the mother exclaimed before all the children, 'Love the governess, my dear!' The lecherous advances of the male members of the household which governesses often had to undergo must have come to many as a welcome relief.

Whether she had been away at boarding-school, or had imbibed such learning as a governess could impart, the Victorian girl of the class which we have been considering continued her education, such as it was, until she married. Nor was this education entirely intellectual, for many young women were physically tortured with an instrument called a backboard, which was a board worn or fastened across the back to give erectness to the figure. It is true that the English girl of the mid-twentieth century often walks badly, but her grandmother was drilled as if she was a grenadier of Frederick William I of Prussia. Miss Pinkerton recommended to Amelia when she left school the 'undeviating use of the backboard for four hours daily during the next three years, for the acquirement of that dignified deportment and carriage so requisite for every young lady of fashion'.

Then there was music, and it was an article of faith with mothers and daughters alike that it was an infallible method of attracting a husband. Once the Victorian girl was seated at the piano with an enraptured swain bending over her, and turning the pages, while she sang, the battle was half-won, so music was a very important weapon in her armoury. The daughters of Sir Pitt Crawley 'took exercise on the pianoforte every morning after breakfast'; Blanche Amory in *Pendennis* to quote her unsympathetic stepfather, was 'screeching from morning till night'; Rosamond Vincy in *Middlemarch* went on studying after she had left school, and practised her repertoire of 'Meet Me

By Moonlight', 'Black-Eyed Susan', and similar songs. Needlework, drawing, and painting flowers were also considered good bait in the husband-fishing business. The Oxford Movement gave great impetus to such activities, and the embroidering of altar-cloths was considered a most ladylike occupation. Many of the goods so produced found their way to church bazaars, where they were sold to helpless young men; much of this female handiwork was known as 'the Jews' basket' because the proceeds of the sale were devoted to the conversion of the Jews. Curates, in particular, especially if they were well-connected, stood to profit by this, and they were the recipients of innumerable purses, pen-wipers, portfolios, and even braces. Honeyman, in *The Newcomes*, is an excellent example, for he received objects so diverse as flowers, grapes, jelly, lozenges, a silk cassock, and even a silver tea-pot filled with sovereigns.

What the eligible bachelor had to put up with was indeed formidable, and Lord Farintosh was no exception. 'Every daughter of Eve was bent on marrying him. . . . Everybody hunted him. The other young ladies, whom we need not mention, languished after him still more longingly. He had little notes from these: presents of purses worked by them; and cigar-cases embroidered with his coronet. They sang to him in cosy boudoirs–mamma went out of the room, and sister Ann forgot something in the drawing-room.'

The real tragedy was that although the Victorian girl was skilled in the art of acquiring a husband, she was, unlike her predecessors in earlier centuries, given no training of any sort in her practical duties as a wife, and this was the case even in many lower middle-class families. She was quite untrained in household management, and generally unable to control her servants. She had no idea of the value of money, and too often squandered what her husband gave her. Even in the very important matter of child-bearing she had to learn by experience with all the physical and psychological shocks which this implies.

The blame for this state of affairs largely rested with the Victorian male. Innocence was what he demanded from the girls of his class, and they must not only be innocent but also give the outward impression of being innocent. White muslin, typical of virginal purity, clothed many a heroine, with delicate shades of blue and pink next in popularity. The stamp of masculine approval was placed upon ignorance of the world, meekness, lack of opinions, general helplessness and weakness; in short, a recognition of female inferiority to the male. David Copperfield's Dora was a 'pretty toy or plaything'; Rosey Mackenzie was a 'pretty little tender nurseling, like a little song-bird . . . a tremulous, fluttering little linnet'. Amelia Sedley's weakness was 'her principal charm–a kind of sweet submission and softness, which seemed to appeal to each man she met for his sympathy and protection'. Men in the presence of women modified their conversation, and there was a definite line drawn concerning what an unmarried girl could hear. The conversation of Queen Elizabeth I would have horrified the female subjects of Queen Victoria. Not only was the impure barred, but also anything requiring intelligence, and, above all, politics were not for women, save in the very highest ranks of the aristocracy. It was little wonder that men took refuge in their clubs from the type of women for whom they were largely responsible.

Most Victorian women accepted almost any sort of marriage that was offered them, and the only relief many of them enjoyed was a prescriptive right to indulge in hysterics in moments of crisis. The number of women who shrieked in fits of hysterics through the pages of novels and poems is legion, and as they were pregnant most of the time they possessed what they considered an excuse. Even when the children came their mothers had no idea of controlling them save by appealing to their emotions.

On her marriage a girl usually passed from dependence upon parents to submission to a husband. Lydgate wanted to find in marriage 'an accomplished creature who venerated his high musings and momentous labours, and would never interfere with them'. The conception of marriage as a partnership was quite unknown, and Charlotte Brontë wrote in *Shirley*, 'A wife could not be her husband's companion, much less his confidante, much less his stay'. One of the favourite scenes with contemporary novelists was the husband waiting until the very eve of ruin to tell his wife of the desperate state of their affairs.

The law reflected this subservience of the female to the male, for it gave women very little protection. In the middle of the nineteenth century an unattached woman of twenty-one could inherit and administer her own property, over which even her father had no power, but on marriage she was legally an infant, and as a wife she had no right to her own clothes. Her personal, as well as her real, property passed into her husband's possession, and without his permission she could not make a will concerning even her personal property, while cases were not unknown where a husband went so far as to will his wife's property to his own illegitimate children. The legal custody of children belonged to the father, and until 1840 a small infant dependent upon a mother could be taken from her. A husband had an absolute right over the person of his wife; he could lock her up, and he could compel her to return home if she ran away from him. On the other hand she did possess a few compensating advantages. Her husband had to support her, and this right could be enforced in both the ecclesiastical and magistrates' courts. He was also liable for her debts, even those contracted before marriage, while she could not sue or be sued for contracts, nor enter into them.

It was exceedingly difficult for a woman to get out of matrimony. It is true that on the ground of adultery, cruelty, or unnatural practices she could obtain a separation *a mensa et thoro*, but a proper divorce with freedom to re-marry was a very different matter. Prior to 1857 it required an Act of Parliament, with an investigation resting by usage with the House of Lords alone, and it was granted to a woman very seldom, and only in cases of aggravated adultery, an isolated act or two apparently not being considered unbecoming in the Victorian husband. Also the price was prohibitive, being in the neighbourhood of six or seven hundred pounds. Of course it was open to a woman to break her chains by committing adultery herself, and so forcing her husband to divorce her, but this was to condemn herself to social ostracism for the rest of her life.

Where women were concerned, as in practically every other aspect of life, the Victorian Age was revolutionary. The change for the better may be said to have started with the nursing profession. In the early years of the reign English nurses were only too often drunken, profligate, violent-tempered, and brutal in language, and Sairy Gamp in *Martin Chuzzlewit* was, it is to be feared, a typical specimen. Florence Nightingale has left it on record that when she informed her parents of her ambition to become a nurse 'it was as if I had wanted to be a kitchen-maid', but her departure for the Crimea lit a torch that was never to be put out. Slowly and surely the status of nursing was raised, and this led women to clamour for professional and business opportunities.

Slowly they got their way. During the latter part of the Victorian Age teaching steadily rose in status through the reforms of secondary schools and the extension of university degrees to women. In 1872 the Girls' Public Day School Company was founded to provide good and cheap day-schools for girls, and six years later the Maria Grey Training College was founded. London University gave a B.A. Degree to women in 1878; Cambridge opened the triposes to them in 1881; and Oxford allowed them to pass the examinations in 1884. In short, the idle and useless middle-class woman of the earlier part of the reign was by the end of it well on her way to becoming what her descendant is to-day.

As the emancipation of women developed the law became cognizant of what was taking place. In 1858 there came divorce legislation of which one of the most important provisions was that which not only protected the earnings of the deserted wife and made arrangements for separate maintenance, but also rendered possible a wife's inheritance and possession of property, and gave her power of contract, of suing, and of being sued in any civil proceeding. In 1882 there was another step forward with the Married Women's Property Act.

It is now necessary to go lower down the social scale, for below the women whom custom and their menfolk protected from any kind of useful employment were others who were notori-

Masculine Fashions, 1847, and the Bloomer Fashions of the 1850's

Victorian Costume of the 'Eighties

ously overworked, and they cannot be omitted from any account of the Victorian Age. Prominent among these were that typical product of the Industrial Revolution, namely the textile worker.

The swift succession of inventions by such people as Hargreaves, Arkwright, and Crompton in spinning, and by Kory, Stell, and Cartwright in weaving created a great demand for labour, and this was in no small measure supplied by women and children. The steady depression in the status of the agricultural community since the fall of the Stuarts paved the way for this great social change. The Enclosure Acts of the eighteenth century drove large numbers of the yeomanry, the country freeholders, and the labourers, formerly with a little land of their own, into the towns and into the mills. Agricultural reforms, such as the reclaiming of waste lands and peat-bogs once used by smallholders, and the enclosure of the commons, where the cattle and pigs had been allowed to feed, created a large class of workers entirely dependent on wages: the custom of gleaning after the harvest was also taken away. Then came the Industrial Revolution to kill the domestic industries which had formerly helped out the earnings of farm workers, whose condition thus became pitiable. Nor was this all, for the steady decline of the old village games since the impulse had been given by Puritanism, combined with the absence of any other popular amusement to take their place, increased the monotony of life in farming communities, and encouraged restless people to flock to the larger centres of population.

This in its turn involved the break-up of the home as a social unit. In the days of the system of domestic industry the parents and children had worked together, with the father as the autocratic head, pocketing the family earnings and directing their expenditure. In these circumstances the home was the stronghold, but under the factory system the members of a family all had their own earnings, they worked in separate departments of the mill, and came home only for food and sleep. Yet in some instances even in these conditions the factory girl contributed generously to the household expenses, and one silk weaver of eighteen, who was a witness before the Royal Commission in

1833, stated that out of her weekly wage of 13s. she gave 7s. to her mother, while another, a reeler of twenty-six, out of 9s. gave her parents 7s. These, however, would seem to have been the exceptions, and there was a general tendency for the father to lose his authority. The Wright family in *Helen Fleetwood* constitute an excellent example of this. The children showed no respect for their parents, and no affection for one another, and even their mother was alienated from them. Esther in *Mary Barton* left John Barton's house for lodgings when he tried to exercise authority over her, and he said of her, 'That's the worst of factory work for girls. They can earn so much when work is plenty, that they can maintain themselves anyhow. . . . You see, Esther spent her money in dress, thinking to set off her pretty face; and got to come home so late at night, that at last I told her my mind. . . . Says I, "Esther, I see what you'll end at with your artificials, and your fly-away veils, and stopping out when honest women are in their beds; you'll be a street-walker, Esther, and then, don't you go to think I'll have you darken my door, though my wife is your sister". . . . So says she, "Don't trouble yourself, John. I'll pack up and be off now, for I'll not stay to hear myself called as you call me".' It was not long before John Barton's prophecy was realized.

Disraeli described such girls as 'gaily dressed, a light handkerchief tied under their chin, their hair scrupulously arranged; they wore coral necklaces and earrings of gold'. The actual counterparts of these literary factory girls, it may be added, appear in the records of Parliament, and when their fathers tried to prevent them from spending their spare time in public-houses they left home.

Contemporary opinion rated the morals of the factory girl very low indeed, at any rate if the literature of the Victorian Age is any guide. Mrs. Tonna puts into the mouth of one of her characters the statement that only one girl in fifty kept her virginity after she went to the mills. Mrs Gaskell does not go quite so far, but she shows John Barton as unwilling to have his daughter so employed, and Esther went from the factory to become mistress of a man who later caused her to become a prostitute. Both authors represent the reputation of factory girls to be so bad that there was no fortune for them in domestic service. When Helen Fleetwood's health was threatened by conditions in the mill in which she worked domestic service was thought of, but too late, 'for there isn't a small tradesman's wife would not think herself disgraced to take a factory girl for a servant'.

These charges are in the main supported by official documents, and as evidence of a general looseness in morals is the number of illegitimate children born to girls in certain mills. On the other hand these figures do not apparently represent the whole picture, for about this time there was a wide circulation of books on birth control by Richard Carlile. Along with this sexual laxity went such vices as theft, excessive smoking, immoderate drinking, and filthy language. Admittedly there was a tendency on the part of those who were not subjected to such temptations to hold up their hands in horror at the behaviour of those who were; for example, there was a borough-reeve of Manchester who counted the number of people entering a certain gin-shop in five minutes during eight successive Saturday nights and at different periods in the evening, and his figures were widely quoted in both Houses of Parliament, though exactly what they were supposed to prove it is not altogether easy to see, more particularly as it was never suggested that heavy drinking was confined to any particular class of the community.

On the other hand it cannot be denied that the conditions in which the textile workers passed their lives were hardly conducive to a virtuous existence. The coarse surroundings of a young girl in the factory; the prevalence of indecent language; the absence of dressing-rooms; the necessity of working in scanty clothing on account of the heat; the precocious sexual development which results from urban life; the long hours and the night-work which made it necessary for her to be out late on the streets alone; the exhaustion which led to thirst; and the monotonous labour which brought in its turn a craving for excitement: these were new and disturbing factors to which the Industrial Revolution had given rise. There can be, too, little doubt but that much of the ill-health and moral degradation of the factory population was due to domestic conditions. Aikin, writing as early as 1795, stated that there were even then in Manchester 'nearly whole streets of houses built of wood, clay, and plaster', and that the town 'unfortunately vies with, or exceeds, the Metropolis in the closeness with which the poor are crowded in offensive, dark, damp, and incommodious habitations, a too fertile source of disease'.[1] With a rapidly increasing population, overcrowding and the lack of sanitation became still more glaring evils, which vitally affected both the moral and the physical condition of the nation.

It is, however, only too easy to read history backwards, and the working-man in the middle of the nineteenth century was far from being *bourgeoisie* like his descendant a hundred years later. His status had been steadily on the decline since the fall of the Stuarts, and it had now reached its nadir. Thus it should be remembered that it was the operatives themselves who were chiefly responsible for such ill-treatment of women as did occur, and that they merely brought into the factory the brutality which the standards of the time permitted the lower classes to practice on their wives and children at home. 'Much cruelty is daily practised in many a cottage, which is not unfit to rank even with the strap and billy roller'.[2]

A prominent figure among the working women was the dressmaker, and the first census of the Queen's reign, namely that of 1841, showed that there were 70,518 of them over, and 18,561 under, the age of twenty. They represented more varied social classes than those employed in the factories. The majority were girls from the country apprenticed to the owner of a shop, like Ann and Frances King in Mrs Tonna's *The Wrongs of Women*, while others were the daughters of mill workers who were unwilling that their children should work in a factory. Not a few were of gentle birth, and Lord Ashley stated that the daughters of poor clergymen and Dissenting ministers, of half-pay officers and of unsuccessful tradesmen, had crowded into

[1] *Description of the Country round Manchester*, p. 192.
[2] *Factory Commission*, 1833, XX, p. cl, 170 (Drinkwater's Report).

this occupation. Whatever their origin they had to work hard in those days when the mass-production of women's clothes was unknown. Hours were closely connected with the rush of work; in London this was during the two 'seasons', April to July and October to Christmas, and in the provinces local festivities, such as hunt balls, brought about the same result.

Girl apprentices began work at five or six in the morning, and sometimes continued until midnight or later. Evidence collected by government inspectors leaves no doubt as to the long hours which existed in the earlier part of the reign. Some witnesses testified that for three months they had worked twenty hours out of the twenty-four, and one of them worked from 4.0 a.m. on Thursday until 10.30 a.m. on the following Sunday because of the orders that came in as the result of the general mourning for William IV, while another girl gave evidence that on the same occasion she did not change her dress for nine days or nights: she rested on a mattress on the floor, and her food was cut up and placed beside her so that she could sew while she ate. In some places the apprentices worked on Sundays, and in others they were kept up late on Saturday night. Even out of the season twelve and thirteen hours, including the time for meals, was the usual working day.

The Song of the Shirt is the most moving picture of the Victorian dressmaker:

With fingers weary and worn,
With eyelids heavy and red,
A woman sat, in unwomanly rags,
Plying her needle and thread.
Stitch! Stitch! Stitch!
In poverty, hunger, and dirt,
And still with a voice of dolorous pitch
She sang The Song of the Shirt!

*

Seam, and gusset, and band,
Band and gusset, and seam,
Work, work, work,
Like the engine that works by steam!

A mere machine of iron and wood
That toils for Mammon's sake –
Without a brain to ponder and craze
Or a heart to feel – and break!

The Victorians were at least as concerned with the moral, as with the physical, condition of those who have been not inappropriately termed 'the slaves of the needle', and the Commissioners reported that immorality was proverbial among dressmakers, though in view of the long hours they worked it is not easy to see how they found the time to be immoral, at any rate upon any extended scale. Indeed, the operative word in the Commissioners' report may well have been 'proverbial'. Certainly the dressmakers had a bad reputation among the novelists of the day. Dobbin, in *Vanity Fair*, assured the mess-room that Osborne was 'not going to run off with a duchess or ruin a milliner', but was going to marry Miss Sedley, 'one of the most charming young women that ever lived'. In the same work Rawdon Crawley is described as amusing himself by 'courtships of milliners, opera-dancers, and the like easy triumphs'. Foker, it will be remembered, when he went to visit his friend Pendennis, 'flattened his little nose against Madame Fribsley's window to see if haply there was a pretty workwoman in her premises'.

A large part of the material dealing with the morals of dressmakers is concerned with those of the young apprentices. Mary Barton's Aunt Esther, herself a sick and weary woman of the streets, when she heard that her niece was learning the dressmaking trade, said, 'I began to be frightened for her; for its a bad life for a girl to be out late at night in the streets, and after many an hour of weary work, they're ready to follow after any novelty that makes a little change'. The writer of an article in *Fraser's Magazine* on 'Milliners' Apprentices' was of the opinion that these young girls did not take to drink like their contemporaries in the factories, but their fondness for clothes, encouraged by their occupation in which the attention centred around nothing else, frequently led to prostitution. It may be added that the working life of these women was estimated at

The Haymarket at Midnight, 1861

not more than three or four years, and only a constant accession of fresh hands from the country 'enabled the business to be carried on'.

Reform was slow in coming, but it came all the same, and by the Queen's death little less than a revolution had been effected, though at first it owed nothing to the attitude of Parliament which was singularly averse from dealing with a problem in which there were clearly votes to be lost rather than gained. In fact the matter very nearly became a party issue, for when the Tories attacked their opponents for their slave-driving methods in the Lancashire mills and the Birmingham workshops the *Edinburgh Review* denounced the nobility and gentry for their carelessness and indifference to the hardship which the London 'season' brought to young girls working at night to finish gowns for presentation at Court. A beginning was made in 1843 by the formation of an 'Association for the Aid and Benefit of Dressmakers and Milliners' with the support of people like the Duchesses of Argyll and Sutherland, but in 1855 Parliament rejected a Private Member's Bill to reduce dressmakers' hours, and in the Press only the *Standard* gave its support to the measure. Gradually, however, public opinion was roused, until by the Factory Act of 1891 the hours of labour for women were limited to twelve a day, with an hour and a half for meals.

The Victorian conscience was more quickly aroused by the horrors attendant upon women working in the mines when this was brought to its notice by the publication of the first *Report on Mines* in May, 1842. On the 7th of that month Lord Ashley noted in his diary, 'The Report of the Commission is out–a noble document. . . . Perhaps even "Civilization" itself never exhibited such a mass of sin and cruelty. The disgust felt is very great, thank God.'

In actual fact the employment of women in the mines was not a result of the Industrial Revolution, as is sometimes stated, for it dates from the earliest days of mining in Great Britain. In the Middle Ages and up to the end of the seventeenth century coal pits were rarely more than shallow holes or slants in which only a few workers with the simplest tools were engaged. The output was small, and it was commonly brought to the surface by the wives and daughters of the miners, who in the earlier days of the industry carried the coal on their backs up ladders, and in later times drew it to the surface in baskets by means of a windlass. While the numbers of both men and women engaged in these somewhat primitive mining operations were very few, it is probable that women were more often employed in the pits than they were after the great expansion of the industry. The introduction of machinery for raising coal and pumping water did away with the necessity for much of this type of labour, and by the nineteenth century the employment of women in mines was unknown in many of the districts in which they had previously worked. According to the Census of 1841 there were 1,185 women over twenty, and 1,165 under that age, in the coal mines of Great Britain, but since the returns made to the Commissioners from East Scotland show that there were 1,189 adult women, and 1,152 girls under eighteen, employed there alone, this would appear to be an understatement of the total number.

One of the earliest references to choke damp is in connection with the death in 1322 of a woman, one Emma, daughter of William Culhare, who was killed by 'le Damp' while drawing water from the '*colepyt*' *at Morley in Derbyshire*,[1] and in 1587 women were mentioned as working the mines at Winlaton 'for lack of men'. In metal mines washing and breaking the ore was from early times done principally by women. During the reign of Edward II they were employed in the Derbyshire lead mines at a wage of a penny a day,[2] a rate of pay which in Stuart times had risen to sixpence. By the end of the seventeenth century a good many women were engaged in the metal mines in various parts: 'There is washing and knocking of Ores, which are Works that many good Men's Daughters are now glad to do, in many places of this Kingdom, for Bread for them and their Children.'[3]

As the mining industry developed and the pits became larger

[1] Salzmann, L. F.: *English Industries in the Middle Ages*, p. 8.
[2] *Victoria County History*, Derbyshire, vol. II, p. 329.
[3] Stringer, H.: *English and Welsh Mines and Minerals*, p. 16.

and deeper, the age of accidents began. Women's names frequently occur in the lists of casualties in the seventeenth and eighteenth centuries, thus indicating the areas in which they were then working, and almost the last mention of a woman employed underground in the Tyne district occurs in an account of a shaft accident in 1772: 'A woman employed in putting at South Biddick (was) riding up one of the pits (when) the other hook, in passing, caught her cloathes. The weight of the rope forced her out of the loop, and she fell to the bottom of the shaft.'[1] Shortly after this, about 1780, women and girls, with a few exceptions, ceased to be employed underground in the pits of Durham and Northumberland. It has been suggested that the northern pits were at this time attracting some of the small farmers displaced by the agrarian revolution, and that this new supply of labour may have had something to do with the disappearance of women from the pits. What is, however, more probable is that the introduction of tramways and horses by the more progressive coalowners proved to be a cheaper means of transport.

By the end of the eighteenth century the windlass and horse gin for raising coal had long been in use in all the coal-fields except East Scotland, where the 'bearing system', that is to say the method of raising coal on the backs of women, was still in use, and was continued into the nineteenth century. The 'bearers' were for the most part the wives and daughters of the miners, who attended their menfolk in the pit, and carried up the coal as it was cut. This continuance of family labour was no doubt due to the system by which in Scotland, up to 1775, all miners, bearers, and their children, if they had ever worked in a colliery, became the property of the coalowner, and they and their services were transferable with the land on any change of proprietor. Until, indeed, the final act of emancipation in 1799 the men and women employed in the Scottish collieries were literally slaves, for they were unable to seek any other work without the permission of the mineowner, and they were liable to be seized and brought back if they attempted to escape.

[1] *Newcastle Journal*, February 8th, 1772.

Their eventual emancipation was designed not so much to remove the reproach of servitude in a free country, as to attract a larger number of men to the mining industry.

Up to this time the employment of women in coal mines does not appear to have invoked any comment. Mining villages were generally isolated, and their occupants, with a dress and dialect peculiar to themselves, and known to indulge in cruel and brutal sports, were often regarded as savages and outcasts. Wesley and his followers made some attempt to call attention to the conditions existing in the mines, but apart from this little was done, chiefly owing to ignorance in the outside world. Hence, while the state of affairs obtaining in some of the early factories roused public attention in industrial centres and led to attempts to remedy the worst abuses, the facts relating to the employment of women and children underground were unknown, and so their sufferings went unrelieved. The first plea on behalf of colliery women was made by Lord Dundonald, who in 1793 called attention to the slavery of women bearers in Scotland, while fifteen years later Robert Bald tried to arouse public indignation by describing the conditions of this class of woman 'whose peculiar situation was but little known to the world'. In England the first protest against the employment of women underground seems to have been made by Ayton in his vivid description of his visit to the Whitehaven mines in 1813.

Another twenty years elapsed before matters came to a head. In 1833 one Tufnell, a Factory Commissioner, made some enquiries into mining conditions in Lancashire with the result that he formed the opinion that 'it must appear to every impartial judge of the two occupations that the hardest labour in the worst room in the worst-conducted factory is less hard, less cruel, and less demoralizing than the labour in the best of coal-mines'. Once again there was no immediate action, but the evidence which Tufnell had collected was used by Shaftesbury in 1840 as the basis of his plea for a Royal Commission to investigate the conditions of employment in the mines. His application was successful; the Commission was appointed; and, as we have seen, it duly reported in 1842.

The evidence of many of the women is more powerful than any comment of the members of the Commission could possibly be. For example, Betty Harris, aged thirty-seven, a drawer in a Lancashire colliery, thus described her work:

> I have a belt round my waist and a chain passing between my legs, and I go on my hands and feet. The road is very steep, and we have to hold by a rope, and when there is no rope, by anything we can catch hold of. There are six women and about six boys in the pit I work in: it is very hard work for a woman. The pit is very wet where I work, and the water comes over our clogs always, and I have seen it up to my thighs: it rains in at the roof terribly; my clothes are wet through almost all day long. I never was ill in my life but when I was lying-in. My cousin looks after my children in the daytime. I am very tired when I get home at night; I fall asleep sometimes before I get washed. I am not so strong as I was, and cannot stand my work so well as I used to do. I have drawn until I have had the skin off me; the belt and chain is worse when we are in the family way. My feller has beaten me many a time for not being ready. I were not used to it at first, and he had little patience. I have known many a man beat his drawer.

Other women told how they worked in the coal-pits until the day their children were born, and then returned a week later. In these circumstances it is not surprising that miscarriages were frequent, and one mother reported that four of her children had been stillborn, while many children died in infancy. A girl of twenty worked for 2s. a day or less, but a man of the same age asked 3s. 6d. A woman was popular as a mine worker because she did not aspire to be a 'coal-getter', that is to say to dig out the coal, which was the work most highly paid, and as a drawer she was steadier than a man and more easy to manage.

Armed with this evidence Lord Ashley delivered on June 7th, 1842, one of the most moving speeches ever made in the House of Commons. 'For two hours', he wrote in his diary, 'the House listened so attentively that you might have heard a pin drop, broken only by loud and repeated marks of approbation.' Many men wept, and Richard Cobden, whose *laissez-faire* views had hitherto kept him hostile to Ashley, now went over to his side. Prince Albert read the speech aloud to the Queen, who was greatly moved. Yet in spite of Ashley's powerful presentation of the physical hardships that the women suffered in the mines, which made them old at forty, and of their constant danger from fire-damp and accidents, it was the part of his speech dealing with the moral aspect of the problem which secured him most support from that Victorian House of Commons. He pointed out that young girls 'hurrying' for men, working beside them in scanty garments, alone with them for hours of the day in an isolated part of the mine, were at their mercy. Covered with black dust, too weary to wash at night, removed from all the decencies of life, they swore and used vile language. They were only too often, Ashley declared, utterly demoralized from childhood. These were the arguments to move an audience in the forties of last century, and results were not slow to follow.

A law was passed without delay which removed all children under ten from the mines and provided that no women should thereafter be employed underground. Legal proceedings arising out of evasions of the Act were, however, frequently necessary in the years that lay ahead, especially round Wigan, and in parts of South Wales and East Scotland, where coalowners continued to connive at the employment of women. So late as 1850 it was estimated that four hundred women and girls were still working in certain collieries in South Wales, and many of them appear to have been only eleven or twelve years of age. However, repeated prosecutions and regular inspection of mines, rendered evasion of the law increasingly difficult, and by the end of the reign the collieries had wholly ceased to be places of employment for women with the exception of the 'pit-brow lassies' who still continued to exist in Lancashire.

In 1841 the Population Returns were, for the first time in the case of women, made on an occupational basis, and they show that no less than 712,493 females were engaged in domestic service, while of these 447,606 were over, and 264,887 were under, twenty years of age. In the case of these women it is, of course, impossible to generalize concerning the conditions in which they worked. On the whole it is probable that in the larger establishments, where many servants were kept, they had little of which to complain. They formed a self-contained community in which service was often hereditary. On the other hand, the general servant was in the vast majority of cases by no means so happily placed. Loneliness was certainly her lot, and 'time off' was very limited, while in the sort of household where only one servant was employed the mistress was more than likely to be a tyrant.

The employer was entitled to dismiss a maid at once for dishonesty, immorality, hopeless incapacity, or flagrant disobedience, and he or she was not obliged to give a character if the servant was adjudged unworthy of one. Domestic servants were usually paid by the quarter or month, and if summarily dismissed they were entitled to a month's wages. In 1897 they were included in the operation of the Workman's Compensation Act, and henceforth they could claim compensation for injuries arising during their employment provided that gross negligence or other wilful misconduct on their part had not caused the injury. At the end of the reign there were 1,641,154 women in domestic service throughout the United Kingdom, and this figure represented a decrease of six per cent on that shown by the previous decennial census. A contemporary comment on this decline was, 'The decrease in the number of servants in the British Isles may be explained partly by the influx of women into factories and business offices, and partly by their emigration to Canada and Australia, where their scarcity leads to the offer of high wages, which naturally attract many girls of enterprise'.

By the middle of the Victorian Age it may be said that the position of women in industry, and their suitability for wage-earning occupations outside the home, had become subjects for public discussion. Reformers and philanthropists, with Lord Ashley at their head, first directed their attention to children, and then passed on to lay a new emphasis on the social value of women and the importance of their influence on the national welfare. The facts revealed by various Commissions of enquiry added strength to the arguments of those who urged that the

State could not remain wholly indifferent to the conditions which were disclosed, and that it must assume some responsibility for women workers. Cracks were already beginning to be visible in the hitherto solid structure of *laissez-faire*, and theories were produced which had not been heard for upwards of two centuries: men, such as Disraeli, were looking back to Stuart paternalism for inspiration. As has been shown, the national conscience had been awakened by accounts of the heavy and unsuitable labour in which women were engaged, and as a result public indignation had brought to an end their work in the mines.

There was, however, another side to the picture. If the earlier Victorians were slow to become aware of the horrors which went on in their midst, their successors were liable to put the wrong construction upon what was brought to their notice. It was a peculiarity of the age to attach excessive importance to the moral aspect of any problem, and where women were involved this is particularly noticeable. We have already seen that it was the morals of the female workers that first aroused the public opinion of the day–had these not been in danger their physical sufferings might have gone unnoticed very much longer, and the upshot was a widespread belief that women had best be withdrawn from all forms of factory labour. The mid-Victorians were themselves too close to the Industrial Revolution to grasp the full significance of its changes and their economic importance for women; and were unmindful of the part which they had played in the past; they were shocked and horrified by the appearance of a new class of women workers in industrial centres, and their only response was to declare that the place of all women, married or unmarried, was in the home.

Of course this was all part and parcel of the belief which held its ground until the last ten years or so of the reign that women were useless creatures except for breeding purposes, and that the more they were shut off from the realities of life the better. Victorian ideas of 'refinement' prescribed a life of idleness for women unless stern necessity ruled otherwise. 'A lady, to be such, must be a mere lady, and nothing else', wrote Margaretta

Greg in her diary in 1853. 'She must not work for profit, or engage in any occupation that money can command, lest she invade the rights of the working classes who live by their labour. Men in want of employment have pressed their way into nearly all the shopping and retail businesses that in my early years were managed in whole, or in part, by women. The conventional barrier that pronounces it ungenteel to be behind a counter, or serving the public in any mercantile capacity, is greatly extended. The same in household economy. Servants must be up to their offices, which is very well; but ladies, dismissed from the dairy, the confectionery, the storeroom, the stillroom, the poultry yard, the kitchen garden, and the orchard, have hardly yet found themselves a sphere equally useful and important in the pursuits of trade and art to which to apply their too abundant leisure.'[1]

The position of women in 1901 was at all levels a great deal more restricted than it was to be fifty years later, but it was almost unrecognizably different from what it had been at the beginning of the Queen's reign, so that it would be hard to cite any sphere of human society in which the Victorian Age was more revolutionary than what concerned the female sex.

[1] Butler, J. E.: *Memoir of John Greg*, pp. 326 *et seq.*

A Midnight Meeting: the Rev. Baptist Noel Preaching, 1861

CHAPTER VIII

Victorian Religion

It is far from easy to define the part played by religion in England in the Victorian Age. In Ireland, violently contrasted religious beliefs, though most sincerely held, were a cause of political division, more particularly after the controversies roused by the First Home Rule Bill; while in Scotland religion, rather than politics, was the pre-occupation of the people. In the case of England one has to dig deeper to get anywhere near the truth.

Trollope concerned himself with the clergy and their problems to a greater extent than any other novelist before or since, yet one would search his pages in vain for even a mention of the controversies by which the Church of England was rent during the period with which he was dealing. Bitterness there might be concerning this or that appointment at Barchester, but his characters, religious and lay alike, were strangely uninterested in theology. Yet the England of Victoria was religious to an extent almost incomprehensible to the subjects of Elizabeth II, even if in many cases the result was that phenomenon described by Chesterton as 'God in a top hat'. In the middle of the twentieth century it may seem slightly ludicrous to find the Victorians looking at social and economic problems from a moral standpoint, but it is evidence of their deep religious feeling.

The heritage from the eighteenth century was deplorable. 'Money was now firmly in the saddle, and money still feared the Church. Convocation was suspended in 1717, and was not summoned again until 1850. After the suppression, the Church had to go hat in hand to Parliament for all that it needed, with bishops in the Lords chosen by the Whigs from men whose beliefs were contrary to the Church's accepted formulas. From the Restoration to the death of Anne, it was the Laudian High Churchmen who had been responsible for the spiritual energy of the Church. To the Whigs, High Churchmen were dangerous Jacobites, the enemies of the new dynasty and the potential supporters of rebellion. All religious zeal was accordingly discouraged, and none but safe men appointed to positions of authority.

Many bishops never went near their dioceses. One Welsh bishop farmed successfully in Westmorland for thirty-four years. The best of the Whig divines were Latitudinarians. In an age of reason they were concerned to prove that religion was reasonable, and they made religion dull and lifeless.'[1] In 1741, Thomas Secker, who was then Bishop of Oxford and later became Archbishop of Canterbury, declared in a charge to his clergy, 'Our liturgy consists of evening as well as of morning prayer, and no inconvenience can arise from attending it, provided persons are within tolerable distance of church. Few have business at that time of day, and amusements ought never to be preferred on the Lord's day before religion, not to say that there is room for both.'

As for the lower clergy, Swift well defined the position of the ordinary country parson when he wrote, 'He liveth like an honest, plain farmer, as his wife is dressed little better than Goody. He is sometimes graciously invited by the squire, where he sitteth at humble distance. If he gets the love of his people they often make him little useful presents. He is happy by being born to no higher expectation, for he is usually the son of some ordinary tradesman or middling farmer. His learning is much of a size with his birth and education, no more of either than what a poor hungry servitor can be expected to bring with him from his college.' A couple of generations after Swift the social standard of the country parson began to rise, and he tended to

[1] Dark, Sidney: *Seven Archbishops*, p. 159.

be a younger son or other relative of the squire, but in the large majority he remained completely unspiritual. The Church of Andrewes and Laud had become the Church of placemen, half believers, and the toadies of the landed gentry.

When the Queen came to the throne William Howley was Archbishop of Canterbury, and he was typical of the prelates of the earlier Victorian Age. Throughout his life he carefully avoided any action that might annoy the comfortable, and he never expressed any opinions that might disturb the indifferent, though he was far from being such a nonentity as some of his immediate predecessors. Howley was educated at Winchester, where he was a contemporary of Sydney Smith, whom, it is said, he 'knocked down with a chess-board for cheeking him': if this is true George Russell has said that it was the only violent action that the future Primate ever took in his life. From Winchester he went to New College, and when he was forty-three he became Regius Professor of Divinity with the comfortable addition of three substantial livings to keep the wolf from the door.

The next step was the bishopric of London, and in the House of Lords he vigorously supported the Bill of Pains and Penalties against Queen Caroline, even going so far as to declare that 'the King can do no wrong either morally or politically'. The First Gentleman was not ungrateful for such a testimonial from such a source, and in 1828 he secured Howley's translation to Lambeth. The new Archbishop for some reason was enthroned at Canterbury by proxy, which prompted Sydney Smith, who may well not have forgotten the incident of the chess-board, to write, 'A proxy sent down in the Canterbury fly, to take the Creator to witness that the Archbishop, detained in town by business or pleasure, will never violate that foundation of piety over which he presides–all this seems to me an act of the most extraordinary indolence ever recorded in history'.

Howley kept up a considerable amount of pomp and circumstance. There were regular banquets at Lambeth at which 'the domestics of the Prelacy stood, with swords and bag-wigs, round pig and turkey and venison'. The Archbishop always drove out in a coach and four,[1] and no woman was allowed in the official apartments of the Palace, while in the evening after service in chapel Howley, preceded by footmen carrying flambeaux, crossed the courtyard to 'Mrs Howley's lodgings'. At the same time the Archbishop never lost a certain innate simplicity of character, and such people as Southey were his guests at his private parties; it was noted 'how capable he was of guiding the conversation into a channel which would call forth the literary powers of his guests, how cultivated a taste he had in old English lore, and how he designedly avoided topics of public agitation'. He was, indeed, naturally modest and good-natured, and Gladstone described him as 'gentle among the gentle and mild among the mild'. Such was the man who may be said to have ushered in the Victorian Age. As Bishop of London he baptised the Princess Victoria: as Archbishop he went in the early hours of a summer morning to Kensington Palace to tell her that her uncle was dead; and he crowned her in Westminster Abbey. He was, in effect, a good, easy-going man, never out for trouble; so much so that when he was mobbed in the streets of Canterbury, and hit in the face by a dead cat, he meekly remarked that he was glad it was not a live cat.

All the same he could not avoid becoming involved in the Hampden controversy, which in one form or another continued for several years. Until 1854 no person could matriculate at Oxford, and until 1871 no one could take a Master's degree at Oxford or become a member of the Senate at Cambridge, without subscribing his belief in the Thirty-Nine Articles. Dr Hampden proposed the abolition of this provision, but Convocation rejected his motion. Two years later, in 1836, Melbourne appointed him to be Regius Professor of Divinity, whereupon Howley and his brother of York waited on the Prime Minister to explain that Hampden was a heretic. This was just the sort of situation in which Melbourne delighted, so

[1] This was probably not regarded by contemporaries as unduly ostentatious, for when the author was an undergraduate at Oxford an old scout assured him that the Church of England had never been the same since the Bishop ceased to drive in from Cuddesdon in a coach and four.

he politely asked the two prelates to point out any particular passages in Hampden's works which could be described as heretical, but this they were unable to do. When Pusey joined in the protest he was informed by Melbourne that 'the danger of religious zeal is the spirit of ill-will, hatred, and malice, of intolerance and persecution, which, in its own warmth and sincerity, it is too apt to engender'. In 1848 Lord John Russell threw down a fresh apple of discord by nominating Hampden to the see of Hereford, and the Dean and Chapter of that cathedral fought hard before obeying the royal mandate to elect him, while Howley was so roused that he declared to the Prime Minister that he would sooner go to the Tower than consecrate him. In that same year Howley died.

If he represented what may be described as the outward and visible form of the Church of England in the earlier Victorian Age there were forces at work behind the scenes which were to prove exceedingly revolutionary in their results. The easy-going attitude of men like Secker and Howley had been typical of most English Christians outside the Roman Church for a number of years, and many Englishmen followed the advice of Sir F. H. Doyle:

For this was still his simple plan,
To have with clergymen to do
As little as a Christian can.

It was small wonder that such should be the case as any reader of Canon Oilard's *Short History of the Oxford Movement* must surely agree. The chaplain of Brownlow North, who was successively Bishop of Lichfield, Worcester, and Winchester, on one occasion examined two candidates for Holy Orders in a tent at a cricket-match while he was waiting to go in to bat; while the chaplain of John Douglas, who held the sees of Carlisle and Salisbury in succession, was in the habit of examining candidates while he was shaving. In 1822 the Hon. George Spencer, son of the then Lord Spencer, who was seeking ordination in order to take up a family living, wrote to the chaplain of the Bishop of Peterborough to ask what books he should read, and the reply he received was, 'As far as I am concerned, it is impossible that I could ever entertain any idea of subjecting a gentleman with whose talents and good qualities I am so well acquainted to any examination except one as a matter of form for which a verse in the Greek Testament and an Article of the Church of England returned into Latin will be amply sufficient'. It is little wonder that Spencer died a clergyman of the Church of Rome. At the other end of the scale Phillpotts declared that he could not accept the bishopric of Exeter with a revenue of £3,000 a year unless he was allowed to hold it in conjunction with the living of Stanhope-in Weardale in Durham which was worth £4,000.

The situation was not much better in Nonconformist circles where the enthusiasm imported by Wesley was dying down. The majority of the English Presbyterians of the seventeenth century had drifted into Unitarianism in the eighteenth, and it was no mere chance that Frederick Maurice should have been born in a Unitarian family. Nor was this all, for the great misfortune of the Dissenting communities during the Victorian Age was that they had comparatively little learning at their disposal, with the exception of Spurgeon, save when they were reinforced from Scotland by divines like Dr Watson (Ian Maclaren).

In these circumstances a reaction was inevitable, and it took the form of the Oxford Movement, of which the starting-point may be said to have been a sermon preached by John Keble in St Mary's in July, 1833. The Movement was founded by four very remarkable men. One of them was Keble himself, who was at that time Professor of Poetry. Another was Edward Bouverie Pusey, who was Regius Professor of Hebrew and a Canon of Christ Church; he was a man of great learning, an ascetic, and a clergyman of unbounded devotion. The third is probably to-day the best-known of all, namely John Henry Newman, of Oriel, who became Vicar of St Mary's in 1828. Although Keble was himself an Oriel man he seems hardly to have been acquainted with Newman until they were brought together by Richard Froude, the brother of J. A. Froude, the historian. Froude was in some ways the most striking of the four, for he was extremely good-looking, a fine rider, a good sailor, and a brilliant conversationalist; at the same time his sense of humour could be an embarrassment to those who were associated with him, as for instance, when he said that there was little good to be recorded of Cranmer except that he burned well. Richard Froude died at the early age of thirty-two.

Shortly after Keble's sermon in St Mary's he and his friends decided to publish a series of *Tracts for the Times* with the laudable desire of awakening the Anglican clergy to a higher conception of their duties. The first of these appeared in September, 1833, and the series continued, chiefly from the pen of Newman, until in 1841 it had reached no. 90, when the storm broke. Four Oxford dons, including Tait, the future Archbishop of Canterbury, published a protest in which they alleged that Newman had contended that the 39 Articles do not condemn the doctrines of Purgatory, the invocation of saints, and the Mass. This protest was posted in Oxford at the gates of the Schools, and in the buttery hatches of all the colleges, of all unexpected places; at once there was a serious outbreak of *odium theologicum*, and one fiery Protestant went so far as to say that he would be sorry to trust Newman with his purse. Abuse of this nature affected Newman deeply: he retired to Littlemore to think matters over, and in 1845 he was received into the Church of Rome.

Even with the great apologist of the Oxford Movement out of the way the battle went merrily on, and both sides gave as good as they got. Already, in 1843, Pusey had been suspended from preaching in the University for two years on account of a sermon on the Holy Eucharist, and in 1850 came the Gorham Judgment by which the Judicial Committee of the Privy Council decided that the denial of the doctrine of Baptismal Regeneration was not contrary or repugnant to the doctrine of the Church of England as by law established. 'Gracious Majesty', wrote Disraeli, 'was much excited, and clapped her hands for joy at the final ruling in the Gorham Case.' This ruling had, however, the effect of sending more Anglicans over to Rome, including the future Cardinal Manning and Archdeacon Wilberforce. Despite these losses the Movement, led by

Rejected Addresses

DR PUSEY 'And, my dear young lady, if I could induce you and your friends to look kindly upon my proposal. . . .'

MISS METHODIST 'But you can't, Sir. I don't want to go to church at all, and if I did, I'm sure I wouldn't go with you.'

(Cartoon from *Punch*, 1868)

Pusey and Keble, continued the fight, and it was joined by new men of distinction such as Church, afterwards Dean of St Paul's, and King, later Bishop of Lincoln.

The lists were now set for the battle which is still being fought in the middle of the twentieth century, but which surely reached its maximum of sound and fury in the Victorian Age, and if the Oxford Movement produced new protagonists at this time so did its opponents. Howley had been succeeded at Lambeth by Sumner, who had no sort of sympathy with what he called Tractarianism or its supporters, and he was encouraged in this attitude by Lord John Russell. In these circumstances it is in no way surprising that Archdeacon Denison should have been charged with the alleged offence of teaching the Real Presence, or that Sumner should have taken advantage of this opportunity to repudiate the Eucharistic doctrine held by his predecessor in the see of Canterbury, William Laud. In 1851 the laity began to take a hand in the controversy, and Lord Shaftesbury founded the Protestant Alliance. In this connection it is important to note that in the reign of Queen Victoria as in that of Queen Elizabeth II the difference between High and Low Church cut across all party allegiances.

Perhaps the most formidable opponent of the Oxford Movement, and certainly not the least hated by its supporters, was Archibald Campbell Tait who was Archbishop of Canterbury from 1868 to 1882. What the High Churchmen thought of him can be gathered from the criticism of one of their more recent apologists, Sidney Dark: 'In the years when the English Church, after generations of lifeless apathy, was recovering its birthright and was acquiring vivid spiritual activity, its chief shepherd regarded the Church as a branch of the Civil Service.'[1] However this may be Tait refused to join the Protestant Alliance on the not unreasonable ground that 'Papacy in this country is better met by every Protestant clergyman and layman zealously doing his duty in the position God has assigned to him than by the agitation which seems implied in the formation of a society for the defence of Protestantism'.

[1] *Seven Archbishops*, p. 197.

Tait's early career was one of promise. He was born in Edinburgh in 1811, and went to Balliol as an Exhibitioner in 1830. On taking his degree he was offered a Fellowship at his own college which he accepted, and in the circumstances of those days this necessitated the taking of Holy Orders. After eight years at Balliol he succeeded Arnold as Headmaster of Rugby, and in 1849 he became Dean of Carlisle. As we have seen, Tait was one of the four Oxford dons who published the protest against Newman, and this certainly did him no harm at Westminster or at Buckingham Palace, where his views were widely held. Lord John Russell at this time set up a Royal Commission to enquire into 'the State, Discipline, Studies, and Revenues of the University of Oxford', and Tait was one of its more active members. This brought him to the notice of the Royal Family, and with the warm approval of the Queen he was appointed Bishop of London. He was consecrated on November 23rd, 1856, and on the 4th of the following month he did homage. In describing this incident in his diary he recalls that when the Bishop of Ripon did homage to William IV, and had just risen from his knees, the King said to him in a loud voice, 'Bishop of Ripon, I charge you, as you shall answer to Almighty God, that you never by word or deed give encouragement to those damned Whigs, who would upset the Church of England'. The supporters of the Oxford Movement doubtless felt that Tait stood much in need of similar instructions from the Sovereign.

At this point the peace of the Church of England was disturbed by two further controversies which must be briefly described. In 1853 the Convocations of Canterbury and York were permitted by the Government to meet again after the lapse of a hundred-and-thirty-five years, and two of their earliest exploits after their revival, were to denounce *Essays and Reviews*, and to fall upon Colenso.

The publication of *Essays and Reviews* took place in 1860, and among the seven contributors to the volume were Frederick Temple, Mark Pattison, and Benjamin Jowett. At once there was a storm of controversy in which both High and Low

Churchmen were not slow to join. What upset the pious most was the suggestion that 'a judgment of eternal misery may not be the purpose of God'. The Episcopal Bench censured the writers; Convocation condemned the publications; and two of the essayists were prosecuted.

Hardly had this tempest died down than another one arose over Colenso, who had in 1853 been consecrated the first Bishop of Natal. No man had set a finer example of care for natives, but he published books of heretical criticism of the Bible, and he protested that he could not use the baptismal service because of its reference to the Flood, in which he did not believe. Truly the heterodox can at times be just as foolish as the orthodox. Anyhow, the fat was in the fire. The English bishops sent Colenso a joint letter begging him to resign, a course which he refused to adopt. He was thereupon tried and condemned by the Bishop of Cape Town, sitting as Metropolitan of South Africa with very doubtful jurisdiction. Colenso was at that time in England, and he took no immediate action, but when he returned to the diocese he was formally excommunicated, a sentence which, however, the English bishops refused to recognize.

The Colenso case raised the whole question of the relations of the colonial churches with the Church of England, and the next step was the convocation of the first Lambeth Conference in 1867, but it was soon apparent that the English bishops had no great enthusiasm for it: six of them refused point-blank to attend, while four others were most conveniently ill. Nevertheless with the votes of the colonial and American bishops the deposition of Colenso was approved, and the Bishop of Cape Town proceeded to consecrate a successor in spite of the fact that the Judicial Committee of the Privy Council held that he had no jurisdiction. Colenso himself retained the endowments of the see until his death, which occurred in 1883.

The Oxford Movement had now been in existence for a generation, but it still aroused the utmost hostility in official circles. Lord John Russell quoted with approval Arnold's statement– 'I look upon a Roman Catholic as an enemy in his uniform. I look upon a Tractarian as an enemy in disguise.' This opinion was shared by the Queen who wrote to her uncle that the Tractarians were doing immense harm, and she told Lord Derby, when he was Prime Minister, that no 'ritualists' were to be recommended for appointments in the Church. The Prince Consort fulminated against those who promulgated 'principles likely to disturb the peace of the Church'. In 1868 there was another vacancy in the see of Canterbury, and Disraeli suggested Tait's name to the Queen, who cordially approved, so Tait duly transferred his residence from Fulham to Lambeth.

It would be at once wearisome and superfluous to carry the story of the struggle between the supporters and the opponents of the Oxford Movement in any detail down to the death of the Queen: it must suffice to have indicated its origins, and to have given some examples of the heat which it engendered. Other instances have also been noticed in earlier chapters in different connections. Of the social position of the Church of England during these years there is considerable difference of opinion. Sidney Dark was very definitely of the opinion that its failure to adopt the principles of the Oxford Movement was its undoing. 'At the beginning of the century (*i.e.* the twentieth century), the English Church had already to a considerable extent become a class church. Its bishops sat with the Lords and were the spiritual ornaments of the Court. The congregations in its often beautiful churches were mostly prosperous and content. Politically it was the valuable ally of the men with money. When the moneyless man was moved to public worship he went to an ugly Methodist conventicle or to an uglier Salvation Army barracks. . . . Much for which Laud died had been recovered, but not for the benefit of the people for whom Laud cared most.'[1] Another authority, C. R. L. Fletcher, while agreeing about the declining influence of the Church of England, would have it that this was due to the Oxford Movement: 'The Early Tractarians had been men of real, if specialist, learning, and had seldom been ritualists; but, from the middle of the century onwards, the learning of the clergy steadily decreased, and a

[1] *Seven Archbishops*, p. 227.

series of elaborate changes in ritual were gradually introduced, many of them in deliberate imitation of Rome, and in ignorance of the probability that much of the ritual of the early Church had been taken over bodily from dying Pagan creeds. The result of the whole Movement has been that large numbers of English laymen, however anxious they may be to co-operate with the clergy in good works, have lost all confidence in their parish ministers and all interest in ecclesiastical matters; and the gulf between clerics and laymen, owing both to the spiritual claims of the former and to their antics in church, has widened every day, and is now probably impassable.'[1]

How far the mass of the people, even of the Church-going people, were affected by these discords it is difficult to say. As we have seen, the close at Barchester was unaffected, and in spite of the deep religious feeling which existed in the Victorian Age religion, in the Scottish sense, was to the English a thing apart. During the whole period the Church of England was in a state of crisis, but there were different crises; the Church of Scotland was also in a state of crisis, but it was always much the same crisis. Contemporaries would appear to have found it as difficult to appreciate the attitude of the Victorians in these matters as does posterity. In June, 1850, Lord John Russell abolished the Sunday delivery of letters, but there was such an outcry that it had to be restored by the end of the year. On the other hand eight years earlier when the shareholders of the Edinburgh-Glasgow Railway had voted in favour of one train each way on Sunday the newspapers attacked the proposal in so violent a fashion–'this is the most momentous day in Scotland for centuries, an object of interest both in Heaven and in Hell'–that it had to be abandoned.

There can also be little doubt, *pace* C. R. L. Fletcher, that until the end of the century, and even until the First World War, the intellectual prestige of the Church of England was very high: men like Stubbs and Creighton would have been an ornament to any body, religious or secular. Stubbs was a High Churchman, and was not always the easiest of guests. Dr G. B.

[1] *Introductory History of England*, vol. V, p. 208.

A Pretty Kettle of Fish: The Puseyite Parson and his Cook

P.P. 'What, want to leave your situation? I thought you were perfectly satisfied.'

COOK 'Well, Sir, the fact is, I ain't equal to all them fast days. For what with a Hegg here and a Hegg there and little bits o' fish for Breakfasts and little bits o' fish for Dinners and the sweet omelicks and the fried and the stewed hoysters and the bashawed lobsterses, there's so much cooking that I ain't even time to make up a cap.'

(Cartoon from *Punch*, 1888)

Grundy relates that Stubbs and his chaplain Holmes called for tea one afternoon, and Mrs Grundy made some remark to the bishop about the weather, only, however, to elicit the somewhat disconcerting reply, 'I always refer questions about the weather to my chaplain, Mr Holmes'.[1]

There can be little doubt but that to some extent the Church of Rome was itself responsible for the feeling roused against it in these years of the Victorian Age. Encouraged by the number of conversions on the one hand, and by the increase of the Catholic working-class population due to Irish immigration on the other, it passed over to the offensive for the first time since the Revolution, and this gave the ordinary Englishman the shock of his life. He had come to believe that so far as his own country was concerned the Church of Rome was down and out, and when it was brought home to him that it was neither down nor out his fury and alarm knew no bounds. Fuel was added to the fire in 1850 when the Pope, Pius IX, issued an Evangelical dividing England into Catholic dioceses, though carefully differentiating them from the Anglican sees. At once there was an outbreak of public-house Protestantism similar to that which had inspired the Popish Plot agitation in the reign of Charles II, and the Gordon Riots in that of George III, and the Government of the day introduced an Ecclesiastical Titles Bill to prohibit Catholic bishops from bearing diocesan titles. It may be added that in the country as a whole this wave of Protestant fanaticism soon died down, but in some quarters the feelings it engendered could still be exploited for political ends as we have seen in the case of Sir Archibald Salvidge's manœuvres in Liverpool at the end of the century.

When the Queen died the position of Catholics in England, whatever their class, was infinitely better than it had been when she ascended the throne, and two quotations from Archbishop Mathew well illustrate the fact:

> A sense of security was induced by the shadow of Arundel, for the Catholic body fully shared in that illusion of social permanence which had gained in English life as the Queen's reign lengthened.

[1] Grundy, G. B.: *Forty-five Years at Oxford*, p. 91.

> The golden contented jubilee of 1887 and the more consciously imperialistic celebrations ten years later enclosed a period of calm. Arundel and Cardiff Castle, Carlton and Allerton brought a suggestion of the Gothic. Memories of a Tennysonian past lingered in the minstrels' galleries, and combined well with the footmen and the silver tea-trays and the formal dinner parties of a leisured present. There were already many Catholics in diplomacy, a considerable number in the services, and none among the new type of defaulting financier.

At the other end of the social scale it was the same:

> The great mass of the Catholics of the working class were now settled in the manufacturing towns and cities . . . (They) remained like their rich coreligionists in a state of stability. . . . It was this generation which built so many of the schools. They would never refuse money for the 'chapel'. Housing conditions were now rather better and employment, though badly paid, was constant. As the families sat in the kitchen at the hot Sunday dinner, with the girls in print dresses and the boys talking of the new League Football and the first boxing successes of Jim Driscoll, they would always have the money ready for the collector coming Sunday after Sunday for the school building.[1]

When one turns from the Church of England and the Church of Rome in the Victorian Age to Nonconformity it is to find the influence of class very strongly marked. Native English Presbyterianism had, as has been shown, almost ceased to exist in the preceding century, but the Scottish invasion had given it a new lease of life, and the Presbyterian churches in the larger centres of population were very flourishing indeed. They drew their congregations almost exclusively from the upper middle-class, as did the Unitarians, who numbered such families as the Chamberlains in their ranks. Only a little lower in the social scale were the Congregationalists, while below them were the Wesleyans, Methodists, and Baptists, who collectively formed that 'Nonconformist Conscience' which was so powerful a factor in national politics. In 1901 these bodies were still forces to be reckoned with, but decay had already set in, and the triumph of secularism, which is so prominent a feature of the twentieth century, was only a question of time.

[1] Mathew, David: *Catholicism in England*, pp. 235–237.

CHAPTER IX

The Services in the Victorian Age

The outstanding characteristic of the Navy and the Army in the Victorian Age was that except during the Crimean War neither was in action against the forces of a European Power. In many respects the Navy was in the worse plight for while the Army had been able to add to its laurels at the Alma, Balaclava, and Inkerman, the Senior Service had not fought a real fleet action against a first-class naval Power since the Basque Roads in 1809, a record which was to remain unbroken until the battle of Jutland in 1916. Furthermore, the Queen herself was by no means partial to the Navy which she never forgave for the obstacles which had been placed in the way of the appointment of the Prince Consort as an Admiral of the Fleet. Above all, it was in the earlier part of the reign that the great change was made from sail to steam.

In these circumstances it is not surprising that by the middle years of the century a torpor had overcome the Service: new guns and ammunition were still included in the Army estimates, and the War Office had the custody of the Navy's war stores. Gunnery was at a very low ebb, and practise-firing was often a mere farce, while black powder was not replaced by smokeless until the very end of the reign. Sight and range-finding equipment were very poor, and the Queen was in her grave before armour-piercing shells were issued. There was a lack of cruisers and destroyers, and the main fleets were without such essential auxiliaries as colliers, ammunition, store-, repair-, and hospital-ships, while even such important overseas bases as Gibraltar were without proper docks and defences. There was no Naval Staff College, and no Naval War Staff at the Admiralty.

The weakness of the Navy was first exposed in September, 1884, in a series of articles which appeared in the *Pall Mall Gazette* from the pen of W. T. Stead under the title of 'The Truth about the Navy'. This not only roused public opinion, but it also had its effect upon the Government, and when Lord Randolph Churchill tried to insist upon further economies he was compelled to resign. Nor was this all, for in 1888 three admirals were appointed to investigate the lessons to be learnt from the recent naval manœuvres, and their report was couched in such terms as to alarm the country. Their verdict was that the Navy was too weak to take the offensive by blockade against even a single enemy, and at the same time carry out all the various duties which would inevitably be thrust upon it in time of war, while in the case of hostilities against two Powers 'the balance of maritime strength would be serious against England'. The report, which was unanimous, continued, 'without particularising her possible antagonist, there can be no doubt that were England involved in a maritime war, and were she to resume her natural rights as a Belligerent which appear to have been voluntarily laid aside by the Declaration of Paris in 1856, complication with Neutral States would inevitably ensue, and her whole commercial position would be jeopardized at the outset were war forced upon her when her Navy was weak'. Naval defeat would mean the loss of India and the British colonies. 'No time should be lost in placing her Navy beyond comparison with that of any two Powers. As there is nothing in our opinion to justify the belief that the days of ironclad battleships are over, we recommend a resumption and a steady continuance of ironclad building.' The danger of invasion, it was stated, would be better met by increased naval expenditure than by costly shore defences.[1]

The result of these recommendations was the Naval Defence

[1] Cf. *The Cambridge History of the British Empire*, vol. III, p. 243.

Act of 1889 which laid down the Two Power Standard, on which the purpose was to ensure that the British Navy was superior to that of any two European Powers. When the Act was passed the navies of France and Russia were what the Admiralty had in mind, but in due course those of Germany and Austria-Hungary became the potential enemy, though this was latent rather than patent when the Queen died.

The development of the Army was, as might be supposed, very different in view of the fact that it had had continuous fighting experience unequalled by that of any contemporary army, though only in the Crimea had it met European troops upon European soil: hence the fact that Lord Wolseley, Lord Roberts, Sir Evelyn Wood, Sir George White, and Sir Redvers Buller, its outstanding figures at the end of the Victorian Age, all of whom had been awarded the Victoria Cross, were specialists only in Asiatic and colonial warfare. All the same the regular soldier of 1890, in spite of much that was antiquated in his weapons, training, and organization was a modern soldier. In this connection tribute must be paid to Edward Cardwell, who was Secretary of State for War from 1868 to 1874. By substituting the short-service system of seven years with the colours for the previous twenty-one he ended the strategic dispersal of the Army about the Empire in what has been described as 'long-service and semi-penal exile'. With the short-service system came also the linking of the infantry battalions in the Line regiments in pairs, which made possible a more reasonable balance between home and foreign service: henceforth one battalion in each pair took its turn to serve abroad, and received drafts from its linked battalion at home, an arrangement which mitigated the hardship of long service in India or the colonies by providing regular reliefs; each battalion serving abroad was also periodically relieved as a whole by the linked battalion at home. On the other hand the critics of the scheme could justifiably point to the great hardship caused to men who, being denied a full career in the Army, found themselves thrown on the labour market too old to adapt themselves satisfactorily to industry; a further ground of criticism was that the poor physique of many of the recruits rendered them unsuitable for training service abroad.

One of the more important of Cardwell's reforms was the abolition of the purchase of commissions, though, as has been shown on an earlier page, the opposition was so strong that he had to persuade the Queen to issue a Royal warrant before he could get his way. Previous to this a Royal Commission had resulted in the revelation of a number of interesting facts regarding the system. There existed a recognized auction room in Charles Street, Mayfair, where competition was keen, and prices were higher than the regulations allowed as the following table will serve to show:

	Regulation	*Real Price*
Cavalry Lieutenant-Colonelcy	£6,175	£14,000
Lieutenant-Colonel, Foot Guards	£9,000	£13,200
A Company of Foot Guards	£4,800	£9,000
Lieutenant-Colonel, Line Regiment	£4,500	£7,000
A Company of Line Regiment	£1,300	£2,400

This system naturally led to every kind of abuse and incongruity, and a typical example is that of a regiment stationed in India in the late forties, in which was serving a captain of forty-seven years' service who had fought at Waterloo, while the only other officer who had been alive in 1815 was the lieutenant-colonel, who had been two years old at the time.

The abolition of purchase was certainly a step in the right direction, but some time was to elapse before its benefits were widely felt. After his experience of the Egyptian campaigns of 1882–5 Lord Wolseley still had grave concern over the inefficiency of many officers, and he has left his feelings on record: he has told how he had seen 'splendid battalions kept in the rear . . . whilst others of inferior quality were sent to the front, because the general commanding did not dare to employ against the enemy a corps whose commanding officer was manifestly incompetent'. He then went on to say, 'It is but right that the nation should obtain in return for the compensation paid to officers for the surrender of commissions the reform that it expected, and had the right to expect, namely, that none but competent and properly educated officers should be selected for the position of Lieutenant-colonel . . . I hold that it is criminal to hand over in action the lives of gallant soldiers to men who are deplorably ignorant of the elements of their profession.' Even so late as the South African War a shrewd French observer could still write, 'The main defect of the British officer is that he is not what the French call *instruit* nor even disposed to become so'. The German official report of that war drives the argument home.

As a commentary on these criticisms Colonel H. de Watteville wrote in 1954, 'The ignorance of its officers . . . could not be laid solely to the charge of the Army. Antipathy to all theory, everything abstract; innate contempt for things that savoured of mere learning or of book-work, had conducted to a lamentable level of education amongst the bulk of that society which provided the army officer. Even as late as two generations ago there still lingered a prejudice against the university candidate in not a few officers' messes–until the newcomer had lost all traces of his undergraduate origin.'[1] Nor was this surprising considering the time that the Duke of Cambridge was Commander-in-Chief, that is to say from 1856 to 1895, and the kind of man he was, for he was heard to say to a distinguished general, 'I don't like Staff College officers. My experience of Staff College officers is that they are conceited, and that they are dirty! Brains! I don't believe in brains. You haven't any I know, Sir!'

To pass from the Victorian officer to the men he commanded is to come across but another aspect of what may be termed the Victorian Social Revolution, for although the status of the private soldier left much to be desired in 1901, it was infinitely higher than it had been when the Queen came to the throne.

After 1859, for example, flogging in both Services was strictly limited to certain classes of offences, and nine years later all corporal punishment was further restricted by the Mutiny Act to crimes committed on active service. On three occasions in the seventies the House of Commons debated the subject, but each

[1] *The British Soldier*, pp. 181–182.

time rejected proposals for its total abolition in either the Navy or the Army. During the Second Afghan War, 1878–80, a few men were flogged, mostly hardened malefactors who looted the medical stores for the sake of the brandy, and there is no evidence to show that this form of punishment aroused any resentment, let alone horror, among their comrades: on the contrary the general opinion seems to have been that it served the culprits right. The final abolition of flogging was brought about by the Army Discipline Act of 1881, when as a substitute there was introduced Field Punishment No. 1 which entailed the lashing of malefactors to a gun wheel for a stated number of hours, but this was awarded on active service only.

Lord Roberts has left on record an account of his feelings on a flogging parade in his earlier years:

> One very painful circumstance stamped itself on my memory. I was obliged to be present at a flogging parade–the only one, I am glad to say, I have ever had to attend, although the barbarous and degrading custom was not done away with until nearly thirty years later. A few years before I joined the service, the number of lashes which might be given was limited to fifty, but even under this restriction the sight was a horrible one to witness. The parade to which I refer was ordered for the punishment of two men who had been sentenced to fifty lashes each for selling their kits, and to a certain term of imprisonment in addition. They were fine, handsome young Horse Artillerymen, and it was hateful to see them thus treated. Besides, one felt it was productive of harm rather than good, for it tended to destroy the men's self-respect, and to make them completely reckless.
>
> In this instance, no sooner had the two men been released from prison than they committed the same offence again. They were a second time tried by Court-Martial, and sentenced as before. How I longed to have the power to remit the fifty lashes, for I felt that selling their kits on this occasion was their way of showing their resentment at the ignominious treatment they had been subjected to, and of proving that flogging was powerless to prevent their repeating the offence.
>
> A parade was ordered, as on the previous occasion. One man was stripped to the waist, and tied to the wheel of a gun. The finding and sentence of the Court-Martial were read out–a trumpeter standing ready the while to inflict the punishment–when the commanding officer, Major Robert Waller, instead of

> ordering him to begin, to the intense relief of, I believe, every officer present, addressed the prisoners, telling them of his distress at finding two soldiers belonging to his troop brought up for corporal punishment twice in a little more than six weeks, and adding that, however little they deserved such leniency, if they would promise not to commit the same offence again, and to behave better for the future, he would remit the flogging part of the sentence. If the prisoners were not happy, I was; but the clemency was evidently appreciated by them, for they promised, and kept their words. I did not lose sight of these two men for some years, and was always gratified to learn that their conduct was uniformly satisfactory, and that they had become good, steady soldiers.[1]

It was, of course, grossly improper to dispose of Government property in this way, but a very high value was attached to it in those days. It is, for example, recorded of a Victorian judge, when sentencing a man to death for stabbing a soldier, said, 'You have hurried a human soul into eternity; and worse than that, you have–for which may God forgive you–protruded a lethal weapon through your victim's trousers, which were the property of Her Majesty.' Perhaps it was the same judge who, on passing the sentence of death on a forger of bank notes, said, 'I can hold out no hope to you of mercy here, and I must urge you to make preparations for another world, where I hope you may obtain that mercy which a due regard to the credit of our paper currency forbids you to hope for here'.

From one handicap all ranks of the Army suffered down to the First World War, and that was unpopularity with the public and ridicule from the Press: the Navy, on the other hand, always commended itself to the man-in-the-street. Colonel de Watteville writes of the soldier of the Victorian Age:

> Too often he was still reckoned as an outcast; too often the King's livery was still regarded as a mark of a lost soul. If Dickens thought more highly of the soldier as a result of his sufferings and courage in the Crimea and the Indian Mutiny, a similar attitude was not adopted by every other artist and writer of the period. In the pages of *Punch*, after the more glorious days of the Crimea and of the Mutiny were past, Titmarsh still remained unable to

[1] *Forty-one Years in India*, vol. I, pp. 25–26.

The Camp at Chobham, 1853

resist belittling the work of the Army in the recent campaign. As for the annual Trooping of the Colour by the Foot Guards he could only see in it a 'magnificent piece of tomfoolery'. His mantle descended upon the caricaturists. John Leach never tired of poking fun at the soldier, fun which might indeed readily turn to ungenerous ridicule. Some of his last drawings for *Punch* were those in which he pilloried the 'Brook Green Volunteers'. The Volunteers undoubtedly deserved better. . . .

Charles Kean inherited the tradition of caricaturing the soldier, and his contributions to *Punch* went on showing the choleric major, the pompous volunteer officer pursued by a string of street urchins, and the guardsmen in shell-jacket, forage-cap, and tight overalls escorting a nursemaid while she trundles her perambulator in the park. Had these types been, only occasionally, interspersed with a more sympathetic figure or slightly more sympathetic letterpress, the conclusion could not have been drawn that the soldier was generally and popularly held in low esteem.[1]

When one passes from a consideration of the Fighting Services to that of the Civil Service, both at home, in India, and abroad it is to light upon another of the real revolutions of the Victorian Age. The way had been paved by Dr Arnold's reforms, for it had long become clear that what may be described as the old Public School system was breaking down, as has been mentioned on an earlier page. Contempt for outside opinion, a pedantic adherence to old customs, and a refusal to consider the boys' point of view frequently brought about insubordination which occasionally broke out into mutiny. Eton and Westminster were notorious in this respect. Open rebellion broke out at Eton in 1743, 1768, 1783, 1810, and 1832, while at Winchester the Riot Act had to be read in 1770, and the same school rebelled in 1774, 1793, and 1818. Similar disorders took place at Harrow in 1771 and 1818, and at Rugby in 1797 and 1822. Above all, in 1851, there was the great rebellion at Marlborough, where after three years of smouldering discontent, of flogging and fighting, and of fiercely repressed insubordination, all authority broke down: for an entire week anarchy, enlivened by fireworks and bonfires, reigned supreme,

[1] *The British Soldier*, pp. 166–167.

and when the rioting was at last quelled it was more by concessions than by strong measures.

There is, unfortunately, no detailed study of the machinery of government, and the type of people who ran it, in the Victorian Age, and the histories of the individual departments have tended to be jejune in the extreme, but there can be no doubt whatever that the reform of the Public Schools, which provided the entrants for the Civil Service, was closely connected with the reform of that Civil Service itself, for previously the one had been as haphazard an affair as the other. Appointments were in the gift of the Government, and were obtained by influence. No qualifying examination was held unless there were more applicants than there were posts vacant, and when an appointment was made it was, as a rule, permanent. The whole approach to life was, indeed, so different from what it was later to become that it is very difficult to understand it at all: Anthony Trollope, for example, after leaving Harrow had seriously thought of joining the Austrian Army, where he had already received the promise of a commission in a cavalry regiment, when he changed his mind, and instead became a Civil Servant.[1]

Sir Algernon West has left on record an account of the way in which appointments were made in those days. He had followed the well-trodden path from Eton to Christ Church, but he only stayed two terms at Oxford for 'about the end of April, 1851, Alfred Montgomery, a Commissioner of Inland Revenue, offered me a small appointment in the Income Tax Office at Somerset House, which I gladly accepted'. The appointment in this case was a temporary one, but it had enabled West to get his feet on the official ladder, albeit on the lowest step, and in due course he was transferred to the permanent establishment of the Admiralty.

The Civil Service of the earlier years of the Queen's reign is almost unrecognizable. Trollope entered the Post Office as a junior clerk in 1834, and for the next six years he had to be at St Martin's-le-Grand daily from ten to six. As might be

[1] Escott, T. H. S.: *Anthony Trollope*, pp. 17–18.

supposed, in view of the way in which the Civil Service was recruited, and of the normal behaviour at the Public Schools from which the vast majority of the entrants came, discipline was lax, and Trollope tells us that the young men with whom he worked counted for lost every half-hour not spent in drinking, smoking, and card-playing; they saw their natural enemies in blue-books and official documents of every kind. The novelist himself was a good deal of an agitator:

> In one of the great rooms of St Martin's-le-Grand, Trollope collected and told malcontents of the place that it was their duty to agitate till, outside office-hours and in all personal relationships, they were as much their own masters as if they had nothing to do with State employ. Mr Secretary Rowland Hill was at once up in arms. The firebrand who had thus tried to inflame the worst passions of the Queen's servants ought, he declared openly, to be dismissed. These words, and the incidents which had led up to them, eventually reached the Postmaster-General, then the second Lord Colchester, a member of the Derby Government. The inflammatory speaker was therefore sent for by the Minister, and told that the authorities of the Department were anxious to be relieved of his services. 'Is your Lordship', meekly asked Trollope, 'prepared to dismiss me?' In reply Lord Colchester, who, with his father's Eldonian Toryism, combined a certain sense of humour that his father did not possess, smiling oracularly, deprecated any recourse to extremities. From that portion of his long duel with Rowland Hill, Trollope consequently came forth with flying colours.[1]

It was not until 1870 that the system of open competition was introduced into the Civil Service, though Queen Victoria continued to regard its members as her own personal servants to the day of her death.

In the Diplomatic Service development during the Victorian Age was on much the same basis, and the professional gradually won the day, at the expense of the amateur. Throughout the eighteenth century, and during the early years of its successor, the British representatives at foreign capitals were usually great nobles who had no special qualifications, beyond a long purse, for the posts to which they were appointed. This custom was

[1] *Ibid.*, p. 118.

not, of course, in any way peculiar to Great Britain, but its defects are obvious, and not the least was the attempted remedy of special envoys who carried on the real negotiations, of which the ambassador himself knew nothing. Louis XV had brought this latter system to a fine art, with results that were equally embarrassing to his ministers and to Foreign Powers. In Great Britain the reforms were originated by George Canning while he was Foreign Secretary between the years 1822 and 1827, and at the end of that period the Foreign Service, as it is now called, was well on its way towards attaining the form in which it exists to-day.

He increased the staff at the Foreign Office, but he delegated very little of the really important work there to other hands. He treated his subordinates at home in the same way as he treated British representatives abroad, that is to say he left them very little latitude indeed; it was, in fact, Canning who began that policy of strict control from Whitehall which in more recent times has changed the whole profession of diplomacy. Difficulty of communication was, however, still the great obstacle in the path of centralization, for the telegraph had not been invented, so that the regulation of details from London was impossible; but the tendency was already at work, and the time was fast passing when an ambassador had any say in the formulation of policy; strangely enough, it was his own cousin, Stratford, who was the last great diplomatist of the old school. That Canning's more rigid discipline was not unnecessary is clear from the fact that the minister at Lisbon had to be reproved not only for his 'slovenly penmanship', but also for the objectionable practice of packing up tea in his official despatches. It had also become a habit with a great many ambassadors to introduce irrelevant and personal topics into their letters and this, too, was censured. Those who did not conform to the new order suffered for their disobedience, however highly placed or well-connected they might be.

In nothing, however, was Canning's zeal for efficiency more marked than in his attitude towards the Consular Service, where he worked in close co-operation with his friend Huskisson at the Board of Trade. When he went to the Foreign Office in 1822 the standing of the vast majority of British consuls left a great deal to be desired. Some of them were, indeed, professional, and others local merchants of substance, but too many were either adventurers, or bankrupt men of fashion like Beau Brummel, who was British consul at Caen. Canning, who may be said without exaggeration to have had the commercial interests of his country more closely at heart than any previous Foreign Secretary, realized that individuals of this type were worse than useless, and that he was most careful in the appointments he made is shown by the case of a Mr Staples. This gentleman had taken up a consular post at Acapulco, in Mexico, after promising, as all Canning's regular consuls were compelled to do, absolutely to renounce trade. It was not long, however, before it transpired that Staples had entered into a contract for a loan to the Mexican Government, and he was accordingly informed that there was no further occasion for his services. This action, it may be noted, was taken in spite of the fact that Staples was the brother-in-law of the Marquess of Ormonde.

At the same time Canning did not hesitate to relax some of the more strict of the existing regulations in the Foreign Office itself. His immediate subordinates, for instance, were summoned to his room by a messenger instead of by a bell, and were not required to stand in his presence except on official occasions, whereas Chatham had never in any circumstances allowed them to be seated.

In 1861 a Select Committee on the Diplomatic Service not only agreed that the previous fifty years had seen the service assume more and more the character of a profession, but the evidence brought before it threw considerable light upon its recruitment and working during the earlier part of the Victorian Age. The Committee was informed that between 1812 and 1860 a total of 119 men had represented Great Britain as heads of missions at foreign courts, but it should be noted that this figure excludes the North African and Asiatic embassies and missions which at that time were on a different footing from the general diplomatic service, and were specially staffed.

These heads of missions fell roughly into four classes corresponding with the routes by which they had entered the service. Sixty-two had come in at the bottom, 26 at various higher levels by way of the Foreign Office, 12 had previously belonged to the Consular Service, and the remaining 19 had been appointed to missions without previous experience of diplomacy.

'The first 62', Professor Bindoff has written, 'were the true *diplomates de carrière*, products of that curious survival, the unpaid attachéship. An eighteenth-century diplomatist often found it convenient to take abroad with him a young son or nephew, or a friend's son, who thus got the opportunity of acquiring Continental 'finish' under a paternal eye. These 'attachés' shared their patron's house and table, and in return assisted with the secretarial work of the mission. They took their duties light-heartedly, the more so as few of them intended to make a diplomatic career. So soon as they had gained whatever insight into public business their simple routine afforded, or had seen enough of the world, they returned home and diplomacy knew them no more.'[1]

Once again it was George Canning who took the first steps to regularize this system. He described the attachés of his day as 'a couple of dozen young men scattered over Europe; owing no allegiance and taking diplomacy only as subsidiary to amusement', while a little earlier, in 1814, there was one young gentleman attached to Lord Clancarty at Frankfort who could not even write. In due course the Foreign Secretary's permission had to be asked before an attaché could be appointed, and from that it was but a short step for the Foreign Secretary to claim priority, and eventually to assert an absolute power of selection. Then in 1853 it became compulsory for would-be attachés to serve a few months' probation at the Foreign Office, and this rule not only enabled the raw recruit to learn the elements of his job before going abroad, but it gave the Foreign Secretary, through his permanent officials, a chance of observing him at work, and, if necessary, of pointing out to him that his future did not lie in diplomacy.

[1] *Royal Historical Society Transactions*, Fourth Series, vol. XVIII, pp. 144–145.

Perhaps the most important development in the creation of a professional Diplomatic Service was the payment of attachés, and this was begun by Canning in 1823. By 1846 there were 24, with salaries ranging from £200 at Mexico to £400 at Paris and St Petersburg, and by 1860, out of a total of 78 attachéships, 34 were paid. On the other hand as the Victorian Age progressed promotion became slower. For attachés who entered between 1812 and 1830 it took nine years to become a secretary of legation and thirteen-and-a-half years to become a secretary of embassy; for those entering between 1831 and 1845 the figures had risen to thirteen and eighteen-and-a-half years, and for those entering between 1846 and 1860 to sixteen and twenty-three years. 'An attaché', writes Professor Bindoff, 'entering early in our period might thus expect to become a secretary of legation at 32 and a secretary of embassy at 36; by the middle of the period the prospect had receded to his 36th and 41st years, and at the end still further to his 39th and 46th years. . . . This situation was only rendered bearable by the distant vision of ambassadorial eminence and emoluments.'[1]

Next we have the group which entered the Service from the Foreign Office, for in spite of the fact that the Committee reported that, save for a rule more honoured in the breach than in the observance, the Foreign Office and the Diplomatic Service were 'entirely distinct' in personnel, there was an exchange between them. The posts concerned in this respect were those of private secretary, précis writer, and clerk, which may be grouped together, and that of Under-Secretary of State.

During the earlier years of the Queen's reign there were only one private secretary and one précis writer in the Office, and both were attached to the Foreign Secretary. The principal task of the private secretary was to copy and file his chief's private letters, while the précis writer dealt similarly with official correspondence. Both were posts for young men in the twenties, though the age-level was tending to rise, and they were rarely held for more than two years, and sometimes only

[1] *Ibid.*, pp. 151–152.

for a few months. They both carried a salary of £300 a year, but while the précis writership originally would appear to have been the superior post the private secretaryship later took the lead. Both posts were in the personal gift of the Foreign Secretary, who followed his own inclination whether he gave them to clerks in the Office or to young men outside it. The Under-Secretary of State, too, was chosen by the Foreign Secretary from among his relations or friends, and he usually held office as long as his patron, or until signs of an approaching change of government rendered it advisable to hasten his translation into diplomacy. For example, Canning's duel with Castlereagh and his resignation in 1809 kept Charles Bagot, his Under-Secretary, waiting until 1815 for the mission which was due to him, while Palmerston's appointment of Shee to Berlin in October, 1834, although announced to the Prussian Government, was cancelled a month later by the incoming Wellington, and when Palmerston did come back to the Foreign Office the best he could do for his friend was Stuttgart.

The third group, that is to say those who entered the Diplomatic from the Consular Service, was the smallest, and that it existed at all was largely due to the advent of a new type of mission, nominally diplomatic, but primarily designed for the protection and furtherance of British commercial interests. Such were the Central and South American posts established by Canning and Palmerston, the North African ones, and those in Asia which had originated with the East India Company but were later taken over by the Crown. Canning himself was opposed to giving diplomatic appointments to consuls, but the obvious advantage of having men with commercial experience and local knowledge at these posts led his successors at the Foreign Office, though neither of set rule nor invariably, to promote consuls of proved ability. In the Central and South American missions the consul was usually made into a diplomatist by easy stages, that is to say that he was first given the label 'and *chargé d'affaires*' as a suffix to his consular rank, and then those words came first in his title, and finally, if he were fortunate, he became a full minister plenipotentiary.

On the appointment as heads of missions of those without any previous experience of diplomacy no special comment is called for as the practice has continued down to the present day, and the arguments for and against it are the same now as they were a century ago. It introduces fresh blood into a profession peculiarly liable to develop rigidity and 'caste', besides enabling the Government of the day to appoint one of its own number, or a man in whom it feels great confidence, and who may therefore be expected to carry special weight abroad. On the other hand there is a danger of its being turned to unworthy ends of patronage, while its too frequent use not unnaturally causes disaffection among the professional diplomatists whose interests it threatens.

Whatever may be the case to-day some of the ambassadors of the Victorian Age were pretty formidable, and their tempers were not always of the best, yet there was a good deal of humanity even in the formal world of those days. One day, for example, Stratford Canning burst out at a young attaché, 'Damn your eyes, Mr Hay', to which came the instantaneous reply, 'Damn your Excellency's eyes, Sir'. There was a pause during which a pin could have been heard to drop, and then the ambassador remarked, 'Quite right, my boy; I had no business to swear at you'.

With the arrival of the telegraph in the middle of the nineteenth century a change came over diplomacy and diplomatists, and it has been going on ever since. Ambassadors became more easily controlled by their respective Governments, and there was no need to give them the wide powers of discretion which they had previously enjoyed when it took the best part of a year to get an answer to a letter sent from the Far East to London. On the other hand it was during the Victorian Age comparatively rare for a conference of the Powers to take place, except at the conclusion of a war or when there was some particular problem to be discussed. British Foreign Secretaries to whatever party they belonged rarely left their own country, and as a result all international business was conducted through the ambassadors, who were thus able to maintain a *façade* of importance even if they were in reality receiving telegraphic instructions from hour to hour.

Down to August, 1914, at any rate in civilized countries, the status of the diplomatist was universally respected: even when war broke out, and ambassadors were withdrawn, the traditional courtesies were observed. On the other hand diplomatists had to be extremely circumspect in their behaviour if they were to preserve their prestige and their privileges, and one thing they had not to do was to interfere in the internal affairs of the nation to which they were accredited. In this respect their virtue, like that of Cæsar's wife, had to be above suspicion. Otherwise they might find themselves recalled, as happened in 1888 to Lord Sackville, who was British ambassador to the United States; he was imprudent enough on the eve of a Presidential election to comply with the request of a correspondent for his opinion as to the merits of the various candidates for the Presidency. Although his letter was strictly confidential it found its way into the Press, and the American Government was so indignant at the ambassador's indiscretion that it at once applied to London for his recall.

Such was the diplomacy of the Victorian Age, and such were the types of men by whom it was conducted. It did not come into existence suddenly, but was the result of a gradual development, and it was admirably suited to the world of orderly progress which generally existed down to the death of the Queen, and indeed until the outbreak of the First World War. The long religious wars of the sixteenth and seventeenth centuries, which were the result of the Reformation, caused something like the law of the jungle to become the order of the day all over Europe. The elaborate procedure of the old diplomacy was an attempt—and a very successful attempt—to restore decency to international relations, and many a war was prevented by this means. Of course this success depended upon the politicians not wrecking the machine by their interference. The diplomatist did his work quietly and unostentatiously, and when he scored a point over an adversary he did not rub it in, or announce his triumph from the house-tops. In effect, the system worked so long as the men in control were determined to make it work; that is to say so long as the politicians were content to transact international business in the main through the professional diplomatists, and with a few exceptions they were prepared to do this not only until the end of the nineteenth century, but down to August, 1914.

Finally there is the Indian Civil Service, and like the other Services in the Victorian Age patronage was the basic principle in 1837 and examination in 1901. The examination was the same as that for Class I in the Home Civil, and the vacancies were limited, but down to the outbreak of the First World War the Indian Civil Service and the Treasury attracted the best brains at Oxford and Cambridge, selection for the Foreign Service at that time being the result of a different examination. From whatever angles the Services, Naval, Military, Diplomatic, Home, or India, be regarded the importance of the revolution effected in the Victorian Age could hardly be exaggerated.

Index

Index